Memories of Jesus

Memories of Jesus

A Journey through Time

Halvor Moxnes

CASCADE *Books* · Eugene, Oregon

MEMORIES OF JESUS
A Journey through Time

Cascade Books
An Imprint of Wipf and Stock Publishers
199 W. 8th Ave., Suite 3
Eugene, OR 97401

www.wipfandstock.com

PAPERBACK ISBN: 978-1-5326-8474-6
HARDCOVER ISBN: 978-1-5326-8475-3
EBOOK ISBN: 978-1-5326-8476-0

Cataloguing-in-Publication data:

Names: Moxnes, Halvor, author.

Title: Memories of Jesus : a journey through time / Halvor Moxnes.

Description: Eugene, OR: Cascade Books, 2021. | Includes bibliographical references and index.

Identifiers: ISBN 978-1-5326-8474-6 (paperback). | ISBN 978-1-5326-8475-3 (hardcover). | ISBN 978-1-5326-8476-0 (ebook).

Subjects: LCSH: Jesus Christ—Person and offices. | Jesus Christ—Historicity | Jesus Christ—History of doctrines. | Jesus Christ—Biography—History and criticism. | Bible. Gospels—Criticism, interpretation, etc. | Jesus Christ—Biography—Apocryphal and legendary literature.

Classification: BT198 M70 2021 (print). | BT198 (ebook).

Figure 1—Map of Palestine at the time of Jesus, Wikimedia Commons, adapted by Johanne Hjorthol. 23 March 2006 (original upload date). Transferred from English Wikipedia to Wikimedia Commons (https://commons.wikimedia.org/wiki/File:First_century_Iudaea_province.gif). Andrew C. at English Wikipedia. Released under the GNU Free Documentation License.

Figure 2—Salvador Dali: *Christ of Saint John of the Cross* (1951). Peter Barritt / Alamy Stock Photo. Used by permission.

Figure 3—Giotto: *The Life of Christ; The Flight into Egypt*, Assisi, 1310–1320. Wikimedia Commons (https://commons.wikimedia.org/wiki/File:Giotto_-_Scrovegni_-_-20-_-_Flight_into_Egypt.jpg/).

Figure 4—*Moses and the Burning Bush* (interior wood panel, Dura Europos Synagogue, 244–45 CE). Wikimedia Commons (https://commons.wikimedia.org/wiki/File:Mose_hasne.jpg)

Figure 5—*The Virgin Mary and Jesus* (old Persian miniature). Historic Images / Alamy Stock Photo. Used by permission.

Figure 6—Giotto: *The Legend of Saint Francis; Renunciation of Worldly Goods* (1297–1299). Wikimedia Commons (https://commons.wikimedia.org/wiki/File:Giotto_di_Bondone_-_Legend_of_St_Francis_-_5._Renunciation_of_Wordly_Goods_-_WGA09123.jpg/).

Figure 7—Matthias Grünewald: *Isenheim Altarpiece* (around 1515, Unterlinden Museum, Colmar). Wikimedia Commons.© Jörgens.mi / CC BY-SA 3.0\ https://commons.wikimedia.org/wiki/File:Matthias_Grünewald_-_Isenheim_Altarpiece_(third_view)_-_WGA10758.jpg/.

Figure 8—Hieronymus Bosch or follower of Bosch (circa 1450–1516): *Christ Carrying the Cross* (1510–1535) Wikimedia Commons https://commons.wikimedia.org/wiki/File:Jheronimus_Bosch_or_follower_001.jpg/.

Figure 9—Marc Chagall: *White Crucifixion* (1938). Peter Barritt / Alamy Stock Photo. Used by permission.

Figure 10—Giorgio de Chirico: *Gesù Divino Lavoratore* (1951), olio su tela (140x102.5 cm), Opera Pro Civtate Christiana 1367. Digital image used by permission of the Galleria d'Arte Contemporanea della Pro Civitate Christiana in Assisi, Italy.

Figure 11—John Petts: *A Black Christ* (2011), stained glass window at the Sixteenth Street Baptist Church in Birmingham, Alabama). Photographer: Jet Lowe. Wikimedia Commons https://commons.wikimedia.org/wiki/File:Stained_glass_window_at_the_16th_Street_Baptist_Church_in_Birmingham.jpg/.

02/05/21

In memory of my teachers in the study of Jesus,

Nils Alstrup Dahl (1911–2001)

Jacob Jervell (1925–2014)

Contents

Illustrations

Preface

THIS BOOK WILL TELL you how the memories of Jesus were transmitted and developed over the centuries, from the first narratives in the Gospels in the New Testament to modern retellings. Jesus is the central figure in Christianity, and in the creeds of the churches he is the divine Jesus Christ. This book, however, focuses on the human person Jesus, and how believers and nonbelievers—Christians, Jews, Muslims, and agnostics—understood him.

Memories of Jesus is a followup to *A Short History of the New Testament* (2014), and it started its life in Norwegian (*Historien om Jesus*). For this publication, it was substantially expanded to integrate perspectives from an international context.

The book is dedicated to the memory of my teachers, Nils Alstrup Dahl (1911–2001) and Jacob Jervell (1925–2014). Dahl was one of the scholars who initiated the Second Quest for the Historical Jesus. Jervell caused great controversy when he introduced the historical and human Jesus into the public debate in Norway in the 1960s.

Preface

Acknowledgments

THE BOOK IS A result of many years of study of the historical Jesus and the reception of Jesus through history, and it is impossible to list all my colleagues, students, and audiences who have contributed in this process. Leif Vaage at Emmanuel College within the University of Toronto and Jonathan C. P. Birch at the University of Glasgow represent many international colleagues.

My New Testament colleagues at the Faculty of Theology at the University of Oslo, especially Marianne Bjelland Kartzow and Anders Runesson, have been helpful discussion partners. I am grateful to Oddbjørn Leirvik, of the University of Oslo, and Susannah Heschel, from Dartmouth College, who have read parts of the manuscript. Parts of the book began as lectures and discussions at various venues in Norway—for instance at the Norwegian Center for Holocaust and Minority Studies.

I am grateful to the Theological Library and the University Library at the University of Oslo for assistance with library searches. Johanne Hjorthol and Rune Selnes have helped with the images and IT support for the book. Forty years after he helped correct the English of my dissertation, my friend Brian McNeil has done the same with this book. I am grateful to Michael Thomson, K. C. Hanson, my editor, and the rest of the staff at Cascade Books (Wipf and Stock Publishers) for their interest in the book and their support in the process from proposal to book. Special thanks go to my copy editor, Jeremy Funk, who has done an extraordinary job in improving language and style.

Introduction

THIS IS A DIFFERENT book about Jesus. The most common way to approach the question "Who was/is Jesus" is to start with the issue of the historical Jesus. This approach has dominated Jesus studies until recently. From this perspective, the Gospels were *sources* for history, and the goal of this kind of study was to reach behind the Gospels to the historical Jesus.

This book instead starts with the Gospels and will study them as *memories* of Jesus. From this perspective, the goal is not to discuss the Gospels as sources of historical information about Jesus but to read them as *stories* and to find the characteristics of each gospel in their narrations of Jesus. These memory narratives present the beginning of the story of Jesus stretching from his time to ours, a story in which he is remembered and renarrated in many different ways. This book thus combines memory studies with another new field of investigation of Jesus and the New Testament: *reception history* and its focus on the role of the recipients of the stories and their cultural contexts. The retellings in the Gospels transmit the memories of Jesus and the way they were shaped by their encounters with the contemporary situation of the recipients.

My attempt to present this history of memories, retellings, and interpretations is of course colored by my own context, standing at the end of the hegemony of historical-critical research, and at the same time being influenced by reception histories of Jesus that reflect their rootedness in the cultural contexts of their times.

Memory Studies

Recent studies of social memory have offered an important perspective within historical studies. These studies begin with Maurice Halbwachs in the first part of the twentieth century.[1] More recently, the German scholars Aleida Assman[2] and Jan Assman,[3] who have developed a theory of cultural and communicative memory, have undertaken important memory studies. Within New Testament scholarship, there are many studies, undertaken (to mention only a few names) by Dale C. Allison,[4] James Dunn,[5] Jens Schröter,[6] Chris Keith, and Anthony Le Donne.[7] Chris Keith has developed a social memory theory in the study of Jesus traditions. This theory emphasizes that memory is a result of social formation, that the individual accesses memory within the framework of society. Therefore, "the primary task of social memory theory is to conceptualize and explain the various manners in which cultures (and individuals as culture-members) appropriate the past in light of, in terms of, and on behalf of the present."[8]

The focus on the *present* is significant; however, it has been developed in two different directions, the presentist and the continuity perspectives. The presentist perspective gives priority to the present in the act of remembrance and is therefore skeptical about its ability to recall historical events trustworthily. The continuity perspective, on the other hand, focuses on the social nature of memory, which transcends the capacity of the individual, and opens a social process of mutual influence between the past and the present. Keith argues that in the study of the Jesus traditions, the appropriation "of collective memory must account not only for the role of the present in shaping the past, but also the role of the past, and past interpretation of the past, in shaping the present."[9] Following Keith, I argue that the continuity perspective presents the best process of memory making.

1. Halbwachs, *On Collective Memory*.
2. Assmann, *Cultural Memory and Western Civilization*.
3. Assmann, *Cultural Memory and Early Civilization*.
4. Allison, *Constructing Jesus*.
5. Dunn, *Jesus Remembered*.
6. Schröter, *Jesus of Nazareth*.
7. Le Donne, *Historical Jesus*.
8. Keith, "Memory and Authenticity," 168.
9. Keith, "Memory and Authenticity," 169.

Memories in History

The Gospels are retellings and interpretations of memories of Jesus that were first transmitted orally. These oral narratives were based on strong impressions of Jesus' life and on convictions that he was still alive as the Son of God. People who had met and remembered Jesus may have told some of these narratives. However, the Gospels present strikingly different ways of telling the life of Jesus; they emphasize different stories and different aspects of Jesus. These retellings and reshapings of memories do not stop with the gospels now in the New Testament. New stories of unknown aspects of Jesus' life were added—for instance childhood stories, stories about his parents and grandparents, and of his descent to Hades after the crucifixion. Many of these stories were collected in the Apocryphal Gospels, which partly fill in gaps in the gospel stories now in the New Testament and partly go in new directions. This was a process that started in the second century and continued for several centuries.

At the same time that Christians continued to create memories of Jesus, the claims of the first memories were contested. Jewish scholars rejected the claims that the Christians made about Jesus. The result was a phenomenon called counterhistory, that is, telling alternative stories, for instance about Jesus' birth and his death, to delegitimize the Christian stories. The seventh century saw the beginning of a third version of stories about Jesus, this time in the Quran. Since Muhammad recognized Jews and Christians as people of the Book, their prophets were also included in the Quran. Thus, the Quran introduced Jesus as an Islamic prophet, rejecting, however, the Christian claims about Jesus' divinity.

These conflicts over the memories of Jesus between Christians, Jews, and Muslims took place mostly in the areas east of the Mediterranean. In the Middle Ages, however, the center of Christianity moved west to present-day Europe. The memories of Jesus shaped the identity of Europe, and Jesus became the symbol of a church that was wealthy and powerful. This image, however, was contested; Francis of Assisi was the main proponent of a spirituality that called people to follow Jesus in poverty. In his criticism of a church that had Christ the heavenly King as its model, Francis preached the human Jesus, the poor Jesus.

This focus on the poor, human Jesus in Francis's criticism of the wealthy church pointed toward a more direct criticism in the beginning Enlightenment. One of the effects of the Enlightenment was the distinction between faith and rational knowledge. As a result, critical thinkers began to distinguish between the divine Christ and the human, historical Jesus. The memories of Jesus were exposed to criticism, and the evolution of modern historical studies in the eighteenth and nineteenth centuries resulted in the search for the historical Jesus. Critics of the traditional teaching of the divine Christ attempted instead to establish the historical figure of Jesus as an alternative and as an ideal for modern societies. I suggest that instead of something very new, this study of the historical Jesus represented a historicizing of the memories of Jesus.

This was the starting point for the research on the historical Jesus that became a dominant trend especially in German universities in the nineteenth century, continuing with full force in the twentieth and into the twenty first century. Even with this new approach, the retellings and interpretations of the historical Jesus continued to be placed within the cultural and social contexts of the interpreters.

This was a context that was shaped by the contrast between "we" and the "others." In a period of colonialism and nationalism, Europeans defined themselves against external others (for instance, East Asians—called Orientals at that time—and Arabs) as well as against internal others (first of all, Jews). Due to the central place that Jesus had in European Christianities, he represented a collective memory that shaped common identities. Jesus was understood to represent the European "we," in contrast to Jews as "the others." The very traditions of the Gospels, of the conflicts between Jesus and the Jewish leaders, which resulted in his death, supported this contrast between Jesus and the Jews in modern Europe. It is a troubling fact that the memories of Jesus contributed to hatred against the Jews in Europe. The retellings of the death of Jesus in the Gospel narratives carry a large responsibility for this situation. Therefore, critical, historical study of these memories was necessary. It was Jewish scholars who first raised this criticism; therefore, Jewish scholarship has been very important to draw a new picture of Jesus, seeing him not in conflict with his Jewish environment but as part of it.

Recent generations have also seen other challenges to hegemonic memories of Jesus. With the recognition that Jesus was a central symbol of identity, it was understandable that discussions of Jesus have played important roles in conflicts over national identities. The beginning of modernity in the nineteenth century saw challenges to gender roles; discussions among theologians in Norway serve as an example of how the masculinity of Jesus influenced the body politic of a nation. Likewise, an Italian art project that aimed at creating an iconography of Jesus as a worker contributed to reconciliation between the church and workers and the Communist Party in postwar Italy. Finally, in a United States torn by race conflicts, the discussion of Jesus' race was bound to enter directly into the consciousness of Americans.

Identity politics is an issue not only on a national level; memories of Jesus are contested also on the level of social and ethnic groups. For these discussions, I have chosen to present memories of Jesus from marginalized groups primarily from the USA. They challenge the hegemonic memories of established groups that have been used to advance their privileges. Instead, marginal groups search the traditions about Jesus for memories of struggle and resistance to oppression. Thus, there are in this process both a deconstruction of hegemony and a construction of new, supportive memories. This is a process that many marginalized groups share—for instance, queer groups, Hispanic *mujeristas*, and migrants attempting to enter the US.

The final question to be addressed is whether it is possible to make a transition from memories to a history of Jesus. This can only be attempted by placing memories in a broader social context and studying them in light of historical and social sciences. Moreover, I will not attempt to sketch a biography of Jesus; there are not sufficient sources for that. The British biographer Hermione Lee suggests instead aiming for *life writing*.[10] Based on the fragments that are left from a life, it may be possible to reconstruct certain activities, sayings, and attitudes that serve to portray the character of a person. Dale Allison, who practices both memory studies and historical studies of Jesus, is careful to draw secure historical conclusions. However, he says, "I find it very difficult to come away from the primary sources doubting that I have somehow met a strikingly original character."[11] This may not be a bad place to end up.

10. Lee, *Body-Parts*.

11. Allison, *Constructing Jesus*, 23.

Abbreviations

ABRL Anchor Bible Reference Library

ATR *Anglican Theological Review*

BibInt *Biblical Interpretation*

BTB *Biblical Theology Bulletin*

CBQ *Catholic Biblical Quarterly*

CHR *Catholic Historical Review*

HTR *Harvard Theological Review*

JAAR *Journal of the American Academy of Religion*

JSHJ *Journal for the Study of the Historical Jesus*

JSJSup Supplement to the Journal for the Study of Jusaism

JTS *Journal of Theological Studies*

LCL Loeb Classical Library

OBT Overtures to Biblical Theology

TS *Theological Studies*

ZNW *Zeitschrift für die neutestamentliche Wissenschaft
und die Kunde der älteren Kirche*

Part 1: Beginnings

THE FIRST THREE CHAPTERS cover the origins of the memories of Jesus, from the first Christian writings and the reactions from Rabbinic and Jewish polemics, to the alternative Jesus stories in the Quran and early Islam. The geographical setting is the modern Middle East and Eastern Mediterranean, and this signals that the Jesus movement, and Early Christianity in this period, was predominantly an Eastern religion.

The beginning was the Christian stories of Jesus, his life, activities and teachings. They are read not as sources for the historical Jesus, but as sources for the memories of Jesus from his first followers. In the present day, they are read as foundational texts for Christian churches and even for Western culture and societies. Therefore, the questions of canon are important: What are the scriptures that belong in the New Testament? However, when we read the gospels as the first memories of Jesus, we find a much more fluid situation. The memories, although fixed as cultural memory in writing, continued as living memories that grew and developed. There is a large literature called apocryphal gospels, which is not clearly defined, and which fills in gaps in the gospel stories, bringing in new persons, e.g., Mary's parents. This process starts in the second century and continues for several centuries.

At the same time as the Christians continued to create memories, the claims of the first memories were contested. The reactions from Jewish scholars and popular polemics rejected the claims that the Christians made about Jesus, and especially the way they used the Bible and Jewish history to support their claims. The situation was one of Christians telling a history of Jesus and of Jews telling counterhistories about Jesus to delegitimize the Christian stories. The seventh century saw the beginning of a third version of stories about Jesus, this time in the Quran. The Quran introduced Jesus as an Islamic prophet, while, however, rejecting the Christian claims about Jesus' divinity.

Part 1 Beginnings

1

Jesus in Early Christian Memory

The Gospels as Biographies of Jesus

"So his fame spread throughout all Syria." —Matt 4:24

THERE CAN BE NO doubt that people told stories about Jesus already during his lifetime. These could have been stories from people who had encountered him, who had themselves experienced healings, or who had heard about such healings. There could also have been stories that people had told synagogue authorities in order to warn them about Jesus' activities. Of course, more stories were told about Jesus after the Romans had executed him. Those who had met him and followed him kept the memories about him alive, especially those who believed that he was risen and that he was still alive. These followers believed that he continued to speak to them and interact with them. The memories of Jesus, of what he had said and done, were told in such a way that they brought him to life for new followers.

After Jesus' death, the memories about him spread quickly, first within the Syria-Palestine area, then further to Asia Minor, Greece, and Rome, and to Egypt in the South. The first Christ followers were often recruited from among members or associates of Jewish synagogues, but they soon established their own groups, meeting in private homes.

Jesus was remembered in two distinctive ways. We find one of them in the letters of Paul or other early Christian letter writers in the form of proclamations of Jesus and his death and resurrection. We do not know how much the early missionaries had actually told about Jesus' life, of what he had said and done. In Paul's letters, we find very few memories about Jesus. Instead, Paul speaks directly to the addressees of his letters to explain the *meaning* of Jesus' death and resurrection for them.

In addition to this way of *reminding* the audience of the meaning of Jesus, there was another way that created memories of Jesus through *narratives* of what he had said and done. We find these narratives in the gospels that were written down thirty to fifty years after Paul's letters. These sayings and stories about Jesus were first transmitted orally within a society with strong oral traditions. This means that these narratives were not only individual memories, but also communal memories shaped by their use in worship and prayer. Readings, preaching, and teachings, as well as the rituals of baptism and the shared meal, together created a shared memory. Through all these events, the memories of Jesus became alive so that the participants experienced that Jesus was present among them, invisible but real. Thus, through the participation in these rituals, the experiences of the presence of Jesus became part of the identity of the Christ believers.

The earliest transmissions of memories of Jesus were in the form of brief sayings and short narratives. Many of them were of a similar type, and they appear quite stereotypical. This is easily understandable when we consider how popular stories were shaped through repeated oral presentations. Furthermore, common patterns of remembering were at work: short sayings, pointed comments, a striking image or parable were easy to remember. The passion narrative is an exception to this pattern of short traditions. It is the longest continuous story in the gospels, and the one that was most painful to narrate. At the same time, it was important to tell the story in such a way that Jesus' life and death did not signify failure but had a positive meaning.

At this oral tradition continued, at the same time sayings and narratives were collected and brought together into larger collections—for instance healing stories—and were probably also written down. Many scholars think that a large collection of sayings of Jesus, called Q (from the German word for "source," *Quelle*), was written down before the first Gospel, Mark. The majority of biblical scholars think that the (anonymous) author of Mark's Gospel was the first to collect the oral traditions about Jesus and to organize them into a chronological framework. The outline, starting with the baptism by John and ending with Jesus' death and resurrection, provided the framework for the sequence of Jesus stories and sayings. In this way, Mark provided a model for a structure that Matthew and Luke to a great extent followed. These three Gospels are called *Synoptic* ("seeing together"), since they have so much material in common. Even the Gospel of John follows the main outline of Jesus' life from baptism to death and resurrection, but within that framework, it has a different structure and much separate material.

Through this process, the memories of Jesus changed in character and acquired a different function. The first oral traditions were based on reports from eyewitnesses or from people who heard about them. These reports were flexible and developed when they were retold in new contexts to respond to new situations. When these memories were written down, however, they were formalized in such a way that it was not up to individuals or a group to change them. The evangelists not only collected and transmitted memories; through the way the memories formed the Gospels, they *shaped* memories for their audiences. When they were written down, the memories gained a greater authority and importance: they became a "cultural memory" for a larger community.[1]

Shortly after the Gospels were written down, some early witnesses describe them as "memories." The first to do so was Papias (ca. 70–120 CE), a bishop in Hierapolis in western Asia Minor. He writes that Mark, who according to tradition was the author of the Gospel of Mark, "became Peter's interpreter and wrote accurately all that he remembered."[2] Around the middle of the second century, the Christian philosopher Justin Martyr (ca. 100–165 CE) wrote a defense of the Christians in which he described the Gospels as "the memoirs of the apostles."[3] In Greek rhetorical handbooks collections of stories or sayings transmitted orally were called *memories*. Within oral cultures such traditions were regarded as trustworthy. These collections of sayings and stories had many similarities to the genre of biography.

Biographies as Models for the Gospels[4]

What forms of writing were available for those who wanted to write down memories of significant persons in Greco-Roman and Jewish societies in antiquity? Jesus was sometimes compared to Socrates. Socrates, too, was a man who gathered disciples around him; he had great influence on those who came after him, and biographies were written about him. Such comparisons between Jesus and Socrates have a history that goes all the way back to the philosopher Justin Martyr (see above).[5]

Justin describes Socrates as a man who shared with Christ the same divine reason. Through this reason, Socrates had a partial knowledge of Christ.

---

1. Assmann, *Cultural Memory and Early Civilization*; Assmann and Czaplicka, "Collective Memory."

2. Papias, *Fragments*, 2.15.

3. Justin Martyr, *Dialogue* 103.6.

4. Burridge, *What Are the Gospels?*

5. Justin Martyr, *Apologia* II, 10.

The writings of Socrates's disciples, and the way they described the impressions that Socrates made, influenced the development of Greek biographies in the fourth century BCE.[6] There were several biographies written about Socrates, partly because different groups competed to be recognized as his true followers. In addition, Socrates's opponents wrote critical presentations of his life. Xenophon's *Memorabilia* (ca. 370 BCE) was a defense of Socrates. It is not a narrative of his life from his birth to his death, but it contains elements of a biography. As part of his defense, Xenophon presented speeches or dialogues by Socrates for the purpose of describing his character. These speeches were not verbatim renderings of what Socrates had said, but they represented what he *could* have said. Such speeches that reflected the character of a person, even if they were not historically true in a modern sense, became a popular element of biographies.

Was biography a literary genre of its own? This question has been much discussed; we may find biographical elements in many different forms of literature. The focus on the *character* of Socrates, his *ethos*, was a central element of *Memorabilia*, which was repeated in many biographies after Xenophon's. Biographies often combined two elements. The first was a chronological narrative of the life and deeds of a person, combined with a presentation of his character. The other focused on the childhood and youth of the hero, detailing the education that he received and pointing toward his role as an adult.

The writings of two Roman authors at the end of the first century CE and the beginning of the second century CE show how biographies developed, with different emphasis on these two elements. Plutarch (45–120 CE) was a Greek historian and biographer. His best-known work was *Parallel Lives* (*Bioi paralleloi*). Plutarch describes Greek and Roman soldiers, legislators, orators, and statesmen and their noble deeds and character. Plutarch was concerned to distinguish biographies from history, which was a more recognized genre. History described a person's deeds whereas a biography reflected the character of a person. The goal of a biography was not to give a complete historical narrative; in a biography, a person's deeds were narrated only if they could illuminate the character of a person. Plutarch chose a form in which he presented the life of a person from his birth to his death, and in the process he introduced evaluations of character traits and important deeds. In the description of the youth of a person, he was especially concerned to point out character traits that shaped his mature life.

Suetonius (whose full name was Gaius Suetonius Tranquillus, 69–122 CE) was a Roman historian. He wrote two series of biographies: *The Life of*

6. Hägg, *Biography*.

the Caesars (*De Vita Caesarum*) and *On Famous Men* (*De Viris Illustribus*). In these works, the historical events are only a framework for Suetonius's discussion of the character of his protagonists. Suetonius used biography both to criticize and to laud his characters; in *The Life of the Caesars*, he evaluated the emperors according to one list of virtues and another list of vices. Both Plutarch and Suetonius used anecdotes as sources for their biographies; their justification was that everyday happenings could be more revealing of character traits than important historical events.

The biographies by Plutarch and Suetonius did not establish a uniform model for biographies; there were many different ways to write a biography. In *The Art of Biography in Antiquity*, Tomas Hägg presents another form of biography in oral traditions about popular, legendary persons—for example, Alexander the Great, Homer, and Aesop with his fables. In contrast to literary *lives* by known authors and with fixed forms, these biographies were anonymous. Hägg characterizes them as "open texts," since they could be changed through transmission. Perhaps we can see similarities here between the evolution of "open texts" and the evolution of the Gospels. From the beginning, they were anonymous; the authorial names were added later. Moreover, Mark, the earliest Gospel, must have been considered an "open text" to which material could be added. The two different stories of Jesus' birth and childhood in Matthew and Luke were probably added from oral traditions. This process continued; in the second century, more biographical stories were added in apocryphal gospels.

Most discussions of possible models for the Gospels have focused on Greek and Roman biographies. However, there is also a Jewish tradition of biographies.[7] In the Hebrew Bible, there are many biographies of prophets, leaders, and kings. Some of them are very short and focus on the calling of a person and on the installation into offices. These biographies often have a stereotypical form: they describe the calling by God and the response and obedience by the one who is called, followed by the installation itself (se 1 Sam 23:1–7). A typical example is the biography of the prophet Isaiah (Isa 61:1–2), which is reused in Jesus' presentation of himself in Luke's Gospel (4:16–18). Other biographies are longer, with a fully developed narrative form. The best example is the life of Moses, from his birth to his death, as narrated in the Pentateuch. This narrative is probably composed from different biographies; most likely each of the main sources of the Pentateuch had a biography of Moses, since he was such an important figure in Israel's history.

---

7. Baltzer, *Biographie*.

Philo of Alexandria (25 BCE–50 CE) wrote his *Life of Moses* to make this great Jewish lawgiver known to the Hellenistic world.[8] Philo was a Hellenistic Jew from a wealthy family in Alexandria, and he wrote many commentaries and allegorical expositions to the Bible in Greek. The two-volume, large biography of Moses builds on the life of Moses in the Pentateuch according to the Septuagint, the Greek translation (with additions) of the Hebrew Bible. Philo's *Life of Moses* displays several elements of Greek and Roman biography traditions. The first volume follows Exodus and Leviticus in a chronological presentation of much of the life of Moses, with Philo's comments added. However, he leaves the chronological presentation to undertake a thematic discussion of Moses's function as a king, his youth and education, and this is material that is not found in the Pentateuch.

The second volume has a very different structure. Only the description of the death of Moses is taken from Deut 33–34. Apart from this section, the volume gives a thematic presentation of Moses as lawgiver, high priest, and prophet. When Philo adds the roles of Moses as prophet and king, which goes beyond the material in the Bible, his intention is to make him understandable to a Hellenistic audience. Most modern studies of Greek biographies do not discuss Philo's *Life of Moses,* but it is obviously an interesting example of how a Jewish hero is described according to the ideals of Greek and Roman biographies.

We have now looked at some presentations of lives of famous people, and their most important elements: deeds, sayings, and character traits. But what is the purpose of such Lives? The persons portrayed were described as ideals and models to be followed—or, if they were bad examples, as warnings to the readers. The purpose could also at times simply be to entertain. In some instances, these Lives could have a direct purpose in relation to disciples and followers. Biographies could be an expression of a wish to preserve the memory of a teacher for oneself and for coming generations. To put the memories down in writing was a way to preserve them and to make them relevant in new settings. They may have been based on memories from a group; but when written down, they became a cultural memory for a larger collective. Contrasting presentations of a leader or a teacher could be used to legitimate different groups of disciples as true followers. It is possible that a similar process resulted in four different presentations of the life of Jesus.

---

8. Philo, *On Moses.*

The Gospels as Lives of Jesus

The immediate impression we get when we read the Gospels is that they are biographies. The Gospels start with the birth of Jesus or his first public appearance, and they all end with his crucifixion and death and the message of his resurrection. The narratives follow a chronological outline that takes place in shifting geographical locations. In the Synoptic Gospels the scenes move from Galilee to Jerusalem. From the earliest times, people regarded the Gospels as Lives of Jesus.[9] This understanding continued through history and was prevalent in the nineteenth century when the first studies of the historical Jesus were called Lives of Jesus.[10]

In the twentieth century, however, scholars became skeptical about describing the Gospels as biographies. Some regarded the Gospels as a unique genre; its purpose was to proclaim the gospel, not to relate history. Other scholars realized that it was strange to speak of a genre that included only four books. They did not agree to speak of them as biographies; instead, they would describe them as history. In particular, this was the case with the Gospel of Luke, the first of a two-volume work, followed by the book of Acts. Others emphasized that the Gospels presented the life of Jesus as salvation history, which was very different from Hellenistic biographies. On the basis of the form of modern biographies, others again were skeptical about attributing the Gospels to the genre of biography since they did not describe the psychology of Jesus or the development of his personality. However, biographies in antiquity were based on a different conception of a human being: a person's character was shaped already in childhood, so the development of a person was traced by the degree to which a person remained true to this character rather than by the realization of a personality.

Recently, new studies have suggested that biographies from antiquity were a plausible model for the Gospels, and have pointed out that we find many aspects of these Lives in the Gospels also.[11] This makes it possible to characterize the Gospels as Lives in a general sense, even if there is no consensus about what constitutes biographies as a genre. Therefore, without being concerned with theoretical definitions, Tomas Hägg suggests that we simply read the Gospels as biographies.[12] After the completion of the Gospels, the biographical elements were strengthened by legendary and apocryphal material that added information about Jesus, his birth, and the

---

9. Justin, *Apology* 1, 67:3.

10. See below, 129–37.

11. Burridge, *What Are the Gospels?*

12. Hägg, *Biography*, 155.

family history of Mary and Joseph. Thus, there is reason to believe that the early audiences for the Gospels read them as "lives of Jesus," on the analogy of the lives of other famous people.

The above presentation of biographies in antiquity will help us to read the Gospels as biographies of Jesus and to prepare the questions we may address to them. Here is a list of questions that I have found useful. The first concerns the structure and content of the biography or gospel. Does it include only the public activity of Jesus, or also the early period of his life? Is the narrative simply chronological, or is it broken up by other elements—for instance, speeches? Moreover, how long was the period of the public activity of Jesus?

The second group of questions concerns how Jesus is described, what type of person he was. We must also address this question to ourselves: How do we understand what it is to be a human being? We might think that this is a superfluous question, but I think it is important, since we find different understandings of what it is to be a person in different societies, cultures, and times. For instance, it is only recently, and because of feminism, that *gender* has become an important issue in analyzing the Gospels. We may consider the fact that Jesus was a man as so obvious that we forget to ask what it meant to be a man in a Mediterranean society in antiquity. Recently, there have been many studies of masculinity and male ideals in Greco-Roman writings; these ideals were also extolled in Jewish literature. This literature primarily reflects the ideals of the elite—for instance in descriptions of Roman emperors.[13] These ideals included courage, self-discipline, wisdom, righteousness, and generosity; they were well known among men with some education—for instance, the authors of the Gospels.

We may suppose that these ideals played a role in their portraits of Jesus, and that they colored the descriptions of Jesus within various social settings, including within his family and household, among his disciples and other followers, and among his critics and opponents. We may also ask whether Jesus was described as a special or unique person; how did the Gospels interpret his sayings and activities? What character traits were ascribed to him? Was he measured according to the Graeco-Roman cultural norms? In addition, how was his role compared with those of important persons from Israel's history and the Bible, such as prophets and kings?

The last group of questions that I will raise concerns the relations between an author and his audience. In what ways do the authors address their audiences? Do they attempt to engage their hearers and readers and to include them in the task of preserving the memories, so that they become

13. Conway, *Behold the Man.*

relevant in their own lives? Can we distinguish between narrations about Jesus as a human person and sections where the authors make their interpretations, attributing a special, even divine character to Jesus?

Mark: Who Was This Man?

The author of Mark's Gospel was the first to write a Life of Jesus by combining many oral traditions into a continuous narrative of Jesus' public life. It starts with Jesus' baptism by John the Baptist and follows his life all the way to his suffering, crucifixion, and the story of the empty tomb. Most readers of Mark's Gospel take it for granted that this was the history of Jesus as it really was, and that we can follow his life from the beginning in Galilee to the end at the Easter festival in Jerusalem, probably within the frame of one year. But in fact, it was not established a priori that the story of Jesus' life should be told in just this way. In their gospels, Matthew and Luke follow the storyline of Mark, but John has a very different story. In John's Gospel, Jesus moves back and forth between Galilee and Jerusalem, and Jesus participates in altogether three Easter festivals, so that John's narrative spans a total of three years. Thus, we cannot take the outline of Jesus' life in Mark as historical fact; it was Mark who, with his written gospel, shaped the memories of Jesus in this way.

Mark's history of Jesus is filled with suspense. In the first part of the story, Jesus is a powerful miracle worker, but in the course of the narrative he is exposed to suffering, and he ends his life as a crucified criminal. How did Mark manage to combine these two aspects in the same story? Mark had to make it plausible that Jesus' suffering was not a coincidence but an expression of God's purpose, and that Jesus not only accepted his suffering but also turned it into the meaning of his life. Mark faced the challenge of explaining how the suffering Jesus was the same as the one he had introduced with the opening words of his gospel: "The beginning of the good news of Jesus Christ, the Son of God."

Mark follows up this contrast between power and powerlessness throughout the gospel. The gospel both starts and ends in a mysterious way. This is how the story of Jesus starts: "In those days Jesus came from Nazareth of Galilee and was baptized by John in the Jordan" (Mark 1:9). Jesus appears without any presentation of who he was, what his history was, or why he came to John to be baptized. The conclusion to his story is likewise mysterious. In the original ending of the gospel (Mark 16:1–8), the women who came to the tomb received the message that Jesus had been raised, but they received no proof (such as an appearance of Jesus to them). Moreover, the gospel ends with this statement, "So they went out and fled from the tomb, for terror and amazement had seized them; and they said nothing to anyone, for they were afraid" (16:8). This is not a triumphant conclusion to the story that started with the proclamation that Jesus was "Jesus Christ, the Son of God;" it sounds rather like a question mark.

Throughout the gospel the disciples, common people, and opponents raise the question: "Who is this man?" In one episode, Mark has Jesus ask his disciples what people think, before he turns directly to the disciples: "But who do you say that I am?" (Mark 8: 29). Jesus is not described as an unambiguous person throughout the history of his life. As a result, listeners to or readers of the story are challenged to respond to the question of who Jesus was, and what that meant for themselves. Throughout the gospel, there is a tension between the memories of the human person Jesus and the attempts to explain the meaning of the memories and to find an answer to who this man was.

Mark seems to have tried to resolve this issue in two different ways. The first is the so-called "Messianic secret," which refers to the way Jesus responded to reactions when he expelled demons or healed the sick. When the demons realized that Jesus was "God's holy one," and the sick were healed, they wanted to proclaim his mighty deeds. However, Jesus forbade this. To proclaim him as the Messiah, according to Mark, apparently would give a wrong picture of who Jesus was. Before his mighty deeds could be proclaimed, the picture of the suffering Jesus had to be inscribed in history.

Mark also had another way to stop misunderstandings of who Jesus was, and that was by the term "Son of Man." Only Jesus himself used this term, referring to a suffering person, but Mark's readers would understand that Jesus referred to himself. In this way, Mark prevented other terms used to refer to Jesus—like "Messiah" and "Son of God"—from being misunderstood as only expressions of power and might. When they were used in combination with "Son of Man," all terms were to be understood in light of suffering.

From Power to Passion: The Structure of Mark's Story

Mark's Gospel gives the impression of being a continuous chronological narrative. However, if we undertake a closer reading of how the different parts are connected, we notice that many of the links between them are rather vague: For instance, "after John was arrested," "again he entered a synagogue" (Mark 1:14; 3:1; 4:1). Mark uses *euthus* ("at once," "immediately") to emphasize that Jesus was in haste to fulfill his task; he uses this adverb no less than six times in the description of Jesus' first days as a teacher and healer. The setting is Galilee, but it is also the border regions. Jesus travels around Galilee with his disciples and ventures into the border areas, to the Gentile districts around Tyre and the Decapolis towns (Mark 7:24–37), and to the land on the east shore of the Lake of Gennesaret. Jesus undertakes most of his activities at this lake, walking along its shores with his disciples or sitting in a boat on the lake. After Jesus left Nazareth, Capernaum came to hold a central place as Jesus' home base.

By combining different stories within a chronological and geographical framework, Mark has succeeded in building a continuous narrative of Jesus' life. Mark's Life of Jesus is only a narrative of his public life; it does not have any stories of Jesus' childhood or youth. The gospel starts with a presentation of John the Baptist and of how Jesus comes to him to be baptized. It is through his baptism that Jesus is chosen by God to be his "Son," with a quotation from Ps 2 about the Israelite king. God's elect withstands tests by the devil, and then he starts to proclaim the kingdom of God and to call disciples. This is the beginning of Jesus' activity in Galilee.

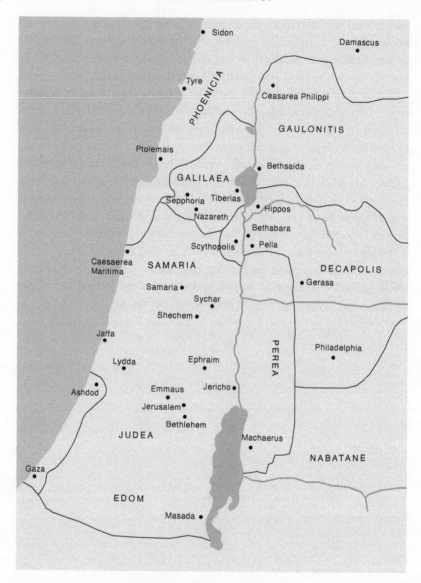

Map of Palestine at the time of Jesus
Wikimedia Commons.[14]

14. 23 March 2006 (original upload date). Transferred from English Wikipedia to Wikimedia Commons (https://commons.wikimedia.org/wiki/File:First_century_Iudaea_province.gif/). Andrew C. at English Wikipedia. Released under the GNU Free Documentation License.

In the first section of the gospel (Mark 1–8) Jesus interacts with people primarily through his miracles. Many of them are healings of the sick or exorcisms, but some are also nature miracles—such as multiplications of fish and bread or the stilling of storms on the Lake of Genesareth. Miracles that protect and renew life characterize Jesus in Mark's Gospel. However, at an early stage among these stories, Mark introduces the conflicts between Jesus and the leaders of the people, pointing toward the passion story at the end of the gospel (Mark 3:6). In this first part of the gospel, Mark introduces a typical element from ancient biographies; chapter 4 interrupts the chronological narrative with a series of parables, first among them the well-known parable of the sower. In this way, Mark combines Jesus' miracles renewing life with Jesus' parables of the kingdom of God.

In the next main section, Mark 8:2—10:52, "the Way to Jerusalem," the gospel changes character. The focus is on Jesus' conversations with, and teaching of, his disciples. This section is introduced by Jesus' questions: "Who do people say that I am?" and "But who do you say that I am?" (Mark 8:27, 29). In a follow-up to the responses from the disciples, Jesus starts to prepare them for what will happen in Jerusalem. Mark attributes great importance to the forewarnings from Jesus; he makes him repeat three times that in Jerusalem he will face suffering and death (Mark 8:31; 9:30–32; 10:32–34). Moreover, he links the fate of Jesus with that of the disciples; they, too, will have to prepare for suffering and death.

In the final section on Jesus' last week in Jerusalem and the passion narrative (Mark 11–16) everything happens in slow motion; the narrative describes in detail everything that happens in these few days. It starts with Jesus' entry into Jerusalem, where people receive him as the Messiah, followed by his provocative acts against the moneychangers. Mark describes in detail how Jesus and his disciples spend their days in the temple and how they return to Bethany to spend the night there (Mark 11:12, 15, 20, 27). The temple scenes give Mark the opportunity to present a series of discussions between Jesus and the priests, the scribes and "the elders," (Mark 11:27—12:44). These debates are followed by the great apocalyptic speech in chapter 13. As a result, this final section of the gospel focuses on Jesus' teaching to his disciples and the conflicts with the Jewish leaders in Jerusalem. They lead up to the passion story with the arrest of Jesus; the interrogations by the Jewish leaders and the Roman prefect, Pilate; the crucifixion; and his death. All this takes place within a few hours.

Jesus and the People around Him

Jesus was not a modern individualist, even if historical Jesus studies might give that impression. Jesus lived in a society and culture where family and the close social group determined who a person was, and made up his or her context. A Jesus' saying in Mark 10:29–30 describes the primary social setting for those who wanted to follow Jesus:

> Truly I tell you, there is no one who has left house or broth-ers or sisters or mother or father or children or fields, for my sake and for the sake of the good news, who will not receive a hundredfold now in this age—houses, brothers and sisters, mothers and children, and fields, with persecutions—and in the age to come eternal life.

This saying describes a family of three generations, who live in the same house and earn their livelihood from their work on the fields. They make up a household—a group of people who form a social and economic unit. This was a group that provided security, but that in return imposed responsibili-ties and obligations on its members. Such groups were based on patriarchy, with strong social control. We must assume that Jesus came from such a household, since this was the form of household found all over the Mediter-ranean. Mark must have taken for granted that since this was the prevalent family structure, it did not need to be described or explained. This may be the reason why it took a while for Mark to give any details about Jesus' fam-ily. We notice that when Jesus is first introduced, there is no mention of his father or his origin; only later does Mark provide some information. When we first hear about Jesus' family in chapter 3, we learn that they shared the criticism of the scribes that Jesus must have gone mad, and that his mother and brothers have come to Capernaum to bring him back home to Nazareth (Mark 3:21, 31–35). However, Jesus rejects them, and proclaims that from now on his disciples are his mother and brothers. In this story, there is no mention of the names of his family members. We learn some of their names only in chapter 6, in a story of how Jesus is rejected when he comes to his hometown. Mark reports what people in his village said about Jesus: "Is not this the carpenter, the son of Mary and brother of James and Joses and Judas and Simon, and are not his sisters here with us?" (Mark 6:3). Interestingly, Mark tells that it was Jesus, not his father, who was a carpenter, and he was known as "the son of Mary," perhaps since he did not have a known father. The names of his brothers are given, but his sisters are not identified. This is the last piece of information about Jesus' family that Mark provides; there is no mention of his family later in the gospel. None of them is mentioned as being present at the crucifixion of Jesus.

Mark presents a very negative picture of Jesus' family. Jesus had broken the ties with his family and had to suffer the consequences. Mediterranean readers who were strongly integrated in a family culture would find this to be a drastic conflict, since Jesus had separated himself from the most important societal institution. Instead, through his baptism. Jesus was associated with John the Baptist as his disciple. John is introduced as a well-known prophetic figure for Mark's readers, and Mark tells that people look upon Jesus as John himself or as a new figure like John (Mark 6:14–18; 8:28).

It is primarily Jesus' disciples who will be his new family (Mark 3:31–35). They are mentioned by name, beginning with the four who are first called to follow him (1:16–20), and then the group of twelve (Mark 3:13–19). In biographies of philosophers such as Socrates, disciples and students have an important role as exemplary followers of their teacher. In Mark, however, the disciples of Jesus do not fulfil these expectations. For his part, Jesus calls and equips his disciples for service; like him, they shall proclaim the good message, they shall heal and shall expel demons (Mark 1:15–20; 3:13–19; 6:7–13). However, in spite of receiving these powers, the disciples soon appear to be afraid and of little faith. Their disbelief is exposed most of all in the stories of the crossing of the Sea of Gennesaret (Mark 4:35–41; 6:45–52). It becomes even more visible in the next major part of the gospel (Mark 8:27—10:52). It starts with Peter's confession that Jesus is the Messiah, but for Peter it is impossible to combine the idea of the Messiah with suffering and death (Mark 8:29–33). Jesus' three predictions of his suffering and death are all followed by his teaching his disciples that they must follow him in service and suffering. However, it is impossible for them to grasp the meaning of this teaching (Mark 8:34–38; 9:30–37; 10:35–45).

These negative pictures of the disciples in the first part of the gospel signal to the readers that there is more to come. In the passion narrative, Judas will betray Jesus to the high priests (Mark 14:10–11, 17–21). Jesus predicts that all the other disciples will fail him and that Peter will disown him (Mark 14:26–31). These predictions quickly come true (Mark 14:32–43, 43–50, 66–72). The picture seems completely dark; how can these men be exemplary followers of Jesus? Moreover, how can they serve as leaders for the groups of Jesus' followers after his death? Thus, Mark's picture of the disciples places readers in a position where they must take responsibility, if the Jesus' movement is to continue.

We may think that the women who accompanied Jesus presented an alternative to the male disciples. Women who heard or read Mark's biography would pay attention to his stories about women. Some of these women

fulfil traditional women roles—like Peter's mother-in-law, who is healed by
Jesus and then "began to serve them" (Mark 1:31). Other women, however,
are more independent and create a role of their own. A Syrophoenician (i.e.,
a non-Jewish) woman dares to talk back to Jesus when he refuses to help her
daughter who is sick, and Jesus finally gives in to her petition (Mark 7:24–
30). The poor widow who puts a penny's worth of coins into the temple
treasury is praised by Jesus (Mark 12:41–44). His greatest praise is bestowed
on the woman who bursts into a dinner party with Jesus and his disciples
in Bethany and anoints Jesus. In response to his disciples' criticism of this
extravagance, Jesus defends her by saying that "she has anointed my body
beforehand for its burial." Furthermore, Mark makes Jesus give room for
her in the memories about himself: "wherever the good news is proclaimed
in the whole world, what she has done will be told in remembrance of her"
(Mark 14:3–9). In Mark's Gospel, Jesus is generally quite traditional in his
relations to women. But when he is confronted by a brave woman, or by a
woman who breaks the conventions of female behavior, Mark shows that
Jesus can reconsider his position.

Outside the close circle of disciples, Jesus is surrounded by large
crowds, especially in Galilee in the first part of the gospel. In these crowds,
there are many people who are ill or possessed by demons, and who are
helped by Jesus. These people are usually without names, and behind them,
there are many who help to bring them to Jesus. In addition, there are many
who come to see and hear Jesus. Mark repeatedly gives the impression that
large crowds follow Jesus.[15] This was the case when Jesus was in Galilee.
In Jerusalem, however, the "crowd" plays a different role. The priests and
the temple authorities stir the "crowd" to demand that Pilate shall release
Barnabas and crucify Jesus (Mark 15:8–15).

Throughout his gospel, Mark describes the leaders of the Jewish people
as opposing Jesus. Already from the beginning, from his first healings and exorcisms, the scribes and the Pharisees criticize Jesus for transgressing various
laws and regulations (Mark 2:6, 16, 18, 24), and they plan to kill him (Mark
3:6). Mark has a clear opinion about who is responsible for the death of Jesus.
In the passion predictions Jesus explicitly says that the chief priests and the
scribes will condemn him to death and hand him over to the "Gentiles," that
is, the Romans (Mark 10:33–34). In this way, Mark lays the foundation for
what became the predominant story of who were responsible for the death
of Jesus. It appears that Mark wrote from a position as an insider in Jewish
society when he describes the leaders of the people, and when he describes
the Romans as "Gentiles." However, in a relatively short time, the majority of

15. Mark 1: 32–34; 2: 2–5; 3: 7–12, 20; 5: 21; 6:53–56.

the readers of Mark's Gospel were non-Jews. When they read Mark's story, the Jewish opponents of Jesus were no longer their own leaders; they were interpreted as "the Jews," that is, the "others," different from themselves. This was the beginning of the dark history when the Christians put the blame for the death of Jesus on all Jews throughout history.

Mighty Deeds

In the previous section, we have presented the social networks that Jesus was part of. But for Mark, this was not enough information to understand who Jesus was. The most important issues surrounded how to find the true meaning of what Jesus did and said. From the very beginning of his narrative, Mark emphasizes that he understands Jesus to be the Christ and the Son of God. This is the perspective from which he understands Jesus' deeds and words. However, this was not the only possible understanding. Mark tells a story of how scribes from Jerusalem accused Jesus of "having Beelzebul." That is, they accuse him of being possessed by the leader of demons and claim that it is through their power that he can expel them. Mark may here have countered an accusation by his opponents. They did not deny that Jesus did exorcisms, but they attributed this to black magic, not to the power of God. In chapter 3, Mark recounts a polemical exchange between some scribes and Jesus, where Jesus exposes the fallacy of their arguments (Mark 3:22–27). This story most likely reflects conflicting views of Jesus in Mark's time. The memories of miracles he performed could be presented in ways very different from the ways Mark describes them. Thus, the readers or hearers of these stories would themselves have to construct their own understandings of who Jesus was: Son of God or possessed by Beelzebul.

The author of Mark's Gospel had recourse to positive models and ideal figures who could help explain the mighty deeds that Jesus did.[16] These could be well-known men from history who had done similar things, and who had special relationships to God. Since Jesus was a man, Mark looks to other men, and foremost among them were powerful men of God from the history of Israel, especially the prophet Elijah and Moses (Mark 8:28; 9:4).

In the first part of his gospel, Mark has collected stories of Jesus as a miracle worker who traveled around Galilee healing the sick, exorcising demons, feeding hungry multitudes and stilling storms at the Lake of Genesaret. Mark sometimes tells individual stories, and in other instances he gives brief summaries of what Jesus used to do when he traveled around Galilee accompanied by large crowds (Mark 1:32–34; 3:7–12; 6:53–56).

16. Conway, *Behold the Man*, 90–96.

Mark's story line in these first chapters gives the impression of a Galilee suffering a crisis.

This sense of a crisis may reflect the situation that Mark experienced when he wrote his gospel.[17] There are several suggestions about the origin and place of the gospel: one is that it was written in Galilee around year 70. The detailed descriptions in chapter 13 of the destruction of the Jerusalem temple may support this hypothesis. This event was a catastrophe in the life of the Jewish people, coming at the end of a long period of internal conflict. Roman rule and the Herodian economic policy, marked by the accumulation of land into large estates, resulted in crises for the peasant population. Peasants lost their land, and they experienced famine; this resulted in families breaking up and in mental breakdowns—for instance in the form of demon-possessions. Mark's narrative of Jesus' exorcisms, healings of the sick, and miraculous feedings of the hungry presents him as responding to crises that many people experienced.

The miracle stories are examples of the function of biographies in antiquity. Recounting the deeds of the protagonist was a way to describe his character. The miracle stories of Jesus show how he reacted to persons he met. These stories present him as a warm human being. When he encounters people who are sick or troubled, he is "moved with pity," and "he [has] compassion for them" (Mark 1:41; 6:34). In other instances, his emotions are expressed through the way he acts—for instance, when he is told that Peter's mother-in-law has a fever, he "took her by the hand and lifted her up" (Mark 1:31).

Another way that Mark interprets Jesus and his miracles is through the framework within which he places them. The miracle stories are linked to Jesus' proclamation of the kingdom of God, and they are signs that the kingdom is close at hand. Jesus does not define the meaning of the kingdom of God, but Mark explains it with his stories of how Jesus and his disciples travel, proclaim the kingdom, heal the sick, and expel demons (1: 39; 3:14–15). The healings of the sick are also put in a meaningful context when they are combined with Jesus' forgiveness of sins (e.g., Mark 2:5). But these interpretations are challenged by the scribes, who criticize Jesus for usurping God's own privileges to forgive sins and for breaking the Sabbath laws (Mark 2:6–12; 3:1–6).

17. Dube, *Storytelling*.

Secret Messiah and Son of Man

The kingdom of God also belonged to a cosmic imagination. In Mark's Gospel, Jesus is fighting against demons that represent the power or kingdom of Satan (Mark 1:13, 23–27; 3:22–27). In this fight, Jesus represents God; the demons called him "the Holy One of God" and "the Son of God" (1:24; 3:11). However, there is something paradoxical here; in Mark, Jesus demands that those whom he has healed not reveal who he is.[18] Among scholars, this phenomenon is termed the "Messianic secret." Since Mark uses the designations "Messiah" and "Son of God" about Jesus, it does seem strange that he makes Jesus forbid others to use these names about him. The historical reason may be that gospel writer Mark was critical of the way these names were understood in relation to Jesus. They attributed power and might to the person who acted on behalf of God; however, for Mark, this power could be misunderstood if it was not corrected by the image of Jesus in the last part of the gospel, his suffering and passion.

This "Messianic secret" has a parallel in the secret of the kingdom of God. In chapter 4 Mark departs from the biographical progression of the life of Jesus to include a collection of Jesus' parables, among which the parable of the sower is the best known (Mark 4:2–9). The disciples are promised an explanation, the secret of the kingdom of God will be revealed to them (Mark 4:13–20). But Jesus describes the crowds who heard the parables as "those outside": they will not understand the parables; their meaning is hidden from them (Mark 4:11–12). However, even with Jesus' explanation, the readers receive little information about the kingdom. Rather, they learn about the different ways of receiving the word of God that Jesus proclaims. Jesus explains how the seed falls on different types of soil: on a path, on a rocky ground, among thorns, and finally into good soil. Jesus then compares these different forms of soil to different people and the ways in which they receive the word. In this way, Mark has Jesus address those who read or hear his gospel, and are challenged about how to respond to his words.

Mark's Gospel describes the life of Jesus as a paradox. He appears with great power and authority to subdue demons, illnesses, storms, and waves of the sea—and at the same time, he repeatedly emphasizes that he is on his way to suffering and death, a fate that he cannot avoid. How can Mark help his audience to understand such a paradoxical figure? For Mark, an obvious solution was to look for comparable figures in the history of Israel. They appear in the response to Jesus' question: "Who do people say that I am?" They were well-known figures like John the Baptist, Elijah,

---

18. Mark 1:34–44; 3:12; 5;43; 7:36; 8:30; 9:9.

or one of the other prophets who spoke the word of God and performed his deeds (Mark 6:14–16; 8:28). Mark himself introduces another figure when he starts his story by naming Jesus "Jesus Christ, Son of God." Here, Mark makes use of a Jewish tradition that designated the Messiah, a savior figure, as "the Son of God." Mark repeatedly uses this title at significant moments in his narrative, at the baptism of Jesus, at the transfiguration, and finally at the death of Jesus.[19]

These epithets show that Mark consciously places Jesus within Jewish tradition. At the same time, he challenges a traditional understanding of these titles. Mark does this partly by the way he develops the narrative of Jesus' life. A period of mighty deeds ends and is replaced by a phase of suffering. Finally, the crucifixion puts an end to any power that Jesus had, and he loses even the presence of God. This transition from might to weakness is also signaled by the epithet Son of Man for Jesus. The origin and meaning of Son of Man have given rise to much discussion. One understanding of the epithet has been that it refers to a figure in Jewish history or mythology, possibly mentioned in the book of Daniel. However, now the most commonly accepted view is that it is a Hebrew term, bar adam, that simply means "man" (i.e. "human being"). Only Jesus uses this term in Mark; other persons do not use it of Jesus. Jesus speaks about the Son of Man in the third person; however, it is likely a cryptic way of referring to himself. In most instances, this epithet contrasts with some of the traditional ones and presents a new perspective on those epithets.

The best example occurs in the episode where Jesus asks his disciples who people say that he is, and finally asks the disciples about their opinion. On behalf of all the disciples, Peter responds: "You are the Messiah" (Mark 8:29). During the time of Jesus, Jews had different images of and expectations for the Messiah. The most widespread was likely a kingly Messiah, a descendant of David who would reestablish David's kingdom and destroy its enemies.[20] It was this concept of a kingly Messiah that Jesus challenges in his response to Peter; he does not use the term "Messiah" but rather "Son of Man" when he speaks of the suffering that awaits him in Jerusalem. The last of the passion predictions provides a positive meaning to Jesus' suffering and death: "For the Son of Man came not to be served but to serve, and to give his life a ransom for many" (Mark 10:45). By replacing "Messiah" with "Son of Man," Mark gives new meaning to the traditional terms. They had been understood in the context of war and power struggles, but now they were put in the context of service and "giving one's life."

19. Mark 1:9; 9:2–8; 15:39.
20. Dunn, *Jesus Remembered*, 619–22.

The Unmanly Sacrifice[21]

The death of the hero receives an important place in biographies: it is in this moment that the significance of his life and character is revealed. This is true also of Mark's story of Jesus' last week in Jerusalem; here narrative and cosmic meaning are combined. The tensions from the beginning of Jesus' public life in Galilee increase. Jesus' entry into Jerusalem is presented as a triumph; Jesus is greeted as the one who will restore the kingdom of David. However, when he expels the moneychangers and the vendors of animals for sacrifices from the temple precincts, the chief priests and the scribes plot to kill him.

Jesus' relation to the temple is a central issue at the end of the story. His conflicts with the scribes lead up to a long speech about the destruction of the temple and the end of time (Mark 13). The destruction of the temple also becomes an issue in the interrogation before the Council; Jesus is accused of saying that he would destroy the temple and in three days and would build a new one not made by hands. Moreover, when Jesus died, the curtain in the temple was torn in two, a clear sign that the time of the temple was over. Thus, Mark presents Jesus as the one who displaces the temple as the place of access to God.

Mark establishes also another context for interpreting events of the passion story. The execution of Jesus takes place during Passover, the celebration of the Israelite memories of the exodus from Egypt—a celebration centered by the blood of the Passover lamb as a sign of the covenant between God and Israel (Mark 14:1–2). It is this tradition that is activated in Mark's report of Jesus' last supper with his disciples (Mark 14:22–25). He describes it as a Passover Seder, and the blood of Jesus, that is, his death, becomes the sign of God's covenant.

The question of who Jesus is, is raised once more in the interrogation by the Council. For the first time, Jesus confesses that he is the Messiah, the Son of God, and at once the Council find Jesus guilty of blasphemy (Mark 14:55–65). However, Jesus continues to speak of himself as the Son of Man. Pilate, however, considers the accusation against Jesus a political one, that he has claimed to be the King of the Jews, and this is also the charge that is posted on the cross (Mark 15:26).

In the passion narrative, Jesus increasingly comes across as a man filled with anxiety. He does not fulfill the expectation of a heroic death, well known from stories of Jewish heroes who encountered persecution.[22] When Jesus

21. Conway, *Behold the Man*, 90–96.

22. The best example is the story of a mother and her seven sons who were executed by Antiochus IV Epiphanes (215–164 BCE) because they refused to renounce their

goes to the garden of Gethsemane to pray, he begins to be "distressed and agitated," and he prays to God that he must "remove this cup from me," even if he is willing to submit to the will of God (Mark 14:33–36). Jesus is not able to carry his cross, so the soldiers force a passerby to carry it for him (Mark 15:21). On the cross, Jesus is suffering passively, and Mark ascribes these last words to him: "My God, my God, why have you forsaken me?" This quotation from Ps 22:2 is the lamentation of a suffering person. Jesus comes across as a man who dies a lonely death, deserted even by God. This end is very far removed from the majestic opening words about "Jesus Christ, Son of God." In Mark's Gospel, Jesus dies a humbled and lonely death, but nevertheless it is this man who is recognized by the Roman centurion: "Truly this man was God's Son!" (Mark 15:39).

In a similarly paradoxical way Mark writes about the women who find the empty tomb (Mark 16:1–8). In the story of the crucifixion and burial of Jesus, the women who had followed him from Galilee, come across as courageous. They witness the crucifixion and watch to see where Jesus is buried, and the next day they come to the tomb to anoint his body. In this way, they fulfill their obligations as women at a burial. When they come to the tomb, they do not find Jesus; instead, they meet a young man (an angel?) who tells them that Jesus has been raised. He reminds them that Jesus had said that he would meet them again in Galilee. The women do not encounter the Risen Jesus; instead, they are pointed to the words of Jesus. The last words of Mark's Gospel are depressing: "So they went out and fled from the tomb, for terror and amazement had seized them; and they said nothing to anyone, for they were afraid" (Mark 16:8). What could be the meaning of ending the memories of Jesus in such an abrupt way? Since it was a story where first the disciples and then the women failed, did Mark want to impress upon his audience their responsibility for spreading the memory of Jesus? Now it depended upon the audience if the message of the resurrection of Jesus and the memories of his deeds and words were to be handed on.

Not only modern readers but also early readers of Mark's Gospel were perplexed at this strange ending. At some later time, an ending parallel to those in Matthew and Luke was added, with stories of how Jesus appeared to Mary Magdalene and two other disciples, and of Jesus' commissioning his disciples.

Jewish faith (2 Macc 4; 4 Macc 16–18).

Matthew: A Teacher like Moses?

Tension persists in the portrayal of Jesus across Matthew's Gospel. Throughout most of the narrative Jesus is a teacher for the Jews; however, in some instances, a picture of Jesus as a universal teacher for the future comes through. The gospel ends with Jesus' commission to his disciples after his resurrection: "All authority in heaven and on earth has been given to me. Go therefore and make disciples of all nations" (Matt 28:18–19). The Christ followers confess a Jesus who is lord of the world, not merely a Messiah for the Jews, but a lord "of all nations."

This appears to contrast with the figure of Jesus, whom Matthew portrays in his gospel as a Jewish insider. This Jesus tells his disciples, "Go nowhere among the Gentiles, and enter no town of the Samaritans, but go rather to the lost sheep of the house of Israel" (Matt 10:5–6). Likewise, he says that he has not come to break with Jewish faith: "Do not think that I have come to abolish the law or the prophets; I have come not to abolish but to fulfill" (Matt 5:17). However, Jesus also gives a sharp criticism of Jewish interpretations of the Law, and establishes his own alternative: "But I say to you . . ." (Matt 5:17–48). Moreover, he crassly criticizes the Jewish leaders when he says they themselves do not follow the Law that they proclaim (Matt 23).

Who are Jesus' addressees in Matthew's Gospel? In his many speeches in the gospel, he seems to address a group that is gathered around him. They are part of the larger Jewish community, but we also get the impression that they are a group of their own, the beginning of a new community on their way to becoming "all nations."[23] This is a complicated picture, so we must read with great attention.

A Biography of "a Great Man"

Matthew follows to a great degree the structure of Mark's Gospel, but he puts more emphasis on Jesus' sayings and on Jesus as a teacher and interpreter of the will of God. Matthew shares much of this material with Luke; it probably comes from the same source, Q. There is one major difference, however. In Luke, this material is spread over large parts of the gospel, but Matthew has combined many of the sayings of Jesus into long speeches; among these, the Sermon on the Mount, Matthew 5–7, is best known. What probably began as many memories of individual Jesus sayings Matthew has shaped into an account of Jesus marked by a number of long speeches. In

23. Stanton, *Gospels and Jesus*, 75–76.

this way, the speeches form a structural element of Matthew's Gospel, parallel to the narrative and chronological sections: the speeches appear in Matt 5–7; 10; 13; 18; and 23–25.[24] Because of these speeches, and in particular the Sermon on the Mount, many scholars have suggested that Matthew wanted to present Jesus as "the New Moses."[25]

In addition to the presence of speeches, Matthew's Gospel differs from Mark's in terms of the elements Matthew included in his Life of Jesus. Greek and Roman biographies often included stories about the birth, childhood, and youth of the protagonist. Biographies of great men often included supernatural events at their births, and in their childhood and youth, education provided the basis for their good character. It was common to narrate how the hero fulfilled prophecies about himself, that he interpreted holy traditions, and that the gods looked upon him with favor. The Roman poet Vergil, for instance, wrote of Augustus that he would save Rome from the sins of their fathers and initiate a period of peace.

It is this type of biography that Matthew writes about Jesus. He starts with the genealogy of Jesus, which takes him all the way back to David and Abraham (Matt 1:1–17). Thus, Jesus' status is secured: he is the heir of Israel's royal family, and he is descended from the ancestor of the people. Compared to Mark's abrupt ending of his gospel, Matthew has added several stories of how Jesus appears to his disciples after the resurrection, the last of which includes the commission to preach to "all nations." These additions not only make Matthew's Gospel much longer than Mark's (Matthew has twenty-eight chapters compared to Mark's sixteen), but they also give it a different character. Mark, too, speaks of Jesus as teacher, but he gives very little information about what Jesus actually taught. In Matthew's Gospel, however, Jesus' teaching contributes much to the understanding of who Jesus is.

A ROYAL BIRTH

The birth narrative serves to legitimate the authority of Jesus already from the beginning of the gospel. The narrative is told from the perspective of Joseph and reflects a masculine culture. It starts with Joseph's wounded honor; he learns that Mary, to whom he is engaged, is expecting a child, and that he is not the father (Matt 1:18–19). Allegations that Jesus was an illegitimate child may have led Matthew to explicitly mention the dubious circumstances surrounding Jesus' birth—and then to refute the speculation.

24. Matthew has created a common structure by ending all speeches by Jesus with "Now when Jesus had finished saying these things," Matt 7:28; 11:1;13:53; 19:1; 26:1.

25. Allison, *New Moses*.

An angel intervenes with the message for Joseph that the conception has been caused by the Holy Spirit. Angels play an important role in the birth narrative in Matthew 1–2; they appear at all important junctures in the story and provide directions from God. For instance, the angel gives Joseph the name of the child: "You are to name him Jesus, for he will save his people from their sins," (Matt 1:21)

The other structural element in Matthew's birth narrative is the frequent use of quotations from the Hebrew Bible. These serve as proof texts and have a fixed introduction: "All this took place to fulfill what had been spoken by the Lord through the prophet" (Matt 1:22). Thus, from the beginning everything that happens to Jesus is legitimized through the sacred authority of the Bible.

The next scene of the birth narrative places Jesus' birth in a political and royal context. Matthew places the birth of Jesus under the rule of Herod the Great—that is, before Herod's death in 4 BCE, and his birth represents a challenge to Herod's power over Israel. However, Matthew provides a wider perspective on Jesus' birth: the wise men from the east who come to pay homage to the child prefigure the end of the gospel when Jesus declares that all power and authority has been given to him.

Angels and dreams also determine the rest of the story of Jesus' childhood and youth. Joseph brings Mary and Jesus to Egypt, and avoids Herod's (historically undocumented) massacre of children in Bethlehem (Matt 2:13–18). After Herod's death, new dreams bring Joseph, Mary, and Jesus back, not to their hometown Bethlehem, but to Nazareth in Galilee. In this way, Matthew brings his story in line with what was historically known about Jesus, namely, that he was a Galilean.

Matthew has succeeded in establishing a memory of Jesus' birth and childhood by combining a genealogy with biblical proof-texts and a creative use of dreams to build a plausible story. All the steps in the history of Jesus are documented by quotations from the prophets: Jesus is the savior of his people, he is the heir of David and born in the town of David. Even his upbringing in Nazareth is documented with a (dubious) quotation from Scripture (Matt 2:23). Compared to Mark, Matthew has established a royal genealogy and a divine conception for Jesus. His Jesus has acquired all the honorable elements of a royal ideal. Matthew has established a "cultural memory" of Jesus' birth and childhood that forms a perfect introduction to his story of Jesus' adult life.

At about the same time, Luke wrote a story of the birth and youth of Jesus that also links him to Bethlehem and Nazareth, but that in other respects is very different. However, this story serves as a preparation for the story of Jesus' adult life in Luke's Gospel. These two different constructions of birth narratives illustrate how cultural memories are developed to serve specific purposes.

Family, Disciples, and Crowds

The infancy narrative in Matthew's Gospel confirmed Jesus' genealogy and his family relations with Mary as his mother and Joseph as his "social father." These family relations are reflected in subtle changes in the way people in Nazareth refer to his family, compared to the Markan version of the episode (Matt 13:55–56). In Mark, they refer to Jesus as "son of Mary," perhaps suggesting that his father was unknown, and as "the carpenter." In Matthew, people speak of him as "the carpenter's son" and they ask, "Is not his mother called Mary?" These subtle but important changes make Jesus a legitimate son of Joseph. Moreover, in Mark's Gospel Jesus' family reacts to accusations that Jesus "had gone out of his mind," when they "went out to restrain him" (Mark 3: 21). In Matthew's version of the story, they are merely "wanting to speak to him" (Matt 12:46). In this way, Matthew has diminished the conflict between Jesus and his family.

This holds true also for Jesus' relations to his disciples. Apart from their betrayal of Jesus in the last conflict in Jerusalem, in the first part of the gospel Matthew presents the disciples in a more positive light than Mark does. In stories where, according to Mark, they do not understand what Jesus tells them, Matthew explicitly says that they do understand him (Mark 4:11, 8:11; cf. Matt 13:16; 16:12; 17:13). The two stories of Jesus stilling the storm on the Lake Gennesaret are good examples of the contrast. In Mark, Jesus reproaches the disciples that they have no faith (Mark 4:40), and Mark comments that "their hearts were hardened" (Mark 6:52). In Matthew's version, the disciples are "of little faith" (Matt 8:26), and instead of reproaching Jesus that he does not care that they are about to perish (Mark 4:39), they cry out: "Lord, save us!" (Matt 8:25; 14:30). This is the *Kyrie eleison* used in liturgical invocations, with the divine name *Kyrios*. With this name, Matthew shows the meaning that he attributes to the story of the stilling of the storm. Jesus is no longer an unknown miracle worker: he is "the Lord," as he was known among Matthew's audience. The disciples are also rehabilitated after their failures and betrayals of Jesus. Their relationship is restored when they meet in Galilee after the resurrection and Jesus gives them a new commission to proclaim his message, this time "to all nations."

Matthew shares with Mark the stories of large crowds that come to hear and to follow Jesus. However, Matthew puts more emphasis on Jesus' compassion for people, for large crowds who have followed him into the wilderness, or for the sick (Matt 15:32; 9:36; 14:14; 20:34). Jesus responds positively to petitions for help from the sick (Matt 20:30–31), with one exception—the Canaanite woman who asks for help with her sick daughter (Matt 15:21–28). Jesus rejects her petition a total of three times before he yields and heals her daughter. Modern readers find it impossible to reconcile such a lack of compassion with our image of Jesus. Why did Matthew tell this story? Was Jesus' behavior in line with the way Jews typically acted toward non-Jews so that it was not considered a problem?

A Teacher with Authority

"Blessed are the poor in spirit, for theirs is the kingdom of heaven" (Matt 5:3) This is Jesus' first saying in the Sermon on the Mount; it is this speech that introduces Jesus' mission and functions as a programmatic statement. The speech is set in a biographical frame: Jesus wants to get away from the crowds and gathers his disciples around him to teach them. However, at the conclusion of the speech, it becomes clear that the crowds have listened in on his teaching and recognize that he has spoken with authority (Matt 7:28–29). In the speech itself, however, Jesus does not appear in person; we hear his voice. In the Beatitudes (Matt 5:3–12), it promises those who are poor, who mourn, who are meek, and who hunger and thirst for righteousness that they will be "blessed." The Beatitudes give the impression of being addressed to disciples who live under pressure in difficult situations, but who at the same time share the values that Jesus represents: peace, mercy, and righteousness.

The purpose of the Sermon on the Mount is to shape the lives of the disciples and a general audience by means of Jesus' interpretation of "the Law and the Prophets" (the two major parts of the Hebrew Bible). The Law and the Prophets were the authorities for Jewish life, and in Matt 5:17–20 Jesus confirms that he will uphold and fulfill them. However, the remaining sections of the Sermon make it clear that Jesus will interpret the Law with his own authority. His focus is not on the externals of the Law, but on its core—the will of God expressed in the double love command to love God and to love one's neighbor. This command is fulfilled in mercy and righteousness. These were the demands made of the disciples and followers of Jesus, in order to separate them from the scribes and the Pharisees, who met with Matthew's criticism. Jesus sums up his admonitions in the words "Be perfect, therefore, as your heavenly Father is perfect" (Matt 5:48). Matthew's Jesus is not concerned with details, but points out what is important: the golden rule (Matt 7:12), and "mercy, not sacrifice" (Matt 9:13; 12:7).

The Sermon on the Mount presupposes that the disciples of Jesus follow Jewish law, tradition, and praxis. However, other speeches in the gospel seem to imply that the followers of Jesus have founded their own fellowships within the Jewish community. In chapter 10, Jesus sends out his disciples to continue his own work: to proclaim the kingdom of heaven, to cure the sick and expel demons. Chapter 18 starts with an exchange between Jesus and his disciples. In response to the question from the disciples about who is the greatest in the kingdom of heaven, Jesus places a small child in front of them. Then the chapter moves from this specific story in the life of Jesus and his disciples to a more general address to Matthew's contemporary audience. Jesus says, "*Whoever* welcomes one such child," and he says, "*If any of you*" brings one of "those little ones" to stumble (Matt 18:5–6). The real-life audience of Matthew's Gospel appears to be a fellowship with some "little ones" who need special care. Another issue that requires a solution is the situation where one member sins against another member of the community (Matt 18:15–17). In response, Jesus tells the parable of the unforgiving servant, who, after the king has forgiven him a large debt, is not willing to forgive a fellow slave a small amount. In response, the king punishes him without mercy (Matt 18:21–35).

This is one of Jesus' kingdom parables,[26] and modern readers may feel uncomfortable at the mention of judgment in the kingdom. However, Matthew's audience would not have reacted negatively to Jesus speaking of judgment. The idea that God ruled over his kingdom included his power to judge; however, it was taken for granted that God was a righteous judge.[27] Matthew has gathered many kingdom parables in chapter 13, including the parable of an enemy who sows weeds in a field with good seed. In the explanation of the parable, the gathering at the harvest is an image of the judgment, when all evildoers will be thrown into "the furnace of fire" (Matt 13:42). There are similarities between these kingdom parables and the speeches and parables of Jesus about the end-time and the judgment (Matt 24–25). This speech starts with a prophecy of the destruction of the temple and the horrible afflictions at the end of time, before the Son of Man will appear and gather the elect ones. This speech is followed by several parables about judgment and the need to be prepared to face it.

One parable tells of a king who judges people according to their behavior toward him when he was deprived—hungry, thirsty, naked, or in prison (Matt 25:34–46). The righteous ones, who gave him food and clothing and

26. Matthew uses the term "kingdom of heaven," in order to avoid using the name of God.

27. Runesson, *Divine Wrath*.

visited him in prison, did not remember that they had done this for him. However, the king says to them, "Truly I tell you, just as you did it to one of the least of these who are members of my family, you did it to me" (Matt 25:40). Therefore, they entered into eternal life. The others, who had neglected to help "one of the least of these," went into eternal punishment, This king and judge must refer to Jesus; his identification with "the least of these" finds a parallel in his saying in Matt 18:5: "Whoever welcomes one such child in my name welcomes me."

This parable in Matt 25 illustrates the truth of the saying "the gospel in parable," namely, that a parable offers the gospel in miniature.[28] In the form of a story, a parable presents the same message to the poor and hungry that we find in the Sermon on the Mount, whether in the Beatitudes or in the demands for righteousness. Most scholars assume that many of the parables originated with Jesus himself. However, the authors of the Gospels have included them in their narratives and used them to express what they found most important in Jesus' message.

AMBIGUOUS MASCULINITY?

As a teacher, Matthew's Jesus expresses strong authority, and people praise him for teaching with power. There are good reasons for his audiences in Matthew to compare Jesus to Moses. Like Jesus after him, Moses too spoke from a mountain (Exod 19–20), and Moses too was rescued from persecution and death as an infant (Exod 2:1–10). Moreover, like Jesus after him, Moses too was called by God to save his people (Exod 3–4). Jesus' mission as a teacher is based on his royal birth within the genealogy of David. Finally, his authority is confirmed at the conclusion of the Matthew's Gospel, when the risen Jesus appears as the all-powerful one and the teacher for all nations.

However, other perspectives in Matthew's portrayal of Jesus might give a different impression, of a more ambiguous masculinity.[29] Jesus' describes himself as homeless (Matt 8:20); he has left his position in his household of origin; moreover, he has also urged his disciples to leave their households (Matt 4:18–22; 9:9; 19:27–29). There is a negative, almost ascetic attitude to family in several instances in the gospel. In what must be one of the strangest sayings of Jesus, he speaks of men who have "who have made themselves eunuchs for the sake of the kingdom of heaven" (Matt 19:12). Eunuchs were regarded as ambiguous, as questioning traditional masculine roles.

28. Donahue, *Gospel in Parable*.

29. Conway, *Behold the Man*, 12–25.

The dominant picture of Jesus in Matthew is that he fulfills the masculine ideals of Jewish tradition, which to a large degree correspond to Greco-Roman ideals. At the same time, however, Matthew's Jesus challenges these ideals with his critical remarks about family, and not least with expressions of ambiguous masculinities.

From Israel to All Nations

The Gospel of Matthew places Jesus fully within an Israelite tradition. Starting with his genealogy, it continues with quotations from the Law and the Prophets, which legitimize him as the one who "will save his people from their sins." The Sermon on the Mount introduces the main points of Jesus' teaching to his disciples and to Matthew's audience: their righteousness must exceed that of the scribes and the Pharisees. Jesus gives a ruthless criticism of the praxis of the scribes and the Pharisees in his long speech in Matt 23. They have only an external relationship to the law; they are full of hypocrisy, concerned with unimportant matters and neglecting "justice and mercy and faith" (Matt 23:23). These false teachers stand in the tradition of the Israelites who killed the prophets whom God sent to them. Jesus concludes with a lament over Jerusalem, and he speaks of himself as a hen that would gather her chicks under her wings, but "you were not willing!" (Matt 23:37). These are words filled with extreme disappointment; now there seems to be no alternative to abandoning Jerusalem and the temple to destruction (Matt 24).

When Jesus first sends out his disciples in Matthew, he tells them not to go to the Gentiles, but to the "lost sheep of the house of Israel" (Matt 10:5–6). Was it the conflicts with the scribes and the elders when Jesus arrived in Jerusalem that caused a drastic turnaround in Jesus' attitude to Israel in Matthew's Gospel? In the parable of the tenants who kill the son of the vineyard owner, the conflict escalates into a full crisis (Matt 21:33–41). The audience draws the conclusion that the vineyard owner will "bring those wretches to a wretched end . . . and he will rent the vineyard to other tenants." Jesus' applies the parable to God's relationship with his people and concludes, "that the kingdom of God will be taken away from you and given to a people who will produce its fruit" (Matt 21:41, 43). So that nobody should be in doubt, Matthew explicates that the scribes and the Pharisees realized that Jesus was speaking about them.

A further development in alienating Jesus from the Jewish people follows in the passion story. Matthew emphasizes that the Jews and their leaders are guilty of Jesus' death. He portrays Pontius Pilate as a weak man who is not strong enough to stand up to the pressure from the Jewish leaders to execute Jesus. He washes his hands and declares that he is innocent of the death of Jesus, whereupon Matthew gives this damning comment: "Then the people as a whole answered, 'His blood be on us and on our children!'" (Matt 27:25). Of course, "the people as a whole" are not present in Jerusalem; rather, those present are a mob that supports the temple leadership. Nevertheless, this saying had a fateful history. When the readership of Matthew's Gospel shifted and became primarily non-Jewish, then readers understood this statement as putting the blame for the death of Jesus upon the Jewish people throughout all generations.[30]

From Death to All Power

For the most part, Matthew follows Mark in the narrative of Jesus' suffering and death, up to Jesus' last words, "My God, my God, why have you forsaken me?" However, Matthew adds reports on dramatic events in nature at both the death and the resurrection of Jesus. At Jesus' death, Matthew says, "The earth shook, and the rocks were split. The tombs also were opened, and many bodies of the saints who had fallen asleep were raised" (Matt 27: 51–52). And likewise on Easter morning, Matthew comes close to describing the resurrection itself; there is a great earthquake and an angel descends from heaven and rolls away the stone before the tomb (Matt 28:2). In this way, Matthew makes heaven and earth participate in the Easter events.

Matthew is also aware that his story of the resurrection of Jesus was contested, that there existed "counterstories" among the Jews that the disciples came and took the body and then claimed that Jesus had been raised from the dead (Matt 27:62–66; 28:11–15). Thus, we have here two different, competing memories. It may be that Matthew tells the story of the Jewish leaders in order to discredit them; he portrays them as liars, and among his own audience his story would have more credibility than the Jewish counterstory.

Matthew can base his credibility on the concluding story in his gospel: Jesus appears to his disciples as risen, with "all authority in heaven and on earth." This is why he can command his disciples to go and "make disciples of all nations," teaching them "to obey everything that I have commanded you" (Matt 28:16–20). With this conclusion, Jesus commands become part of the message his disciples are to proclaim, with the same authority as "the Law and the Prophets." The gospel started as a story of Jesus who was born as a Jewish king; and it concludes with his universal kingdom. No

30. See chapter 6 and Cohen, *Christ Killers*, 17–32.

wonder that Matthew ends with a mission to "all nations." This makes it possible, and even plausible, that Matthew addresses his gospel to a group of Christ believers who have left Palestine and who live somewhere in the greater Roman Empire.

Luke: Prophet for the Poor[31]

Luke is the historian among the evangelists. His introduction to his gospel is similar to that used by Hellenistic history writers. He wants to write a history based on examination of sources, and he will write it from a holistic perspective (Luke 1:1–4). This introduction suggests that Luke wants to write a new "memory story" that is different from those of Mark and Matthew. Three aspects illustrate Luke's main purpose with his Life of Jesus.

First, Jesus' public career starts with a programmatic speech; its main point is "good news for the poor." Second, Jesus' life is put in the context of the Roman Empire: Jesus is born under Caesar Augustus. Third, Luke adds a central section to his gospel. In Mark's Gospel, Jesus and his disciples spend one chapter on the journey from Galilee to the passion in Jerusalem (Mark 11); Luke has extended it to ten chapters (Luke 9:52—19:28?). Thus, following Jesus on "the Journey to Jerusalem" is not only a geographical journey: it becomes the way for the disciples and for Luke's audience to learn what discipleship means.

A Programmatic Speech: Good News for the Poor

Luke introduces a totally new start to Jesus' public career. Mark and Matthew start with Jesus' proclamation that "the Kingdom of God has come near" and his calling of the first disciples. Luke, instead, starts with the story of how Jesus was rejected in his home town, Nazareth, following his programmatic speech about "good news for the poor" (Luke 4:16–30). This is an interesting case of how the same story can be used to create different memories. In Mark (6:1–6) and Matthew (13:53–58), Jesus' visit to Nazareth follows after a longer period of preaching and healing in different parts of Galilee. When he is rejected in Nazareth, Jesus comments (in Mark): "Prophets are not without honor, except in their hometown, and among their own kin, and in their own house" (Mark 6:4). Breaking with one's own household and village community was a serious matter. Luke has preserved this aspect, but he has given the story a totally new meaning. He turns the

---

31. For this section on Luke, see Moxnes, *Economy of the Kingdom*.

story into the very starting point for Jesus' public career. In antiquity, biographers often rendered speeches of what the protagonist typically would have said in a certain situation, without great concern for the historical accuracy of the speech. For the sermon in the synagogue in Nazareth, Luke chose a text from the prophet Isaiah:

> The Spirit of the Lord is upon me,
>
> > because he has anointed me
> >
> > to bring good news to the poor.
>
> He has sent me to proclaim release to the captives
>
> > and recovery of sight to the blind,
>
> to let the oppressed go free,
>
> > to proclaim the year of the Lord's favor
> >
> > (Isa 61:1–2; Luke 4:18–19).

Jesus gives a very short sermon: "Today this scripture has been fulfilled in your hearing" (Luke 4:21). Jesus' message is that with him starts the time of salvation that God had promised, and throughout the gospel, Luke emphasizes that Jesus is empowered by the Spirit of God. Moreover, his care for the poor, the sick, and the marginalized is a prominent feature in the gospel.

The word "poor" is of signal importance in Luke's Gospel; he uses it in a way that might remind us of a Marxist analysis of society (although Luke, of course, lived in a time that did not know Marxism), with a contrast between "rich" and "poor." For instance, unlike Matthew, Luke combines the Beatitudes for the poor with condemnations of the rich (Luke 6:20, 24). The parables and sayings of Jesus present a society dominated by the rich, supported by a Hellenistic ideology and value system. The Lukan Jesus represents a reversal of these values; he proclaims salvation for the poor and solidarity within the village community.

Initially, Jesus' sermon in Nazareth is well received by people in the synagogue, until he provokes their anger when he rejects their expectations that he should cure the sick also in his hometown. He says, "No prophet is accepted in the prophet's hometown" (Luke 4:24), and proceeds to tell of two instances of crises in which God helped only Gentiles, not Israelites. The first was a famine, when God sent the prophet Elijah to help a widow in Zarephath in Sidon, but not to any of the widows in Israel (Luke 4:25–26). In another instance, the prophet Elisah was sent to cleanse the Syrian Naaman from leprosy, although there were many lepers in Israel (Luke 4:27).

These stories make people in the synagogue angry, and they want to kill Jesus. With these stories Luke has escalated the conflict between Jesus and those in his hometown; the incident no longer represents only disappointment at a village son (who had created great expectations!). Luke turns it into a conflict over the boundaries of Jesus' mission and those of his followers in Luke's own time. Jesus' message of the God who sends prophets to Gentiles points forward to the stories of Paul's mission in Acts. When his proclamation is rejected in the synagogues, Paul turns to the Gentiles (Acts 13:46). The programmatic sermon in Luke 4 announces that Jesus will direct his mission to the poor and the marginalized among the Jewish people, at the same time as it signals his care for the suffering outside these boundaries, among the non-Jews.

Savior and Bringer of Peace—Jesus, not Augustus

Like Matthew, Luke starts his gospel with the birth and childhood of Jesus; however, there are few similarities between their stories.[32] Jesus is descended from David; therefore, he must be born in Bethlehem. Furthermore, his mother and father are Mary and Joseph; apart from that, the stories are very different. In Matthew's story, the protagonists are King Herod and the three magi from the East; Luke, however, tells of Caesar Augustus and a group of poor shepherds. A miraculous birth was a common motif in Greco-Roman biographies; Luke follows that tradition and tells of the conception by the Holy Spirit. Luke's story clearly comes from a Jewish tradition; it is written in an archaizing style that reminds readers of the Septuagint, the Greek translation of the Hebrew Bible. In this Bible too are stories of miraculous births by barren women, whether the women are old, like Sarah (Gen 18), or young, like Hannah (1 Sam 1).

Unique to Luke, the nativity story is a double biography, not just of Jesus, but also of John the Baptist. He was an important figure in the life of Jesus in all the Gospels; however, theirs was also a problematic relationship. Did Jesus' baptism by John imply that Jesus became a disciple of John, so that John was his master? Both Matthew and John discussed this issue, and both reject the possibility that John the Baptist was the master (Matt 3: 14–15; John 1:19–34). However, Luke is the first to bring the discussion of the relationship between Jesus and John back to its very beginning, their births and childhoods (Luke 1:5–80). Thus, Luke emphasizes that already before he was born, John was subordinate to Jesus (Luke 1:41–44).

32. For a comparison, see Brown, *Birth of the Messiah*.

At one level, the story of Joseph and Mary and of Jesus' birth and up-bringing is a story of a Jewish household that was obedient to the require-ments of the Law concerning circumcision, offerings in the temple, and pilgrimages to Jerusalem. At another level, this story told of an unusual birth and an unusual family. Messages from angels and canticles similar to the Psalms of David provided interpretations of the events: Jesus is to inherit the throne of David and be a king like him. God himself will provide for him, and he is to be called "Son of the Highest" and "Son of God" (Luke 1:30–35). These expressions were used of the kings of Israel, for instance in the Psalms; however, they could also be used of individuals. For instance, when Jesus was in the temple when he was twelve years old, he said, "I must be in my Father's house" (Luke 2: 49). This is an ideal story that explains that already from his childhood, Jesus was conscious of his special relationship to God. Mary too gives an interpretation of the life of Jesus in the Magnificat. She praises God, who reverses the relations between the powerful and the poor (Luke 1:51–53), and points towards Jesus' programmatic sermon in the synagogue in Nazareth, that he is to bring "good news to the poor."

To inherit the kingdom of David, Jesus must be born in the hometown of David, Bethlehem. It was Joseph, Jesus' social father, who was a descen-dant of David and who ensured that the birth took place in Bethlehem. This story cannot be historically verified; however, a census by the governor Quirinius in Syria did take place several years after the death of Herod the Great, during whose reign Matthew places the birth of Jesus. What is impor-tant, however, is that Luke makes use of memories of censuses imposed by Caesar Augustus in order to place Jesus in the context of world politics. The message of the angel to the shepherds is that now is born a "Savior, who is the Messiah, the Lord," who brings God's peace (Luke 2:12, 14).

How would Luke's audience understand the message of Jesus as a sav-ior who would bring peace? Luke wrote his story as a Hellenistic historian who knew both Greco-Roman and Jewish culture and literature. In Rome in the first century, "savior" was a much-used designation for the emperor, to describe his superior power and authority.[33] Augustus, for instance, was praised as "the Savior of the Common Race of Men."[34] He received this and similar titles on the basis of his victories in war; he was victorious over the enemies of Rome, and established peace and security for Rome and the inhabitants of the Roman Empire. Peace was therefore associated with warfare, and implied an absence of war. Augustus was very successful in

33. Seo, *Luke's Jesus*, 116–30.

34. Inscription in Halicarnassus in Asia Minor (quoted in Winter, *Divine Honours*, 40).

establishing peace through warfare; he was praised for having established the Pax Romana, and this was the reason for his Savior title.

When Luke speaks of Jesus as "Savior" (Luke 2:11; Acts 5:31; 13:23), his audience will have associated that title with the emperor. Thus, Luke may have adapted his message to the ideology of the Roman Empire and the expression of masculine power in the title. Another possibility is that Luke used the title Savior for Jesus in order to criticize its Roman use, as a protest against the dominant culture. Roman senators and powerful men proclaimed the Roman emperor; in Luke's story, poor shepherds receive the message of Jesus as Savior.[35] Moreover, in contrast to the emperor, Jesus is not victorious over his opponents by means of violence. When he was tempted by the devil in the desert, he triumphs by the word of God. The Lukan Jesus is countercultural; he rejects the use of violence in confrontations (Luke 9:52–56; 22:51); it is with peaceful means that he creates peace. Most explicitly, Jesus shows his nonviolent attitude in his saying about loving one's enemies (Luke 6:27–30).

A Double Message for Women

Many aspects in the birth narrative in Luke 1–2 point towards the main part of the gospel. One of them concerns the role that women play in the narrative. In contrast to Matthew, where Joseph is the main protagonist in the birth narrative, in Luke Mary plays the main part. She receives the message from the angel Gabriel; she is obedient to the message, and she sings a song of praise to God as the protector of the poor (Magnificat, Luke 1:46–55). Twice Luke says that "Mary treasured all these words and pondered them in her heart" (Luke 2:19, 51). Thus, Mary is portrayed as a role model for all believers. Consequently, the conflict between Jesus and his mother and his siblings, which was so strong in Mark's Gospel, is toned down by Luke (Luke 8:19–21). Luke gives his readers insight into the women's world, separate from that of men, when he describes the meeting between Mary and her relative, Elizabeth, the mother of John the Baptist (Luke 1:39–45).

In is in Luke's Gospel that Jesus has most contact with women; they support him and show him hospitality (Luke 8:1–3; 10:38–42). In several passages, Luke points to women as good examples of self-sacrifice (Luke 21:1–4) and love (Luke 7:36–50). In Luke's stories, Jesus is more open towards women than was common in a society as segregated by gender as Jewish society in the first century. However, despite a generally positive view of women, Luke presents them as those who serve, not as leaders for the

35. Brown, *Birth of the Messiah*, 420–21.

community.[36] It is only at the very end of the gospel, in the narrative of the women who come to visit the tomb of Jesus, that they become witnesses of the resurrection. However, when they bring their message to the male disciples, these describe their message as "idle talk," and they do not believe the women (Luke 24:11).

The Kingdom of God as Household

The kingdom of God in the proclamation of Jesus in Luke's Gospel signals what we, in modern terminology, would speak of as a new economic world order. "Good news for the poor" implies a break with social structures and with an economic system that threatens the cohesion of fellowship in village communities in Galilee. The word *economy* originates from the Greek *oikonomia*, from *oikos* ("house"), and carries the meaning of keeping a house, or larger units like towns and cities, in order. To be poor was not only a matter of money; it meant to be at the bottom of or outside of the household and community. Many such marginalized groups are named in the quotation fro Isaiah that precedes Jesus' sermon (Luke 4:16–18): the poor, the captives, the blind, and the oppressed. In Luke's stories of village life, members of these groups make appearances as sick, as demon-possessed, or as tax collectors and sinners.

Jesus' proclamation of good news for the poor is at the same time a criticism of the rich. Luke combines the Beatitudes to the poor with woes to the rich, who have already received their consolation (Luke 6:20–26). The economic rationale was that if somebody had more than others, the person with more had taken it from someone else—for instance by exhortation on the part of soldiers and toll collectors (Luke 3:12–14; 19:8). The idea was that the economy was of a limited size, like a cake. If somebody took a large share, there was less to divide among the others who were left. The parable of the rich man and Lazarus illustrates this mentality (Luke 16:19–25). The story gives an example of the contrast between the beatitude "Blessed are you who are hungry now, for you will be filled," and the woe, "Woe to you who are full now, for you will be hungry" (Luke 6: 21, 25). Wealth showed itself in meals, feasts, and hospitality (Luke 12:19; 16:19). The rich shared their wealth through reciprocity with other rich people, so that they kept their wealth within their own circles.

Luke's Jesus describes these social and economic exchanges in terms that Greeks used to describe the exchange economy based on reciprocity between equals:

36. Seim, *Double Message.*

> When you give a luncheon or a dinner, do not invite your friends
> or your brothers or your relatives or rich neighbors, in case they
> may invite you in return, and you would be repaid. But when
> you give a banquet, invite the poor, the crippled, the lame, and
> the blind. And you will be blessed, because they cannot repay
> you, for you will be repaid at the resurrection of the righteous.
> (Luke 14:12–14)

Here, Jesus criticizes the typical forms of social relations within Hellenistic culture; instead he proposes as an alternative "the economy of the kingdom." This is a social economy based on giving without expectations of return. Jesus develops a similar argument in the Sermon on the Plain. In the exhortation to love one's enemies, he adds "do good, and lend, expecting nothing in return." This type of behavior will earn a great reward by God, because he is kind even to the ungrateful and the wicked! (Luke 6:31–36).

Jesus as Storyteller

Luke uses various literary forms to express Jesus' message to the poor: sayings, parables and biographical stories of Jesus' encounters with people. Where the Matthean Jesus is a teacher who speaks with authority, the Lukan Jesus is a storyteller who tells parables. Luke has many more parables than the other Gospels, and some of the best-known ones are found only in Luke: the parables of the good Samaritan (10:25–37), the rich fool (12:16–21), the father and his two sons (15:11–32), the rich man and Lazarus (16:19–31), and the Pharisee and the tax collector (18:9–14). These parables are stories have rhetorical heft: they tell dramatic events, feature exquisite characters, and include artistic details. Often they take surprising turns, challenging the status quo (what is taken for granted) and establishing an alternative to the present world order.[37]

Parables often follow up on a dialogue or a discussion between Jesus and some scribes or Pharisees. In one instance, when they have criticized Jesus because he eats with sinners, he tells them three parables, among them the parable of the father and his two sons (Luke 15:11–32). Most modern readers of this parable have focused on the relationship between the father and the younger son (the prodigal son), who spent his inheritance in "a distant country," but who, against all expectations, was met with his father's mercy (Luke 15:11–24). People in Luke's audience, however, may have been just as concerned with the relationship between the father and the elder son in the last part of the parable (Luke 15:25–31). He had met

37. Crossan, *In Parables*, 52–76.

every expectation of an obedient son, without receiving any reward, and now he was asked to participate in the celebration his father held for his wasteful, disobedient brother. Would he participate, and so accept his father's boundless generosity? The parable ends before we know the answer, and that may be on purpose. Indirectly, Jesus addresses the audience and asks, How would you react? The immediate audience for the story were the scribes and the Pharisees. Would they accept that Jesus shared meals with sinners? In the next instance, the question was directed at Luke's audience, and ultimately, at all later readers.

The parable of the prodigal son and his brother addresses the question of how Jesus received "internal outsiders" in Israel. The parable of the good Samaritan raises the question of "external outsiders," the Samaritans. They were semi-Judeans; they had a separate temple and their own version of the Law. Luke has Jesus tell this parable in response to the question from a scribe, "Who is my neighbor?" The scribe had already quoted the double love commandment, of love toward the neighbor, so his question concerned who was included in this commandment (Luke 10:25–28). Then Jesus tells the parable of the man who fell into the hands of robbers, and the parable turns the expectations of obedience to the law upside down. A priest and a Levite pass him by, before the despised Samaritan enters and shows himself to be the exemplary helper. Jesus does not offer an interpretation of the parable, but asks the scribe: "Which of these three, do you think, was a neighbor to the man who fell into the hands of the robbers?" (Luke 10:37). The scribe must, of course, answer, "The one who showed him mercy." Thus, with this parable Jesus has turned the scribe's question around—from Who is my neighbor? to Am I a good neighbor? The self-confidence of the scribe, who was satisfied that he fulfilled the requirements of his religion, is challenged, and that by a Samaritan. There is almost something Socratic about Jesus in the way Luke has combined dialogues with parables; they challenge the hearer—or reader—to examine oneself, and to confront one's prejudices.

On the Way to Jerusalem

The third structural element that Luke has introduced in his gospel, in contrast to Mark's structure, is the long journey to Jerusalem. With short intervals, in chapters 8, 9, and 10 of Mark Jesus announces three consecutive predictions of his suffering and death in Jerusalem, but the journey itself fills only chapter 10. Luke, too, has these three predictions; however, between the second (9:43–45) and the third (18:31–34), he has introduced a total of ten chapters on Jesus' journey with his disciples from Galilee to Jerusalem. It has a solemn beginning, "When the days drew near for him to be taken up, he set his face to go to Jerusalem" (Luke 9:51). This introduction announces that Jesus knows that the way to Jerusalem is a way toward suffering and death. At uneven intervals follow remarks that Jesus is on his way to Jerusalem (13:22; 17:11; 19:28), but Luke does not describe it as a continuous journey. The "way" toward Jerusalem is not so much a geographical distance as the "way" where the disciples follow Jesus. In Acts, the followers of Jesus are those who "belong to the Way" (Acts 9:2; 19:9). Since the leaders have the power to judge Jesus, Jerusalem is place that represents a threat to him. On the other hand, Jesus' triumphant entry into the city is a sign that he will conquer Jerusalem and the temple and establish a new form of rule.

Luke follows Mark and Matthew in the passion narrative, however, with some important additions. The first occurs at the Last Supper, and shows Luke as a Hellenistic history writer. The last item in Greco-Roman biographies often was a farewell meal and a farewell speech from the hero before he died. Here he speaks about his impending death and about the future; and he gives his friends advice about what they should do after his death. In Jesus' speech in Luke 22:24–38, he confronts his disciples and their ambitions; he raises criticism of kings and those in authority and the way they use their power. Jesus confers on his disciples authority to rule over Israel; he emphasizes, however, that the leaders must be like servants, and that they must be prepared for suffering.

In Luke's Gospel, Jesus suffers the death of a martyr. In the trial before Pontius Pilate, the governor three times declares that Jesus is innocent (Luke 22:4, 14–15, 22). Herod, the ruler of Galilee, whom Luke brought into the passion story, likewise declares Jesus' innocence. This verdict is repeated by one of the criminals who were crucified together with Jesus, as well as by the Roman centurion who witnessed his death (Luke 22:41, 44). Throughout the suffering and crucifixion, Jesus maintains his character: he shows compassion for the women who weep for him, for the soldiers who crucify him, and for the repentant criminal crucified with him (Luke 3:27–32, 34, 43). Jesus' last word on the cross is an expression of confidence in God, from Psalm 31:5, "Father, into your hands I commend my spirit" (Luke 23:46). During his passion, Jesus shows the same characteristics as he has shown throughout his life: compassion for women, for the marginalized and the poor; and a prayerful attitude to God.

Moments of Recognition

The resurrection narratives in Luke are not so much narratives of miracles, as of *memories*. The women at the tomb and the disciples are admonished to remember the sayings of Jesus and quotations from Scripture, and it is by remembering that they start believing. These stories are primarily memories of how the disciples came to believe that Jesus was raised from the dead. The stories are told in such a way that the audience may participate in the process towards this belief. Luke reminds his audience of Jesus' sayings and of the prophecies in Scripture. The two men at the tomb remind the women of what Jesus had said to them when he was in Galilee—that the Son of Man must be crucified, and then rise again on the third day. Luke reports: "Then they remembered his words," i.e., they remembered and believed (Luke 24:8).

The story of the two disciples who encountered Jesus, without recognizing him, on their way to Emmaus is the most detailed story of how the disciples came to belief in his resurrection (Luke 24:13–35). The disciples tell Jesus their memories of him, about how they had put their hope in him, and about their disappointment when he was crucified, and their confusion at the report from the women at the tomb (Luke 24:18–24). Jesus, who is still unknown to them, explains what Scripture says about the Messiah and his suffering before he is taken up into glory (Luke 24:25–27). This is an instance where we must say that Luke has created a memory; nobody has been able to find any evidence of such a prophecy in the Hebrew Scriptures.

It is only at the meal in Emmaus, when Jesus breaks bread, that the disciples recognize him. However, at that very moment Jesus vanishes. Then they remember that their hearts had been burning within them when Jesus had explained the Scriptures for them on the way (Luke 24:29–32). In Jerusalem, Jesus appears to the skeptical disciples and eats together with them. Most importantly, however, he "opened their minds to understand the Scriptures," and what they say about the Messiah (Luke 24:44–46). In contrast to Matthew, Luke does not embellish his story with miracles and signs in nature. Instead, he describes how skepticism and disbelief are overcome in ways that hearers or readers of the gospel might recognize. Luke reminds hearers of Jesus' sayings, and prophecies in the Scriptures that lead to memories and recognition. Such moments of recognition could happen when Christ believers gathered for readings and expositions of the Scriptures. Not least during the celebration of the sacred meal, they can share the experiences of the disciples at Emmaus and recognize Jesus when he breaks the bread.

The way Luke presents these stories makes me think that he is aware that faith in the resurrection is not based on indisputable proofs, but rather on recognition and memories of what Jesus has said, or of stories from the Scriptures. The ultimate admonition from Jesus to his disciples in Luke's Gospel is the command to proclaim conversion and forgiveness of sins "to all nations"; they must only await the Spirit that is promised to them (Luke 24:44–49). This conclusion points towards the future of Luke's story in the Acts of the Apostles and to the start of the mission from Jerusalem "to the ends of the earth" (Acts 1:8).

John: The Son from Heaven

Christ of Saint John of the Cross, the famous painting by the Spanish painter Salvador Dali, captures the main point of the presentation of Jesus in John's Gospel. The painting shows the crucified Jesus from above, looking down upon the world, majestically elevated above it. It illustrates John's main point: Jesus has come down from heaven, that is, from God.[38]

In the Gospel of John, the unique relationship between God and Jesus is expressed with the terms of "Father" and "Son." Jesus is always "from above," even when he is on earth. The gospel is characterized by the use of binary terms; on the one side, we find "from above," "heaven," and "light"; on the other side, "from below," "the world," and "darkness." There is actually only one topic in John's Gospel. The characters in the gospel as well as the audience are faced with one question: do you believe that Jesus is "from above," that he is sent by the Father to do his works? Their response to that question determines whether humans, originally "from below," may through faith in Christ begin abiding ("above," so to speak), with the Son in union with the Father.

---

38. For an introduction to John, see Culpepper, *Anatomy of the Fourth Gospel.*

Salvador Dali: *Christ of Saint John of the Cross* (1951).
Peter Barritt / Alamy Stock Photo. Used by permission.

In the Beginning was the Son

Biographies frequently described the birth of the hero and his extraordinary characteristics, often including a divine ancestry. In John's Gospel this element has a unique form; Jesus' ancestry is traced all the way back to creation. John's Gospel starts with the so-called Prologue: "In the beginning was the Word, and the Word was with God, and the Word was God" (John 1:1). This phrase refers back to the beginning of the creation story in Genesis 1: "In the beginning when God created . . ." By choosing the term "Word," John chose a Greek word, *logos*, that had a symbolic meaning both in Jewish theology and Greek philosophy. For Stoic philosophers, the "word" was the rational principle behind the very existence of the world. In the Hebrew Bible, "the Word of God" was the life-giving means through which God communicated with humans. A term related to "Word" was *wisdom*, which also expresses God's activity in creation. In Proverbs 8:22–31, Wisdom appears as an independent agent in the creation of the world.

John's Prologue makes a transition from creation to the human birth of Jesus; "And the Word became flesh and lived among us, and we have seen his glory, the glory as of a father's only son, full of grace and truth" (John 1:14). This human Jesus was the same as he who was present at creation; however, John does not make any references to Mary or a birth in Bethlehem. To place Jesus in the cosmic context of creation is a dramatic expansion of the importance and meaning attributed to Jesus, when compared to the Synoptic Gospels.

With this interpretation, John has established himself as the philosopher among the writers of the Gospels. In the Prologue, he introduces almost all of the main themes of the gospel, so that it becomes a prism through which to see the rest of the gospel. John's statement in 1:11–12 introduces the main plot of the gospel: "He came to what was his own, and his own people did not accept him. But to all who received him, who believed in his name, he gave power to become children of God." This comment expresses in a poetic form the conflict between Jesus and the Jewish leaders that is the driving force in the gospel. The Prologue concludes with the unity between Father and Son, which sums up John's understanding of Jesus: "No one has ever seen God. It is God the only Son, who is close to the Father's heart, who has made him known" (John 1:18).

A Minimalist Biography

How might John's audience have reacted to this memory story of Jesus? The question of whether or to what degree John knew or used the other, earlier gospels has been much discussed. We do not know if John's first readers knew Mark, Matthew, or Luke. If they did, John's Gospel must have come as a great surprise.

Granted, it follows the main structures of a biography: Jesus' public career takes up chapters 1–12; his discourses with his disciples follow in chapters 13–17, before the passion narrative and the resurrection and Jesus' appearances to the disciples in chapters 18–21. However, the gospel does not include the birth narratives, the temptation in the desert, the commissioning of the twelve disciples, or the story of the transfiguration. A few healing stories are included, but none of the exorcisms. Even more surprisingly, the parables of the kingdom of God with their pictures from nature and folklore are not included. In his speeches in Matthew and Luke, Jesus addresses many issues related to interpretation of the Law (e.g., marriage, family life, and relations between neighbors). In these speeches Jesus comes across as concerned about people and their everyday lives. The speeches in John's Gospel have a very different character. Although John records many speeches, they all either present Jesus himself or promise the presence and guidance of his Spirit to the disciples after he has left them. The structure and the form of the speeches are also different. The speeches and parables in the Synoptic Gospels create the impression that Jesus is an actively involved teacher who uses many images and a variety of expressions. The speeches in John appear to have the same form and the same theme; they appear to be more shaped by the author of the gospel than by memories of Jesus transmitted through oral narrators. There is very little progress in these sections of discourses and speeches; instead, they seem to move in a circle. The same themes and the same confrontations reappear with some modifications.

When John is so selective in what he chooses to include in his gospel, it must be because he has a specific purpose in telling his audience these memories. In the original ending of his gospel, John explains the purpose behind which of Jesus' signs he included: "these are written so that you may come to believe that Jesus is the Messiah, the Son of God, and that through believing you may have life in his name" (John 20:31). His contemporary situation determined the shape of John's memory narrative. This will be seen clearly when we look in more detail at how John shaped his memory of Jesus.

Time, Place, and People

John's Gospel presents memories of the life of Jesus; however, his biography is different from those in the other Gospels with regard to its time frame, its primary setting, and the people who surround Jesus. In a strong contrast with the Synoptic Gospels, which foreground a mission in Galilee and only at the end bring Jesus to Jerusalem, John's Gospel places Jesus in Jerusalem at the beginning of his public career (John 2:13–25). Moreover, it is during his first visit there that Jesus cleanses of the temple. (In the Synoptic Gospels, this provocation leads to Jesus' arrest and crucifixion.) But in Jon's Gospel, after Jesus' first pilgrimage to Jerusalem, he is constantly on the move between Jerusalem, Judea, Samaria, and Galilee. The festivals celebrated in the Temple in Jerusalem often determine the scenes of Jesus' activities. Jesus is a conscientious Jew who regularly goes to Jerusalem, especially for Passover.[39] John mentions a total of three times that Jesus goes to Jerusalem for Passover; consequently, John presupposes a three-year public mission for Jesus, in contrast to the one year in Mark's Gospel. Thus in John's Gospel, when Jesus comes to Jerusalem for his last Passover, he is already a well-known public figure, both among people at large (by "the crowds") and among the Jewish leadership.

Among the minor characters in the gospel, John introduces some who were previously unknown, and he gives new information about persons already known from the Synoptic Gospels. Mary, mother of Jesus, is present with him at the wedding in Cana (John 2:1–11), where Jesus appears to be critical of her. As the only witness, John tells that she is also present at the cross, together with the disciple "whom Jesus loved" (John 19:25–28). The brothers of Jesus take part in some episodes; however, they do not believe in him (John 7:1–9). The unmarried sisters Martha and Mary are known from Luke's Gospel; in John, they have a brother, Lazarus, whom Jesus raises from the dead (John 11:1–44). Nicodemus, one of the Jewish leaders, appears as a secret follower of Jesus in a nighttime conversation (John 3:1–16; 38–40), and he reappears together with Joseph of Arimathea to bury Jesus (John 19:38–42).

How does John portray Jesus and his emotions and human characteristics? Whereas the Synoptics, and especially Matthew, emphasize that Jesus showed compassion to people who were suffering or seemed to be lost, this is not the case in John's Gospel. Neither does John depict Jesus together with children. Only Martha, Mary, and Lazarus are singled out; John repeatedly says that Jesus "loved them" or "loved him" (John 11:3, 5,

---

39. The festivals described, are first and foremost Passover, 2:13; 6:4; 11:59; 12:4; Sukkoth (Tabernacles), 7:2; and Hanukkah (Dedication of the Temple), 10:22.

36). Among the disciples, the "disciple whom Jesus loved" has a special relationship to Jesus (John 13:23).

When they describe Jesus' activities in Galilee, Mark, Matthew, and Luke typically report that large crowds gather around him; they turn up outside the house where he lives, they follow him along the road, or they come to meet him when he enters a village. These stories create the impression that Jesus is well received in Galilee, in contrast to the situation in Jerusalem when he arrives there at the end of his life. John's story, however, creates a different impression. He rarely tells about large crowds coming to Jesus. The festivals in Jerusalem are the settings for many of John's stories; and the festivals, not Jesus, are the reasons for large gatherings of people. The settings for Jesus' discourses are often Jerusalem and the temple area. Only rarely do people assemble because Jesus performs a healing or a sign, and the crowds that do gather around Jesus at festivals are often divided in their opinion of Jesus. Negative opinions of some in the crowds may reflect objections that believers in Christ during John's time actually encountered. Yet John's community likely either themselves held or found support from viewpoints expressed by other members of divided crowds.

In John, the theme of Jesus' speeches and discourses is always the same: who is Jesus, and what is his relationship to God? Take, for example, the discussion that follows the miracle of Jesus' feeding a large crowd with a few loaves of bread and some small fish (John 6:1–15). Many in the crowd are provoked when Jesus says, "I am the bread of life," and identifies the bread of life with his own body, which he will give for the life of the world (John 6:41–65). Likewise, when Jesus says that he gives living water, that is, the Spirit (John 7:37–38), the result is a conflict in the crowd about whether Jesus might be the Messiah. Such splits in the crowd occur also in several other places in John's Gospel.[40]

Who Are the Jews in John's Gospel?

One group consistently has a negative opinion of Jesus—(almost) all the leaders of the people, the Pharisees, the high priests, and the Council members.[41] However, there is a problem with the vocabulary that John employs; it must have confused his original readers or hearers, and it certainly has created problem for modern readers of and commentators on his gospel. The problem is John's use of the word *Ioudaioi* ("Jews" or "Judeans").[42] Mark, Matthew,

40. John 7:11–13; 25–31; 8:48; 10:19–21.

41. John 7:32; 45–52; 8:13; 9:13–17; 11:45–54.

42. Reinhartz, "Jews," 126–28. For historical reasons, the translation "Judeans," i.e.

and Luke use it only a few times each; John, in contrast, uses *Ioudaioi* seventy times, and mostly with a negative connotation.[43] "The Jews" are responsible for opposition to Jesus that gradually increases from chapter 5 until the passion narrative. The "Jews" make plans to kill Jesus (John 5:18; 7:19; 11:53), and they want to stone him (John 10:31). These same rejections and plans are attributed to the leaders of the people; therefore, the most probable solution is that "the Jews" refers to these leaders. When Jesus is brought before Pilate, Mark, Matthew, and Luke distinguish between the leaders of the people who voice the accusations against Jesus, and the crowd who cries, "Crucify!" John, however, does not make this distinction; they are all "the Jews" (John 18:31; 19:12). Since the crowd most likely is a mob of clients and dependents of temple leaders, it is understandable that John speaks of "the Jews," meaning the leaders and their clients.

Although John's Gospel can be understood by interpreting his use of *Ioudaioi* historically (as has been done above), another path to understanding comes through examining John's rhetoric within the symbolic world of the gospel.[44] Binary oppositions characterize this symbolic world; it is divided into light or darkness, into heaven and the world, and by the acceptance or rejection of Jesus. The *Ioudaioi* belong on the negative side in this cosmology, so that there is a parallel between their role in John's symbolic world and their role in a historical understanding of the gospel. John's use of *Ioudaioi* thus remains complex.

We can try to explain John's intentions when using the term "the Jews"; it is another matter how John's audience—not to speak of later audiences—might have understood "the Jews." It is possible that John wrote his gospel at a time when Christ believers separated or were excluded from synagogues (John 9:22; 16:2). Increasingly more and more members of the Christ groups were non-Jews, and the social distance between Christians and Jews increased. As a consequence, Jews increasingly became the "others"; as a result, "the Jews" took on the meaning of all Jews, in all periods. Therefore John's accusations against "the Jews" became dangerous; that Jews were "Christ killers" became a common viewpoint in Europe during the Middle Ages.[45]

"the people of Judea," may be more accurate; however, "Jews" are more commonly understood, so I shall use that.

43. Reinhartz, "Jews," 123–24.

44. Reinhartz, "Jews," 125–30.

45. Cohen, *Christ Killers*.

The Son Makes the Father Known

In John's Gospel, John the Baptist is the first to confess who Jesus is: "Here is the Lamb of God who takes away the sin of the world!" and "This is the Son of God" (John 1:29, 34). The first disciples too, almost before they have met him, confess that Jesus is the Messiah, the Son of God and the King of Israel (John 1:35–51). They all confer titles of honor from the history of Israel upon Jesus. These titles appear throughout the gospel, and they do in fact sum up the gospel's conclusion: John's goal is that readers "come to believe that Jesus is the Messiah, the Son of God (John 20:31). It is not these titles, however, that are most important when John speaks of the relationship between Jesus and God. The most pervasive terminology is that of Father and Son. The father-son relationship was the strongest family relationship in Greco-Roman and Jewish cultures in antiquity.[46] The son was like the father: he represented the father and could undertake responsibilities on behalf of his father. Since this was part of the cultural context, John's audience would have recognized the implications of Israel's God and Jesus enjoying a father-son relationship.

It is the known assumptions of a father-son relationship that John makes Jesus employ in his defense against his opponents who accuse him of calling God his father and of making himself equal to God (John 5:18; 10:33). Jesus defends himself by claiming that he does the works of God, and that these can be recognized as the works of God since they provide life. At the same time, however, John rejects the accusation that this implies that Jesus makes himself like God. Jesus points to a central aspect of the father-son relationship: a son does not act on his own; he is *sent* by his father. The son does the works that his father has shown him; therefore, they are the same as those his father does. In the same manner, when Jesus speaks, he does not speak on his own initiative; his father has commanded him what to say (John 12:49). Thus, Jesus sums up the first part of John's Gospel when he says, "whoever sees me sees him who sent me" (John 12:45).

On the basis of his father-son relationship to God, Jesus criticizes the Jews and their claims to a special relationship with God. In response to accusations that Jesus commits blasphemy, Jesus accuses the Jews of having the devil, not God, as their father. They do not listen when Jesus speaks the words of God to them, because they are not of God. To modern readers, chapter 8 in John's Gospel comes across as a brutal verbal battle; it is an example of a type of exchange well known from so-called honor-shame societies: the exchange

---

46. Murray, "Elite Father and Son Relationships."

of challenge and riposte.[47] It is a competition to gain honor and recognition, and to avoid losing face. John's audience would have known this cultural context, so they would not have been so shocked as many modern readers are by Jesus' entering into this form of exchange. (Still today there are cultures where these forms of verbal battle are acceptable.)

Another characteristic of how John's Jesus speaks of himself is that he applies to himself terms that the Hebrew Bible reserved for God. When God commissions Moses at the burning bush to bring the Israelites out of Egypt, Moses asks God by what name God should be called by the Israelites. God responds: "I AM WHO I AM" (Exod 3:14). Jesus adopts the formula "I am" and combines it with "light," "bread," and "water." These are the most important symbols in John's Gospel, and are frequently repeated. "Light" appears first in the Prologue; it is combined with "life" and contrasted with "darkness" and "death." When Jesus introduces himself as "light" (John 9:5), the significance of this symbol is expressed in the story of Jesus' healing a blind man and the subsequent controversy with the Pharisees. As the "Light," Jesus makes it possible for the blind man to see, to enter into the light from darkness, and that makes it possible for the blind man to believe in Jesus. The Pharisees, who criticize Jesus' healing on a Sabbath, claim to see, but Jesus declared that they are blind (John 9:39–41). Thus, physical eyesight becomes a sign of "seeing," like believing. In a similar way, the story of the feeding of the multitudes in the desert leads into Jesus' discourse about himself as the true "bread of life" (John 6). This discourse is also part of the controversy with "the Jews" over the true meaning of Israelite traditions, in this case the miracle of manna during the Israelites' forty years in the desert. Jesus proclaims that he is the true bread (i.e., manna) from heaven that gives eternal life.

In a dry Mediterranean landscape, water was an obvious symbol for life, and it occurs several times in John's Gospel. Water provided the occasion for Jesus' dialogue with a Samaritan woman at the well. This dialogue too centers on the association between water as a life-giving source and the "living water" that Jesus will give, as a source of eternal life. Water becomes a symbol of new life through the Spirit, and of spiritual worship (John 4:7–26).

In John's Gospel light, water, and bread are symbols of how Jesus does God's work to give life. It is significant that these symbols are so corporeal; they are what people need in order to live. John reminds his audience that light, water, and bread are means by which the Father and the Son support human, physical life, at the same time as they are symbols of eternal life.

---

47. Moxnes, "Honor and Shame."

How Do You Come to Believe?

John's Gospel has several stories of individuals who encounter Jesus and respond either with belief or with rejection. These figures become ideals or prototypes of different reactions to Jesus: Nicodemus, in chapter 3; the Samaritan woman in chapter 4; and the man born blind in chapter 9. These individuals come across as "real people," so that readers get involved in their interactions with Jesus. They are what literary theory calls "round figures"—not stereotypical but as people who in the course of the story undergo change and development. The individual narratives are similar to "recognition scenes" from classical Greek drama.[48] In these stories, the identity of the protagonist is hidden from those who encounter him, but through the story, they are brought from ignorance to knowledge. The spectators—or readers—know the identity of the protagonist; the question is whether the characters in the play will reach this insight.

Nicodemus, a Pharisee and a member of the Council, is an example of a figure who does not attain full faith. The dialogue between Jesus and Nicodemus also illustrates how John uses double meanings and misunderstandings. When Jesus tells Nicodemus that he must be born *anothen* (John 3:3), this is an example of double meaning. This Greek word can mean both "anew" and "from above." However, Nicodemus understands it to mean "anew, again," and he responds that another biological birth is impossible. He cannot understand that Jesus uses the word in the meaning "from above," that is, from heaven, and by the Spirit. Nicodemus remains at the stage of the physical, biological meaning, and cannot proceed to the heavenly meaning of Jesus and the true believers.

The Samaritan woman at the well, however, succeeds where Nicodemus failed. Socially and religiously, she is the antitype to Nicodemus: a woman of bad reputation and from a people despised by the Jews. However, she follows when Jesus leads her, gradually, to more insight. Initially, she (mis)understands Jesus' request for a drink to refer to water from the well, and she does not comprehend the meaning of the "living water" that Jesus will give her. Gradually, when Jesus reveals that he knows about the many men she has had, she recognizes that he is a prophet. When Jesus speaks to her about worshiping God in spirit and truth, regardless of place and temple, she realizes that he must be the Messiah. She has now reached insight, and becomes a missionary to her village.

The beggar born blind is a similar example of a man who gradually moves towards faith in Jesus. As he gains more and more of his sight, he also

---

48. Culpepper, *Gospel and Letters*, 72–86.

gains more and more faith, in contrast to the Pharisees, who are revealed as blind with regard to faith, even if they have full use of their eyesight.

These stories of individuals who become believers illustrate the words of the Prologue about becoming "children of God" (John 1:12). This does not happen by a natural birth, "of blood or of the will of the flesh or of the will of man," but "of God" (John 1:13). The contrast here is between a natural birth and a birth by the Spirit, similar to the contrast in the dialogue with Nicodemus. The Spirit is from heaven, and through the Spirit, believers can share in heaven, they become "from above." This emphasis upon the spiritual, in contrast to being "of the body," which is so characteristic of John's Gospel, made this gospel very popular in Christian groups of a gnostic type in antiquity.

Lifted up in Glory

The passion narrative and the story of the empty tomb are the part of the Life of Jesus where the Gospels are most similar. This suggests that there was a shared memory tradition behind these narratives. However, the evangelists bring—or shape—separate memories too. Jesus' last supper with his disciples introduces the passion narrative in John's Gospel (13:1–17). However, unlike in the Synoptic Gospels, in John's Gospel it is celebrated on an unspecified day "before the festival of the Passover," not on the day of the paschal meal itself. Thus, Jesus and his disciples do not celebrate a paschal meal; there are no formal blessings of the bread and the cup(s). Instead, Jesus performs a footwashing ritual for his disciples as an example of serving. Moreover, Jesus gives a long farewell address, which he introduces with what he terms "a new commandment": to love one another (John 13:31–35). The address continues in chapters 14–17; however, I have chosen to discuss it after the passion narrative, since it deals with the disciples and their life after Jesus has left them.

Jesus is a divine presence throughout the Gospel of John and is thus in full control of events in the passion narrative too. The Roman authorities have no power over him; they may crucify him, but he preserves his authority even on the cross. Jesus does not cry out to God in Gethsemane to be rescued from death. In John's Gospel, the garden is merely the place where Jesus is arrested while he is in full command of events (John 18:4–9). Jesus is not in the least subdued at the interrogation by the high priest, and he takes the leading role in his interrogation by Pontius Pilate about whether he is the king of the Jews. Pilate appears submissive in his dialogue with Jesus, and he is very weak in his attempts to convince the Jewish crowds to release Jesus instead of Barnabas (John 18:33–40). Jesus rejects Pilate's attempts to exercise power; he claims that Pilate has his power only "from above," that is, what God has granted him. Moreover, it becomes obvious that Pilate has no power of his own; the Jewish leaders cleverly play on his total dependence on the emperor (John 19:12).

In the brief story of Jesus on his way to Golgotha, John deletes any mention of Simon of Cyrene, who in the Synoptic Gospels is forced to carry the cross, presumably because Jesus is too weak to carry it. Not so in John's Gospel, which proudly asserts that Jesus was "carrying the cross by himself" (John 19:17). In contrast to the crucifixion scene in the Synoptic Gospels, in John Jesus is surrounded by his mother, Mary, and two other women, and the "disciple whom he loved." Jesus' final act of love is to entrust his mother and the disciple whom he loved to one another as mother and son (John 19:26–27). Moreover, Jesus does not die with a cry of fear and despair; rather, he utters a majestic "It is finished" (*tetelestai*, John 19:30) in the sense of "fulfilled" or "completed." The Greek word is the same in John 4:34 and 17:4, where Jesus speaks of fulfilling the works with which his Father had entrusted him. Jesus' death as "fulfilment" means that crucifixion also is Jesus' ascent to heaven, whence he came (John 3:13–14). To add to the symbolism of crucifixion, in John's reckoning, it took place on the very day when the Passover lamb was slaughtered. Within this symbolic universe, the crucified Jesus fulfills John the Baptist's prediction when John first met Jesus: "Here is the Lamb of God who takes away the sin of the world!" (John 1:29).

The story of the empty tomb in John is reduced to the bare minimum: there are no earthquakes, no angels, no group of women who have come to anoint Jesus' dead body. There is only an empty tomb, linen wrappings, and three bewildered disciples—Mary Magdalene, Peter, and the disciple whom Jesus loved. For Mary Magdalene, it is the voice and the words of Jesus that cause her to recognize him; and she receives his message to the disciples: "I am ascending to my Father and your Father, to my God and your God" (John 20:17).

This means that the message of the resurrection is part of the main theme of John's Gospel: Jesus was with God from the beginning; he descended to the world and ascended again to God (John 3:13; 6:62; 16:28). Careful readers of the gospel will recognize this theme in John's editorial comments at the beginning of the Passover narrative: Jesus knew that "his hour had come to depart from this world and go to the Father" (John 13:1). The disciples ought not to have been surprised at the empty tomb; however, it was only the disciple whom Jesus loved who "saw and believed;" the other disciples needed more signs in order to believe (John 20: 8, 19–25).

Do Not Let Your Hearts Be Troubled! A Future with Jesus

In his farewell speech in John 14–17, Jesus speaks to his disciples about their life after he has left them "to go to the Father." Its combination of speech and dialogue is a form that was developed in the later apocryphal, so-called "dialogue-Gospels."[49]

The speech starts with an encouragement not to be troubled. In this speech, the enemy is no longer "the Jews," as it was in the earlier parts of the Gospel, but "the world."[50] However, it appears to be the same or a similar force. Chapter 16 predicts that Jesus' disciples will be expelled from synagogues and will even be killed. It is difficult from these general threats to guess how Christ believers experienced this hate, and what social realities lay behind the fear that Jesus addresses in his farewell speech. We get the impression that there was an urgent fear among the disciples of being abandoned once Jesus had left them and was no longer physically among them.

In his speech, Jesus reminds his disciples that he has ascended to his Father, so he and the Father have reached a complete unity. This unity between the Father and the Son can also be established with the Christ believers, and between the believers (John 17:21–23). The basis of their unity is that they must keep the commandments God has given them through Jesus. However, in John's Gospel, Jesus does not exemplify these commands; they are all summed up in the one great commandment: to love (13:34–35; 14:15–26).

The criterion for love is to hold on to the words of Jesus and to remain in them. This entails more than just remembering the words of Jesus. Memory is a dynamic event; it is linked to the Spirit that Jesus has promised to send to his disciples. In John's Gospel the Spirit has a special form. In Greek it is called *parakletos*, and various attempts have been made to translate the word: "advocate," "intercessor," and "comforter" are three. However, when we look at the tasks of Spirit, they include to speak the words of Jesus and to remind the Christ followers of what Jesus has said. This gives John's way of speaking about the Spirit a different profile from other presentations of the Spirit in Christian antiquity. As a religious type, early Christianity was characterized by charismatic elements; Paul speaks of different gifts of the Spirit, including speaking in tongues. John's audiences no doubt also knew these forms of the Spirit's gifts. However, John chooses to speak of the gifts of the Spirit in a different way, in a way more strongly linked to the words of Jesus, to expressions of love—that is, to social and emotional relationships.

---

49. See below, 77–80.

50. John 14:17–18; 15:18–23; 16:25–33.

Four Memories of Jesus

We started by saying that the Gospels are memories of Jesus, and we have seen how the individual gospels shaped their memories of Jesus from their specific perspectives. The Synoptic Gospels base their structure on Mark's construction of a Life of Jesus; John, however, has a separate structure of the memories of Jesus. To summarize the results of comparing the memories of Jesus in these four Gospels, we will focus on the way they describe the death of Jesus. The passion narrative with the crucifixion of Jesus appears as the most stable and earliest established part of the memories of Jesus. Nevertheless, although each gospel includes a passion narrative, even within these narratives important differences appear between the separate gospels, especially in the last words of Christ on the cross.

Many will be surprised at this observation, since they know and remember a tradition of memories that bring together all of Jesus' sayings on the cross in a unit called "the Seven last words of Jesus on the Cross." This collection of the seven words of Jesus on the cross first appeared in devotional literature in the late Middle Ages. Words from the various gospels were brought together: one from Mark and Matthew, three from Luke, and three from John.[51] This collection was based on the idea that the passion narratives from all four Gospels could be combined into a single, coherent passion narrative.

The tradition of Jesus' seven last words on the cross became part of the shared cultural memory in Christian churches of many confessions, since Christ's words became part of the music for the passion period. The composition by Joseph Haydn from 1785 for the cathedral in Cadiz, a choral masterpiece, is probably the setting of Jesus' last words most performed today.[52] On the basis of this performance, it is easy to imagine that these seven words are part of a continuous story of what Jesus said on the cross; however, they are a composition of sayings from the four different Gospels.

---

51. The traditional order of the words are

  1. Luke 23:34: Father, forgive them; for they do not know what they are doing.

  2. Luke 23:43: Truly, I say to you, today you will be with me in Paradise."

  3. John 19:26–27: "Woman, here is your son." "Son, Here is your mother."

  4. Matthew 27:46 & Mark 15:34: My God, My God, why have you forsaken me?

  5. John 19:28: I am thirsty.

  6. John 19:30: It is finished

  7. Luke 23:46: Father, into your hands I commend my spirit.

52 Other compositions setting Jesus' seven words on the cross are, e.g., by Heinrich Schütz, 1645; César Franck, 1859; Sofia Gubaidulina, 1982; and James MacMillan, 1993.

This means that the various last words of Jesus are expressions of how each gospel understands his death, and of how it stands in the context of the totality of Jesus' life. In Mark, Jesus' last word is "My God, my God, why have you forsaken me?" (Mark 15:34). This saying is taken from a psalm of lament, Psalm 22:2, and is a desperate cry to God. Those who know this psalm will know that it concludes with an expression of confidence in God—that he will lend help; however, Jesus' word is one of Godforsakenness. This expression of despair comes at the end of Mark's description of a weak and passive Jesus. This interpretation of the last part of Jesus' passion was probably established early on; it was taken over by Matthew as well (Matt 27:46).

Jesus' last word in Luke 23:46, "Father, into your hands I commend my spirit," is taken from Ps 31:6, a psalm of lament over dangers from enemies, but with expressions of confidence and trust that God will redeem the psalmist. This last word shares similarities with other words of Jesus that are unique to Luke's Gospel. For instance, Jesus prays for the soldiers who have crucified him: "Father, forgive them; for they do not know what they are doing" (Luke 23:34). Moreover, even in Jesus' own death agony, he shows compassion for the criminal who repents: "today you will be with me in Paradise" (Luke 24:43). These words sum up Luke's perspective on Jesus throughout the gospel, starting with Luke's presentation of the start of Jesus' ministry: Jesus had God's spirit to proclaim good news to the poor, to the blind, to captives and to the oppressed (Luke 4:16–18).

In John's Gospel, Jesus' last word, "It is finished" (John 19:30), points to a central aspect of Jesus' works in John; Jesus finishes (that is, fulfills) the work of God that he is sent to perform.[53] This is part of John's description of Jesus throughout the gospel; it is summed up in Jesus' high priestly prayer: "I glorified you on earth by finishing the work that you gave me to do" (John 17:4). In John's Gospel, Jesus' crucifixion is at the same time his glorification; he is lifted up on the cross, towards God (cf. John 3:14). Accordingly, Jesus' death on the cross is not a failure; rather, it fulfills his life of doing the work of God.

It does not make sense to undertake a historical discussion of these different last words of Jesus in order to identify the oldest or most original. Rather, we should consider them as expressions of various memory traditions; the writers make Jesus himself express the meaning of his life in the moment of his death. These words combine the historical event of Jesus' execution with memories that bring forth the meanings attributed to his death—meanings that believers can identify with in their lives.

---

53. The Greek *tetelestai* can also be translated "It is accomplished," or "It is complete."

2

Growing Memories

The Apocryphal Jesus

THE GROWTH OF MEMORIES of Jesus did not end with the writing down of the original four Gospels in the last part of the first century. Rather, there were a great many new memories that were told and written down, many in the second century, but this process continued into the fifth and sixth centuries as well. These writings go by the name *apocryphal gospels*, and lately there has been much discussion of their role and importance in Early Christianity. For instance, Bart Ehrman, a recognized expert on the New Testament and Early Christianity, suggests that they represent "a lost Christianity" that was suppressed by bishops and church leaders who established the New Testament canon with the four Gospels.[1] He and many other scholars argue that this was a decision based on power, supported by Emperor Constantine. According to them, Christianity would have been very different if the apocryphal gospels had been included. This position has been strongly contested by conservative Evangelical scholars, who argue that the church did not freely choose which gospels to include, but accepted the four, now canonical, Gospels as Scripture.[2] Moreover, they argue that the apocryphal writings were not much used and therefore did not have the central importance that Ehrman and others ascribe to them.

There is something to be said for both sides in this debate. With regard to Ehrman's position, I think it is commonly recognized that there was a great diversity among early Christian groups, and different positions on Jesus. Many Jews who believed in Jesus as the Messiah understood him as a human being, and rejected the idea that he was divine. Writings by so-called Jewish

1. Ehrman, *Lost Christianities*, 159–80.
2. Moxnes, "History of the Canon."

Christians, such as the Gospel according to the Hebrews, were strongly criticized by bishops who were regarded as church authorities.

On the opposite side of the spectrum were groups who emphasized
the divinity of Jesus and who rejected his physical humanity. Such a priori-
tizing of the spiritual over the material world was common in antiquity; it
was part of a philosophical and religious system that included cosmology,
theology and anthropology. Such systems have been described as gnostic.
However, there is a discussion around whether Gnosticism existed as a
single cluster of beliefs and practices or whether Gnosticism influenced
tendencies of many Christian groups. Those who held that Jesus was both
divine and human became the strongest, and were to consider themselves
orthodox and the others heretics.

On the other side of the contemporary debate, it is correct to say that
there is less evidence for the use of the apocryphal gospels than for the use
of those that became part of the canon. However, there are obvious reasons
for this. Groups of Jewish Christians that composed what are called apocryphal gospels did not survive for very long, so their writings were no longer
copied; therefore they have disappeared and are only known through the
polemics of their opponents.

What Are the Apocryphal Gospels?

The word *apocryphal* for these contested writings had different meanings according to which side you took in the conflict. *Apocryphal* means
"hidden" or "secret," and the orthodox church authorities used the term
to give a negative meaning to these scriptures: they were not accepted
and were to be kept hidden. Many of these scriptures have disappeared,
and therefore we only know them from the writings of orthodox church
leaders. However, for the authors and users of these writings, *apocryphal*
had a positive meaning: they imparted a knowledge that was hidden from
outsiders—from ordinary Christians.

Because of these disputes, there never was a defined group of writings
with the name New Testament Apocrypha.[3] Moreover, a great variety of
writings are described by this term. In this chapter, I will discuss not all the
different forms of apocryphal writings adjacent to the New Testament,[4] but
only the apocryphal gospels. The term *apocryphal gospels* may be misleading;
for the most part, they do not belong to the same genre as the four (now

3. However, there is a fixed collection of writings called the Old Testament
Apocrypha.

4. There are also many apocryphal Acts of the Apostles.

canonical) Gospels, which give a full life of Jesus. Most of them are short and give only a fragment of the life of Jesus or a particular aspect of it. Their common denominator is that they are interpretations of, or make use of, narratives and traditions about Jesus. So far, we have discussed the theologically contested writings. However, the writing of new memories about Jesus was not only a result of theological conflicts; many of the stories in apocryphal gospels were popular narratives that played a central role in developing Christian spirituality in late antiquity and the Middle Ages.

There were many reasons why Christians wanted to know more about Jesus and his life. One reason was simple curiosity: people wanted to know more about Jesus and his family than the Gospels reported. Another reason had to do with interest in linking personal religious experiences to the history and life of Jesus. These are some reasons for the growth of a popular literature that both was religious in character and also served as entertainment. These writings do not give us new historical information about Jesus; rather, they offer retellings and embellishments of earlier stories. For this reason, many of the apocryphal gospels may be described as "legends."[5] However, this is a literary characterization only. From a social point of view, these narratives reflect the values of Christians and the meaning of Jesus for their lives in particular situations. Thus, this development illustrates one trend within memory studies, namely, the emphasis on how the present situation shapes memories.

Take the memories of Jesus' birth and his family background. New stories were told to fill in the gaps in the existing stories and to support faith in the miraculous aspect of his birth. Many felt a need to know more about Mary and Joseph: Who were they, and what was their history before Jesus? There was also a great gap in the history of Jesus between his birth and his emergence as a prophet as an adult. Likewise, in the passion narrative: what did Jesus do in the days between his crucifixion and his resurrection? However, these questions were more than a matter of ordinary curiosity; they were theologically significant. Was Jesus' birth really a miracle, or was he illegitimately conceived? What was the significance of Jesus' death on the cross? Moreover, did Jesus have miraculous powers to heal illnesses?

Responses from the apocryphal gospels to these questions varied; they reflected different social and cultural contexts. There were differences between Rome and Egypt, and even more differences between the culture of urban elites and the culture of ordinary people in peasant villages. For many, incantations and other forms of magic were believed to bring about healings and supernatural events. For others, physical objects, such as

5. See the subtitle of Elliott, *Apocryphal Jesus: Legends of the Early Church.*

clothes or other items that belonged to a holy person, were imbued with holiness and so were precious. These are examples of elements from the apocryphal gospels. The four canonical Gospels are quite reserved about such details, and they were primarily read aloud and heard in Christian common worship. Many of the stories in the apocryphal gospels, however, reflect a narrative culture and were probably read aloud and heard in social gatherings in households or in villages.

It is impossible to present all the apocryphal gospels in a short review, so I will concentrate on four groups of texts:[6]

1. Jesus' birth, his family and childhood: The Protevangelium of James, the Gospel of Pseudo-Matthew, the Arabic Infancy Gospel, the Infancy Gospel of Thomas.

2. Jesus' sayings and his appearance: The Gospel of Thomas, the Acts of John.

3. The death of Jesus and his descent to Hades: The Gospel of Peter, the Acts of John, the Gospel of Nicodemus.

4. Jesus' revelations to his disciples, before and after his death: The Gospel of Judas, the Gospel of Mary Magdalene.

Jesus' Birth, Family History, and Childhood

The histories of Jesus' birth and childhood have never been apocryphal in the sense that they were kept secret or were forbidden by church authorities. Quite the opposite, they were very popular at the time; they have been translated into many languages and are preserved in numerous manuscripts. They were very popular throughout antiquity and the Middle Ages and played an important role in the development of popular spirituality. In particular, they were an important source for Christian art in many churches.[7] These writings are tentatively dated to the last part of the second century. Of course, this is only an estimate, but clearly they represent early and developing traditions that continued in the following centuries.

Both the Protevangelium of James, from the end of the second century, and the much later Pseudo-Matthew build on the nativity narratives in the Gospels of Matthew and Luke, and they combine material from both into a new unity. However, before the beginning of the history of Jesus, the Protevangelium of James introduces the history of Mary and her

6. For the texts, see Ehrman and Plese, *The Apocryphal Gospels*.

7. Cartlidge and Elliott, *Art*.

parents, Joachim and Anna, giving an ideal portrait of Mary. Such praise of a person that includes the description of her family and her character was a characteristic aspect of ancient biographies. Joachim and Anna are described, on the analogy of Abraham and Sarah in the Bible, as too old to bear children. Accordingly, the birth of Mary is described as a miracle. Moreover, as a child she already shows a unique character and piety. Therefore, her parents commit her to the temple so that she will be brought up in purity and in the fear of God. The temple authorities commission Joseph, an elderly widower, with the responsibility to protect Mary. It is thus a very serious matter when Mary becomes pregnant. Only by drinking poisoned water from the priest and showing no ill effects from it are they able to clear themselves of the accusation that they had had sexual intercourse. Thus, Mary's miraculous conception of Jesus is defended. Moreover, Jesus' brothers and sisters, mentioned in Mark 6:3, are said to be the children of Joseph from his previous marriage.

The sexual purity of Mary, both before and after the birth of Jesus, is of great concern to the Protevangelium of James. This determines the additions the gospel makes to the nativity story in Luke. The birth of Jesus brings the world to a halt. Joseph walks into Bethlehem to secure the assistance of a midwife. She arrives, and after the birth of Jesus another woman, Salome, comes to the scene. Salome refuses to believe the story that the child is born by a woman who remains a virgin even after giving birth. She claims that she will not believe this without testing it herself. However, when she puts her hand into Mary's body, her arm withers, and she is healed only by touching the baby Jesus.

In its final form, the Gospel of Pseudo-Matthew is much later than the Protevanglium of James, perhaps as late as the seventh century, but it contains material that is much older. It follows the tendencies to elaborate the miraculous aspects of the birth of Jesus. However, an increasingly negative attitude to the Jews is a new element in Pseudo-Matthew. On their way to Bethlehem, Mary sees in a vision one people that weeps and one that rejoices. An angel explains that the people that weeps are the Jews, because they have abandoned God. The other people are the Gentiles, who rejoice since they have been brought near to God. They were now included in the promises to Abraham, that in his inheritance all peoples should be blessed. This explanation corresponds to an early anti-Jewish interpretation of the promise to Abraham—that it now applied only to Gentiles, not to the Jews.[8]

8. See Letter of Barnabas, 13.7.

A Combined Birth Narrative

A common trait in these retellings of the nativity of Jesus is that they combine the two separate narratives in Matthew and Luke. The story of Jesus' birth from the Protevangelium of James starts with Augustus's decree of a census from Luke's Gospel before it adds the miracle of unnatural stillness at Jesus' birth and the test of Mary's virginity. Then the narrative continues, a bit strained, with King Herod and the magi from the east, according to Matthew, without paying attention to the fact that Augustus and Herod represent different chronologies for the birth of Jesus. Pseudo-Matthew gives a shorter version of Matthew's narrative and adds from Luke's narrative the story of the shepherds who receive the message from the angels.

Thus, already from the end of the second century, a new narrative of the birth of Jesus combined elements from the two very different stories in Matthew and Luke. Theological interest in the miraculous birth of Jesus and popular veneration combined to establish a new tradition. The result was what we now consider "the cultural memory" of the birth of Jesus, which has shaped Christian tradition for centuries. Moreover, new memories continued to be added. One way to create new memories was to turn quotations from the Bible into real events. We can understand how this happened by looking at the birth narrative in Matthew's Gospel, which supports everything that happened to Jesus with quotations from Scripture. Pseudo-Matthew continues this practice when it describes how Mary carried the baby Jesus from the cave where he was born, into a stable and put him in a crib where he was worshiped by an ox and a donkey. Pseudo-Matthew adds that in this way the word by the prophet Isaiah was fulfilled, that "the ox knows its owner, and the donkey its master's crib" (Isa 1:3). This example of quotation shows how a passage from Scripture can be turned into historical reality, without a basis in the canonical birth stories from Matthew and Luke. With Pseudo-Matthew, the ox and donkey became a fixed feature in the now common birth narrative, visualized in Christian art and immortalized in the twelfth-century Latin hymn "Puer natus est in Bethlehem," with the stanza "The ox and ass in neighbouring stall, See in that Child the Lord of all. Alleluia."[9]

This combined nativity tradition gained an enormous popularity; the Protevangelium of James and the Gospel of the Pseudo-Matthew are transmitted through innumerable manuscripts and translations into many

---

9. There is an early relief showing a nativity scene with only the child and an ox and donkey, from Naxos, possibly fourth century. In the Byzantine and Christian museum, Athens.

languages in antiquity and the Middle Ages. It is also widely documented in art history.

The Infancy Gospel of Thomas

The purpose behind the Infancy Gospel of Thomas is to fill out the great lacuna in the history of the life of Jesus, between his birth and the story of him as a twelve-year-old in the temple. The writing consists of many short narratives of miracles that Jesus performs as a child. Other stories show how intelligent Jesus was, and how he put his teachers to shame and made it impossible for them to teach him anything. However, there is something very troubling about many of these stories. They portray Jesus as a very aggressive boy who uses his miraculous powers to kill other children if they cross him. Taken together, these aspects have made many scholars think that the Infancy Gospel of Thomas is a popular, folkloristic narrative, without any theological relevance.

Recently, however, the biblical scholar Reidar Aasgaard has made an interesting interpretation of the gospel and suggested a theological relevance of its stories.[10] Aasgaard argues that many aspects of the gospel can be understood in light of ideas about masculinity in antiquity. Part of being masculine is protecting and defending one's honor against challenges from others, even with force. Several of these stories make references to quotations from the canonical Gospels that confirm Jesus' divine rights. Especially interesting is Aasgaard's suggestion that the gospel is directed toward children. This, of course, cannot be proven, but it is a fascinating theory that the Infancy Gospel of Thomas is a narrative of how Jesus is both God and child.

The Infancy Gospel of Thomas probably dates from the mid-second century, and the world of the stories most likely reflects the values of a non-elite, village population. The gospel quickly became very popular, especially in the eastern parts of the Roman Empire, and it was translated into many languages.

10. Aasgaard, *Childhood of Jesus.*

Giotto: *The Life of Christ; The Flight into Egypt* (Assisi, 1310–1320)
Wikimedia Commons[11]

The Arabic Infancy Gospel

The Infancy narrative in Matthew briefly relates that an angel warns Joseph
to take refuge with Mary and Jesus in Egypt, to escape from the persecution by King Herod (Matt 2:13–15). No details are given about the sojourn
in Egypt; however, this barest of stories inspired many new memories.
Among these are stories of miracles that happened in Egypt, of fruits that
fell from palm trees and of springs that suddenly came up in the desert.
Many of these stories are collected in the Arabic Infancy Gospel; it was
probably written down in the sixth century, but with many older sources.
The narratives show characteristic aspects of Christianity in an Arabic society; for instance, it attributes great importance to relics and visible signs
of miracles. The infant Jesus performs the miracles; however, in many instances Mary acts as the intermediary between the supplicant and Jesus.
Many of the miracles are localized to specific places in Egypt, often villages
or churches and monasteries. These stories have been and still are of great
importance for the Coptic Church. They serve as founding stories of the

11. https://commons.wikimedia.org/wiki/File:Giotto_-_Scrovegni_-_-20-_-_
Flight_into_Egypt.jpg/.

church in Egypt and as proofs that Christianity in Egypt goes all the way back to Jesus' stay in Egypt as an infant. The miracle stories have been associated with churches and monasteries that are placed along a trajectory of the travels of the Holy Family in Egypt, especially up and down the Nile. Thus, the memories of Jesus' journey through Egypt are inscribed and preserved in "a holy geography" of the land.

Jesus' Sayings and His Appearance

The Gospel of Thomas

The Gospel of Thomas is the only apocryphal writing that may go back to the first century, and thus is possibly as old as the transmission of the sayings of Jesus in the gospels.[12] This text contains only sayings attributed to Jesus. There are almost no stories about Jesus, which play such an important role in the Gospels in the New Testament. The sayings are divided into 114 short units (called "Sayings"). About half of these words are the same as or quite similar to sayings of Jesus that are shared by Matthew and Luke. Thus, the sayings of Jesus in the Gospel of Thomas resemble the so-called Q source, which is a (hypothetical) collection of sayings, with very little narrative material about Jesus. This similarity with the Q source has led to discussions of the possible date for the Gospel of Thomas: is it from the same period as the Q source, that is, earlier than Matthew and Luke? Alternatively, did the Gospel of Thomas borrow these sayings from Matthew and Luke so that it is of a later date? Most of Jesus' sayings here that do not have a parallel in Matthew and Luke probably have a later origin. This suggests that the Gospel of Thomas as such dates from the second century. These other sayings of Jesus have often been characterized as gnostic; that is, they show traces of a dualism between a spiritual world and the material world. Probably this aspect led bishops and other church authorities in the last part of the second century to label the Gospel of Thomas heretical. This rejection may have been the reason the Gospel of Thomas was no longer copied and gradually disappeared from the church's memory. Then, suddenly, it reappeared among the writings of the Nag Hammadi collection, which was found in 1945.[13] These writings had belonged to a Christian monastery in the Nile Valley, and were probably hidden in a cave to protect them from plunderers.

When the Gospel of Thomas reappeared, it was possible go get an impression of how the sayings of Jesus that were not integrated in a narrative setting presented a very different picture of Jesus from that in the Gospels in

12. Ehrman, *Lost Christianities*, 47–65.

13. Robinson, *Nag Hammadi Library*.

the New Testament. Only a very few of the sayings of Jesus in the Gospel of Thomas have traces of a narrative setting.[14] Thus, unlike the narrative Gospels in the New Testament, the Gospel of Thomas is not a Life of Jesus. There is no mention of the baptism of Jesus or of his calling disciples; neither are there traces of a passion narrative—of the crucifixion or the resurrection. There are no references to Jesus' mission in Galilee or to his encounters in Jerusalem. However, there are some sayings in which Jesus is very critical of the Pharisees; other sayings are negative about Jewish customs of fasting, almsgiving, circumcision, and purity rules (6, 14, 53, and 89). This distancing from a Jewish society and its traditions and customs is also indicated by the fact that the gospel does not use any Jewish designations for Jesus, such as Messiah, Son of David, or Son of God.

The Gospel of Thomas opens this way: "These are the secret words that the living Jesus spoke and which Didymos Judas Thomas wrote down." The very first saying is, "And he said: 'Whoever finds the interpretation of these sayings will not experience death.'" It is "the living Jesus" who speaks in these words that will give life to those who find the meaning of these "secret words." The words that Jesus speaks, not his death and resurrection, give life. These words convey not just an ordinary meaning but also a secret wisdom. What is important is to "seek and find"; and what is to be found is the kingdom of heaven, which is "both inside you and outside of you." That the kingdom is inside you means that the kingdom emerges "when you recognize yourselves. . ." (3). Another way to express that "you are sons of the living Father" is to say, "We have come from the Light" (50). The ideal hearers of the Gospel of Thomas belong to the world of the Spirit, and therefore they must abstain ("fast") from the material world.

The Gospel of Thomas comes close to announcing that human beings have their origin in God and are destined to return to God. In the Gospel of Thomas this understanding of the person as coming from God and returning to God is combined with praise for an ascetic lifestyle; according to Thomas, the followers of Jesus should live as itinerants, without a fixed abode or a permanent household. This is a radical form of tendencies also present in the narrative Gospels, where they have been modified by the narrative framework. In the narrative Gospels, Jesus is a social critic of abuse and exploitation; in the Gospel of Thomas, he turns away from the world. Even the body is looked upon as negative in itself.

It is possible that the Gospel of Thomas had its origin in Syria, where the apostle Thomas had a special authority. This is reflected in saying 13, where Jesus asks his disciples whom he is like. Only Thomas succeeds in giving the right answer, namely that it is impossible to express whom Jesus is like. As a reward, Thomas gets to partake in Jesus' revelations.

14. Sayings 22, 60, 72, 79, 99.

The very last saying in the collection, number 114, reflects a negative attitude toward women among male leaders. Peter says that Mary (i.e., Mary of Magdala) must leave the community because "women are not worthy of life." Jesus defends Mary, but to modern readers the reasons he gives sounds like discrimination: "I myself shall lead her in order to make her male, so that she too may become a living spirit resembling you males." The idea that a woman could become masculine reflects an understanding that is very different from the modern view that a man and a woman belong to two different genders. The idea in antiquity was that man and woman belonged to the same gender, but at different stages of development. Of course, the man was at the higher stage of development. However, it was possible for a woman to advance to become more masculine, and thereby more spiritual. The division between masculine and feminine corresponded to the division between spiritual and material. These categories were not exclusively linked to man and woman as sexes; therefore, women could advance and become more masculine and spiritual. In a similar manner, a man who did not fulfill the obligations of masculinity and spirituality might sink down to a lower level of femininity. Within this ideological context we can understand Jesus' words about Mary of Magdala as a positive statement, as a recognition of the role she could play as a leader among Christ followers. The conflict where male leaders tried to exclude women from leadership positions is discussed in greater length in the Gospel of Mary Magdalene.

In the Gospel of Thomas, Jesus represents the spiritual principle. Many of the sayings that Thomas shares with Matthew and Luke appear more radical when they stand alone, without any modifications through a narrative context. This radical tendency is also enhanced by other sayings, added later, that emphasize that Jesus belonged to the divine, spiritual sphere, filled with light, in contrast to the material and earthly sphere.

What Did Jesus Look Like? The Apocryphal Acts of John

We do not know what Jesus looked like. The Gospels do not give any information about his physical appearance. In a book titled *What Did Jesus Look Like?*[15] the British historian and biblical scholar Joan Taylor has explored all evidence that we have about Jesus' appearance. Most of it is from a time much later than Jesus and reflects the imaginations of the various historical periods. The most useful evidence is circumstantial, for instance DNA information about what an ordinary Near Eastern man in the first century looked like. We also know that a non-elite Jewish man at the time wore a short tunic, and we must presume that this held true for Jesus also. Since there was much continuity in

15. Taylor, *What Did Jesus Look Like?*

terms of clothing, a mid-third-century fresco of Moses as a young man from the Dura Europos synagogue in present-day Syria may give us an idea of how Jesus dressed. The fact that the earliest memories about Jesus do not give any specific information of what Jesus looked like makes it likely that there was nothing exceptional about him in terms of his appearance.

Moses and the Burning Bush (interior wood panel, Dura Europos Synagogue, 244–245 CE). Wikimedia Commons.[16]

16. https://commons.wikimedia.org/wiki/File:Mose_hasne.jpg.

The closest the Gospels come to a description of Jesus' appearance is in describing an extraordinary event, the Transfiguration scene, when "the appearance of his face changed, and his clothes became dazzling white" (Luke 9:29). Not even the stories of how Jesus appeared to the women and the disciples after his resurrection provide a physical description of him. They recognize him, but that is not only because they recognize his body; sometimes they even have his body before their eyes, without recognizing him. Most of the times there was more than Jesus' body that made the disciples recognize him: for instance, that he performed an act they knew from their history together with him, such as the breaking of the bread at a meal (Luke 24:31) or a miracle (John 21:7). In these appearances Jesus' body sometimes is immaterial so that he can walk through closed doors (John 20:19), but at other times it is physical so that he can eat food (Luke 24:41–43) and the disciples could touch his body (John 20:27).

The only early Christian writing that does describe Jesus' appearance, the Apocryphal Acts of John,[17] illustrates the difficulties in giving a clear picture of what Jesus looked. Scholars have tentatively dated this writing to the mid-second century. The Apocryphal Acts of John was one of the writings that orthodox church leaders criticized and tried to suppress. They regarded it as conveying a dangerous form of spirituality. The presumed author of the Acts of John was the beloved disciple of Jesus in John's Gospel.

A section of the Apocryphal Acts of John (87–93) provides examples of how Jesus appeared differently to different disciples. For instance, a story of the disciples as fishermen in a boat on the Sea of Gennesaret describes how they all saw Jesus on the shore but perceived him in different ways. For James he appeared as a small child whereas John saw him as a handsome man with a friendly appearance. When they came ashore and started following him, John saw a bald man with a long beard; James, however, saw a young man who had just started to grow a beard. A permanent feature, however, was that Jesus had wide-open eyes. In other respects, he appeared in very different ways: sometimes as a small and ugly man, at other times so big that he reached into heaven. John, the beloved disciple, had different experiences when he rested at the bosom of Jesus: sometimes it was soft, and at other times it was hard as stone. When he sums up his impressions of Jesus, he says that when he touched Jesus, his body sometimes was a solid, physical body; at other times, it was immaterial, without any bodily substance.

It is not easy to characterize the pictures of Jesus in the Apocryphal Acts of John. They may be expressions of a docetic theology, that is, a teaching that emphasized the exclusive divinity of Jesus, so that his human body was a mere appearance. However, the descriptions might also be just a development of the appearance stories in the canonical Gospels, with their different

17. Elliott, *Apocryphal Jesus*, 57–58.

presentations of Jesus. The Apocryphal Acts of John has two more texts about Jesus; one goes by the name the Jesus hymn. This hymn probably was part of a ritual of a dance around the cross.[18] The other is a mystical presentation of the crucifixion of Jesus (see below); this text makes it apparent why many considered the Acts of John to be a heretical text.

Crucifixion and Resurrection

The crucifixion was the most dramatic event in the memories of Jesus, and the seismic point for establishing a position on how to understand Jesus. For the first Christ followers, finding a meaning in Jesus' death was a great challenge. The narrative of Jesus' arrest, interrogation, judgement and crucifixion was among the first stories about Jesus to be established as a "cultural memory"; and that gave little room for new interpretations. With this well-known story so early fixed, it was impossible to tell a very different story of these events. To a large degree, the four Gospels follow the same structure and progression of the passion narrative. There are smaller differences between the gospels, above all in the characterization of Jesus' death. In Mark, Jesus dies alone, in fear. Luke presents Jesus as the martyr caring for others; in John, Jesus is the lord of events, even unto death.

In addition, with regard to the responsibility for the death of Jesus, there are differences between the gospels. They all attribute great responsibility to the Jewish leaders, some also to the people of Jerusalem; however, to varying degrees they excuse Pilate (i.e., the Romans) from responsibility. In the retellings of the memories about the death of Jesus in the second and third centuries, these two issues—the guilt of the Jewish leaders and innocence of the Romans—recur.

The Gospel of Peter

We find mentions of the Gospel of Peter from the third century; it was later lost and was recovered only in a manuscript that was found at the end of the nineteenth century. It is possible that it originally contained a longer history of the life of Jesus; however, the part of the narrative that has been preserved starts with the interrogation by Pilate and ends with the resurrection.[19] The fragment starts with a disclaimer: about Jesus' death the Jews and Herod did not want to wash their hands. This is a reference to Pilate's handwashing in

18. Elliott, *Apocryphal Jesus*, 60–62.
19. Elliott, *Apocryphal Jesus*, 69–72.

Matthew's Gospel, indicating that he was not a guilty party in Jesus' death (Matt 27:24). Also, as in Matthew, so also in the Gospel of Peter Pilate supplied a guard of soldiers for Jesus' tomb (cf. Matt 27:62–66).

The picture of Jesus in the Gospel of Peter shows many similarities with that in John's Gospel. When the crowd insults Jesus, places him in the judgment seat, and shouts: "Judge justly, King of Israel" (3:7), they inadvertently speak the truth about Jesus. When Jesus is crucified, he does not utter a word, "because he did not feel any pain" (4:11). This was an expression of Jesus' self-control, a masculine ideal in antiquity, and of his spiritual character. Jesus' last words on the cross are, "My power, O power, you have forsaken me." Jesus did not die; he was "lifted up" (4:19). In the same manner, the young man at the empty tomb does not say that Jesus had gone ahead of the women to Galilee, but instead he says, "For he is risen and gone to the place from which he was sent" (13:56). This expression is similar to the language in the Gospel of John, which speaks of Jesus as the one who came from heaven, who ascends to heaven, and who is sent by God (John 3:13–17).

Because of Jesus' death, the Jews and their leaders acknowledge the evil they have committed, and they mourn the judgement that has come over Jerusalem. What is extraordinary about the Gospel of Peter is that it ventures to describe the resurrection itself. Here the Gospels in the New Testament are very reticent; they limit themselves to describing the empty tomb and the messengers who speak to the women who have come out to the tomb. The Gospel of Peter, however, describes how three men walk out from the tomb. Two of them are so tall that they reach up to heaven, and the head of the third one reaches above heaven. Moreover, a cross follows them. A voice is heard from heaven: "Have you preached for those who sleep?" and the cross responds, "Yes" (10:41–42). The question whether Jesus had made proclamation to the dead is a reference to a statement in 1 Peter 3:18–19: "He was put to death in the flesh, but made alive in the spirit, in which also he went and made a proclamation to the spirits in prison."

The statement that Jesus "did not feel any pain," and the notion that he did not die but "was taken up" suggests that the Gospel of Peter understands Jesus' death as a spiritual event; this understanding diminishes Jesus' physical, human suffering. According to the Gospel of Peter, crucifixion equals resurrection, since at the resurrection Jesus went "to the place from which he was sent."

Apocryphal Acts of John: A Spiritual Crucifixion

In the Apocryphal Acts of John 97–102,[20] crucifixion is even more of a spiritual event than in the Gospel of Peter. Jesus' crucifixion is seen from the perspective of John, the disciple of Jesus. John explains that he hid in a cave when the body of Jesus was hanging on the cross. However, the real Jesus appears to John and tells him the truth about crucifixion. To the people of Jerusalem it appeared that Jesus was bodily crucified and "pierced with lances and reeds." However, Jesus shows John a cross of light where Jesus is present, not as a body, but as a voice. The true cross was not the one made from wood, and the true Jesus was not the one hanging on that cross. Furthermore, according to the Apocryphal Acts of John, Jesus did not suffer what people said that he had suffered. Suffering is a mystery, and it is the Word that was crucified. Therefore, Jesus urges John to understand the Word so that he will understand the Lord, and finally "the Man," that is, Jesus, and what he had suffered (Apocryphal Acts of John 101).

This understanding of the cross creates a division among people. In his vision, John sees a great crowd gathered around the wooden cross, but they are people without a form; they belong to the lower nature. In addition, others are inside the cross; they will at some time in the future become united with the Lord into one form.

The Apocryphal Acts of John presents a form of Christianity in which the physical crucifixion of Jesus is not important. Indeed, it is a total misunderstanding since it is the revelation of the spiritual Word that is the decisive event. Accordingly, the cross that gives spiritual illumination is the true cross. John concludes his story of the cross by saying that for the Lord everything is symbolic, and the cross was given for humanity, for their conversion and salvation. "Conversion" and "salvation" were well-known terms; they had a socially recognizable meaning for ordinary Christians. However, in the Apocryphal Acts of John they have a different meaning. Salvation represents an alternative to the bodily form of Christianity, and conversion means choosing a life illuminated by spiritual insight.

The Gospel of Nicodemus: Polemics against the Jews

The Gospel of Peter and the Apocryphal Acts of John share the characteristics of many writings in the category *apocryphal*: these gospels were probably used only in a few groups; they have been preserved in only a few manuscripts. Moreover, they represent an alternative view of Jesus' death on the cross from

20. Elliott, *Apocryphal Jesus*, 60–64.

the Gospels in the New Testament. The Gospel of Nicodemus,[21] however, was a very popular piece of writing: it was not esoteric, but it represented a broad religious tradition. It was spread in many manuscripts and translations and exerted a great influence for centuries.

The Gospel of Nicodemus is made up of several different writings. The first part, about the passion of Jesus, his death and resurrection, also goes by the name the Acts of Pilate, and may have originated in the fourth century. The name indicates the purpose of this writing: to acquit Pilate from any guilt for the crucifixion of Jesus, and to put the blame one-sidedly upon the Jews. The last part of the Gospel of Nicodemus tells the story of Jesus' descent to Hades; the two parts were probably put together in the sixth century.

The scene of Pilate's interrogation of Jesus is greatly expanded from the Gospels in the New Testament; its main motive is to emphasize the guilt of the Jews. False accusations by Jewish leaders take a prominent place. The accusations reflect Jewish polemics in response to Christian claims in late antiquity: Jesus was born out of wedlock; his birth caused the massacre of the innocents in Bethlehem; Joseph and Mary fled to Egypt to escape the bad reputation they had taken on among their neighbors. Furthermore, in Egypt Jesus was taught to become a sorcerer. These accusations are examples of the genre of counterhistories (see chapter 3). In response to these accusations, the Gospel of Nicodemus introduces other witnesses in order to show how the Jewish people was divided over Jesus. Twelve well-respected men counter the accusations: Jesus was not illegitimately born; they had been present at the betrothal of Joseph and Mary.

Furthermore, other figures from the canonical Gospels are brought in as character witnesses for Jesus. First among them is Nicodemus, the council member who came to Jesus at night. Other witnesses are many of the men and women healed by Jesus. Pilate is consistent in his wish to acquit Jesus of the accusations against him; but then the Jewish crowds use their trump card: they accuse Pilate of recognizing Jesus as King, and that would amount to treason against the Emperor.

The power and authority of Jesus are emphasized throughout the Gospel of Nicodemus. For instance, the Roman legionaries carry the standards of the emperor, and when they pass Jesus, they bow down by themselves to show him due respect. As it is in John's Gospel, Pilate's interrogation of Jesus in the Gospel of Nicodemus turns into a conversation about truth, an arena where Jesus has full authority. At the end, Pilate asks in despair, "What shall I do with you?" Jesus responds: "As it was given to you." To Pilate's follow-up-question—"How was it given?"—Jesus responds: "Moses

21. Elliott, *Apocryphal Jesus*, 73–79, 81–88.

and the Prophets foretold my death and resurrection." Thus, Jesus himself gives the verdict. Throughout this process, the Jewish leaders are delegitimized. At the conclusion of this narrative, Jesus is innocent; however, he must die because his death must happen as it is foretold by Moses and the Prophets. Pilate is only God's tool.

"Descended into Hell"

Jesus' proclamation for those who were in hell became a very popular topic within Christianity in antiquity, although it was barely alluded to in the New Testament (1 Pet 3:19). It became part of an early version of the Apostles' Creed.[22] Christian teaching about hell builds on ideas about a realm of the dead, in Greek tradition called Hades, a place where the dead live under the rule of Hades, the God of the underworld. In Jewish and Christian cosmology, the ruler of this realm of the dead was named Satan. Christian ideas about death go back to the notion, found in Paul's letters—that since the progenitor of human beings, Adam, sinned and was punished with death, all human beings suffered death, since they all sinned (Rom 5). However, with his death, Christ had conquered death and its power, and he had restored life. In some of the apocryphal gospels, these dogmatic expressions are transformed into dramatic narratives (for instance, the story of how Jesus preached to and liberated the dead in hell).

This development probably happened quite early. The Gospel of Bartholomew may have been an early case, most often dated to the late second century. It belongs to a genre of revelatory texts in which the resurrected Jesus reveals secrets to his disciples. In most cases, these revelations concern their future life; in this case, however, it deals with what happened in the past. It starts with Bartholomew addressing a question to Jesus. He had noticed that at the crucifixion Jesus had disappeared from the cross. He had also heard voices speaking, so he wondered to where Jesus had disappeared. Jesus responds that he had gone to Hades to bring out Adam and all who were together with him; the voices Bartholomew had heard had been those of Hades, and Satan. Bartholomew's main interest is in Jesus' opponents, who go by various names: the Dragon, Beliar, and Satan. Moreover, Bartholomew wants to know how Beliar punishes those who had committed varies types of sins. Since Jesus had conquered Satan, Bartholomew can address these questions directly to Beliar. Empowered by the cross of Jesus, Bartholomew can tread Beliar under his feet and force him to respond.

22. *"descendit ad inferos,"* English translation: "he descended into hell"; or, "he descended to the dead."

The history of how Jesus conquered Satan is dramatically narrated in *Christ's Descent to Hell*, which makes up the last section of the Gospel of Nicodemus. This section dates from a much later period than the Gospel of Bartholomew. The story is told as a dialogue between Hades, the ruler of Hades, and Satan. The proclamation from Psalm 24:7 signals the arrival of Christ to hell:

> "Lift up your heads, O gates!
>
> and be lifted up, O ancient doors!
>
> that the King of glory may come in."

Christ conquers Satan and liberates Adam and all who follow him in death. Whereas Adam died because he ate from the tree of knowledge, Jesus brought all to life through the tree of the cross, which mediates salvation. According to the Gospel of Bartholomew, those who are rescued are the prophets in ancient Israel and the brigand who turned to Jesus on the cross; he was a very popular exemplary figure of conversion.

This early Christian story of how Jesus conquered Satan has had a strong and long lasting influence throughout the history of the Christian church. It is reflected in church doctrine, in private meditation, in iconography and in church art, as well as in Christian drama, especially in medieval mystery plays. A large series of paintings on the Apostles' Creed in the Protestant Cathedral in Oslo, by the Norwegian painter Hugo Lous Mohr, shows the dramatic motif of Christ who kills the dragon.[23]

Jesus' Revelations to His Disciples

In the four original Gospels, we find teachings of Jesus to his disciples about what will happen to them after his death. Mark 13 is an apocalyptic vision of persecutions, and of terror and destruction on a large, cosmic level. In the setting of the Last Supper, Jesus gives a farewell speech in the Hellenistic tradition to his disciples at Luke 22:24–38. In John's Gospel, the farewell speech is developed into a dialogue between Jesus and his disciples, and it extends over three chapters; its main point is how Jesus will send them the Spirit, the Intercessor.

This form was developed further and became an important part of the apocryphal writings, particularly in order to convey the secret teachings of Jesus that were restricted to those with special insight. Because of the role

23. https://kirken.no/nb-NO/fellesrad/kirkeneioslo/menigheter/oslo-domkirken/om-domkirken/om-oslo-domkike/les-mer-om-oslo-domkirke/takmaleriene.

that dialogues between Jesus and the disciples play in these writings, they are often called *dialogue gospels*. Several of these writings have disciples as their protagonists and develop or reinterpret their roles from the canonical Gospels. This holds true of the two writings I have chosen to present from among a large number, the Gospel of Judas and the Gospel of Mary Magdalene. The special nature of these texts that convey Jesus' secret teachings means that they all belong to those apocryphal writings that were contested and looked upon with suspicion by those who later would be called orthodox.

THE GOSPEL OF JUDAS

Popular reception history around the Gospel of Judas shows how the apocryphal writings, like thriller novels, are often surrounded by mystery, suspense, and sensationalism. It was at Easter 2006 that *National Geographic* presented an ancient manuscript it claimed showed that Judas did not betray Jesus. According to this manuscript, it was Jesus himself who had asked Judas, his most trusted disciple, to hand him over to the authorities to be crucified, so that Jesus might be liberated from his body. It was of course perfect timing for a sensational claim, which brought much publicity. However, later studies of the manuscript showed that the claims about what it said were overblown. But the history of the manuscript was truly a mystery story. Like so many other manuscripts from antiquity, it was found in a desert in Egypt in the 1970s. It went through many different hands and various antique dealers, who all wanted to make big money from the manuscript. For instance, it was kept in a freezer for many years, which almost destroyed it. Finally, *National Geographic* acquired the right to publish the manuscript.

The Gospel of Judas was known in antiquity; at the end of the second century, Bishop Irenaeus included it in a book about heresies. In its form, it is a dialogue gospel.[24] This is indicated already from its start: "The secret account of the revelation that Jesus spoke in conversation with Judas Iscariot during a week three days before he celebrated Passover." This document assumes that its audience knows the narratives about Judas in what would become the canonical Gospels and Acts, where he is portrayed as the great betrayer and even as a tool of Satan (Luke 22:3). The Gospel of Judas presents a different image of him; he, not Peter, is the leader among the apostles. This is similar to the situation described by the Gospel of Thomas, where Thomas is the leading apostle. Furthermore, the Gospel of John and Paul's letters indicate that there were conflicts among early Christian groups,

24. Kasser et al., eds., *Gospel of Judas*.

which claimed different apostles as their leaders. Each group wanted to include new memories of Jesus and the disciples in their particular gospels and to replace the memories of Peter's hegemony in the earliest (and eventually canonical) Gospels.

The Gospel of Judas is very critical of the other disciples, who are portrayed as "ordinary Christians," without insight. Jesus criticizes them for belonging to an earthly sphere where they are ruled by a false, earthly god. Judas is the only one who can approach Jesus, and Jesus reveals to him "the secrets of the Kingdom" and the secrets of all the spheres above the earth. However, not even Judas may enter the highest, that is, the heavenly sphere. In the end, Judas is lifted up in a cloud; however, it is unclear (partly because the manuscript is damaged) whether he actually enters into the heavenly sphere.

Although Jesus entrusts Judas with his revelations, this gospel has preserved the traditions about Judas's betrayal of Jesus. However, it is expressed by the following words of Jesus: "But you will exceed all of them. For you will sacrifice the man that clothes me" (Judas 56). The idea that Jesus' body only "clothed" him, so that the body was not his true self, reflects a dualistic split between the spiritual and the material. We find this dualism in writings that often are called gnostic; however, they might better be called *gnostic Christian*, in order not to put too much weight on the differences among early Christian groups.

At the publication of the Gospel of Judas, *National Geographic* claimed that it presented a new picture of the "historical Judas." However, we might rather say that it presents a different memory of Judas from those in the first Gospels. The stories of Judas in the (canonical) Gospels show a struggle within each gospel to explain Judas's role in the story of Jesus' passion. Judas is a trusted disciple who ends up with betraying Jesus; however, his betrayal is also instrumental in the fulfilment of Jesus' prophecies about his death. In the Gospel of Judas, the fact that Judas receives revelations proves the close relationship between him and Jesus on a spiritual level. However, on human level, the Gospel of Judas paints an ambivalent picture of Judas and his betrayal of Jesus.

The Gospel of Mary of Magdala

The Gospel of Mary of Magdala may have originated as early as the first half of the second century.[25] A Coptic manuscript was found in the end of the nineteenth century; however, it was not published until 1955. In addition,

25. King, *Gospel of Mary of Magdala.*

two small Greek fragments of the gospel have been preserved. Unfortunately, several pages of the first part of the gospel, which contained the conversations between Jesus and the disciples, are lost.

Mary of Magdala is one of those persons in the group around Jesus whose memory was continuously developed, with new perspectives and new stories added on. In Luke's Gospel, she is one of several elite women who, after she is healed from evil spirits, supports Jesus and his male disciples (Luke 8:1–3). In John's Gospel, she is the central figure who encounters Jesus at the empty tomb; she is entrusted with his message to the disciples that he will ascend to his Father (John 20:1–18). In the Gospel of Mary of Magdala, she has even greater responsibilities; she is the central person in the group of disciples when Jesus reveals himself to them after his resurrection. Jesus' message is that the material world will perish, and that sin as such does not exist. The disciples themselves create sin when they engage in mixing the material and spiritual worlds. This message confuses the disciples, so that they start doubting and become uncertain about Jesus' command to proclaim the good message of the kingdom. Mary of Magdala comforts them in their crisis, and they beg her to tell them what Jesus has revealed to her. Jesus blesses her because she is not "wavering" but has remained steadfast. Moreover, he explains to her how the soul can be liberated from the powers that keep it imprisoned in the world, unaware of its true spiritual nature.

However, when Mary brings this message to the male disciples, she is met with rejection and incredulity: this was not what Jesus had told them. Peter asserts male superiority and doubts that Jesus would have told this to a woman in secret rather than openly to the apostles. In the end, one of the other male apostles castigates Peter; if the Savior knew Mary fully and loved her, who was Peter to reject her?

The Gospel of Mary of Magdala reflects several conflict areas between and within early groups of Christ followers. The role of women and the inclusion of women in leadership was obviously a contentious issue. In this conflict, Mary of Magdala was an important model of women's leadership. However, this issue apparently competed with others, including the divide between the spiritual and the material, the understanding of what constitutes sin, and the understanding of ways to attain salvation.

Conflicting Memories

Maurice Halbwachs, who is recognized as the founding father of memory studies, suggested that a group that selected and elaborated its records in order to shape its identity in the present produced collective memory.[26] This

---

26. Halbwachs, *On Collective Memory*.

is what happened with the apocryphal gospels. They build upon existing memories of Jesus found in the first Gospels. These gospels (either all or some of them) were known to many Christian groups in the second century, and in some instances they were combined into one collection. Building on these memories, the new writings adapted existing memories and added new ones, with the purpose of making them useful to the present situation.

Jesus of Nazareth was the focus for all groups of Christ-followers, and the basis for their identity, or rather identities, since the elaborations and additions of memories about him showed great diversity. The most important memories were associated with Jesus' birth, and with his passion, death, and resurrection. The great interest in his family history and especially in Mary and Joseph served to support the claims of Jesus' miraculous birth. Thus, these stories were important means to defend Jesus' unique status. Likewise, the added memories in the passion and resurrection narratives reflected discussions and conflicts going on during the period when the Gospels were written. Their accusations against the Jewish leaders—that the leaders alone were responsible for the crucifixion of Jesus—may reflect external conflicts with Jews in various local communities, and also apologetics vis-à-vis Roman authorities, on whose goodwill Christians depended.

In some of the gospels, conflicts within and between Christian groups come to the fore in the competition between apostles. The memories of the apostles played into discussions about leadership and identity within the various groups. Apparently, groups linked their identities and positions on religious issues to various apostles. It is striking that Peter's leadership, which was so important in the first Gospels, and which become dominant in the tradition of Peter for the bishops in Rome, was contested in several of the apocryphal gospels: in the Gospel of Thomas, the Gospel of Judas, and the Gospel of Mary of Magdala. Here, rewritings and additions of new stories show the importance of memories for legitimation and delegitimation.

One aspect of the apocryphal writings that is often overlooked by those who want to see them as a liberal alternative to the dogmatic, traditional Christianity[27] is the dominance of magic and (what moderns would speak of as) superstition, which is an integral part of their worldview. In the apocryphal writings, we enter a world of miracles, magic, and sorcery: a world filled with evil powers. This is, of course, also true of the writings included in the New Testament; however, they are much more reserved about it. This is partly, I suggest, because in many of the apocryphal writings we enter into a non-elite world, into the everyday life of ordinary people. However, since the elite too harbored many of the same ideas as the non-elite, it is difficult to disentangle elite cultural presuppositions from their more lofty religious ideas.

27. E.g., Ehrman, *Lost Christianities*.

3

Counterhistories about Jesus

Jesus-Stories in Jewish Sources
and in the Quran

THE GOSPELS AND SOME of the apocryphal narratives were memory stories about Jesus, and for the Christ believers they were expressions of their identities. When the stories were retold or repeated as events, for instance in the Eucharistic meal, the participants experienced a fellowship with Jesus, and he became present among them. This chapter will introduce examples of criticisms of these memory stories; they presented alternative stories and alternative readings of narratives about Jesus. I will use the term *counterhistories* for these alternative stories.

Counterhistory is a separate genre of history. It reworks narratives that are well known from an already-established history; its purpose is to create an alternative history that subverts the former. The historian Amos Funkenstein has given the name to this form of polemical history writing, taking as his example presentations of the conflicts between Israelis and Palestinians.[1] Counterhistory, says Funkenstein, means exploiting the most important sources that one's opponents use to support their position, and reading them "against the grain," that is, in a negative meaning. The purpose of a counterhistory is to deprive an opponent of his/her positive identity and instead to put up a negative picture. There are many examples of such counterhistories. A well-known example is The *City of God* by the Christian theologian Augustine (354–430), who challenged the official history of Rome as an ideal of peace and justice. Augustine used the sources of the history of Rome to present an alternative picture of greed and desire

---

1. Funkenstein, "History, Counterhistory, and Narrative."

for power. In Jewish sources and in the Quran, we find counterhistories to the memories of Jesus in the Gospels.

Jewish Counterhistories

All the Gospels describe people who did not accept Jesus. They are part of the stories about Jesus, but they also represent later readers or listeners to the stories. The criticisms coming from scribes, Pharisees and priests in polemical discussions with Jesus also reflect opinions held by opponents of the gospel writers. We find an interesting example of such polemics, combining an account of a historical event with a contemporary conflict, in Matthew's version of the story of Jesus' death and resurrection. Matthew places his story alongside the story of Jesus' Jewish opponents (Matt 27:62—28:15). Following the Markan story, Matthew tells how Jesus is buried in a tomb (27:57–61). Then he adds a story of how Jewish leaders make Pilate put guards at Jesus' grave to prevent the disciples from stealing the dead body of Jesus so that they could claim that Jesus was raised form the dead (27:62–66). Next, Matthew continues with Mark's story of the women who come to the tomb and encounter an angel (28:1, 5–7). However, Matthew adds a story of how the plot of the Jewish leaders failed: at the resurrection, there was a strong earthquake and an angel appeared like lightening before the soldiers, who fell to the ground like dead men (28:2–4). Then Matthew combines the story of the women who meet Jesus, and with great joy go into Jerusalem to bring the news of the resurrection to the disciples (28:8–10) with a parallel counterstory. In that story, the guards go into Jerusalem and tell the priests what has happened to them. The priests, however, do not give up their plan: they pay bribes to the guards and order them to tell that the disciples came and stole Jesus' body while they were asleep. The result, according to Matthew, is this: "And this story is still told among the Jews to this day" (28:11–15).

It is very interesting that Matthew openly tells a counterstory to his own story of how Jesus is raised from the dead. This story of the Jewish leaders is a typical example of a counterhistory. It has a polemical purpose, to challenge the trustworthiness of the story of Jesus' followers. For Christ believers, the story of Jesus' resurrection was the very basis of their faith; this means that a challenge to this story challenges their very identity. The Jewish leaders took the central parts of the "faith story" and turn them upside down. The Christ believers and their opponents agree on one point: the tomb was found empty. Matthew explains this by means of the memories of how Jesus had appeared to the women and the disciples. The opponents, however, undermine this story with their counterstory of how the disciples stole the body of Jesus. If Matthew spends so much time exposing the Jewish story as lies, it must be because many people found the Jewish alternative explanation of the empty tomb trustworthy.

Matthew's combination of the story of Jesus' resurrection and its counterstory is unusual at such an early time of the history of writings about Jesus. There are not many early examples of Jewish counterhistories to the Christian histories. One reason may be that Jews were not so preoccupied with the Christ believers as the other way around. Christ-believing groups took over the Jewish Bible and read it as prophecies about Jesus. They saw themselves as heirs to these prophecies and held that they had superseded the Jews as the people of God. Most of the Jews were spread all over the Roman Empire, and into Arabia and Persia in the East; accordingly, the Christian groups were not so important to them. Judaism was an old and recognized religion, whereas the Christians were newcomers. It was not until a later period, when the emperor Constantine made Christianity an accepted religion in the Roman Empire, that the Jews felt the pressure to react to the Christian stories.

The most important Jewish writings in this period were the Talmud, which in modern editions fill many volumes. The Talmud comprises the Mishnah, a Jewish law codex from about 200 CE, and comments and expositions by rabbinical scholars, frequently in sharp discussions with one another. There are two different versions of the Talmud, the shorter Palestinian one, and the longer Babylonian Talmud from circa 500 CE. Jesus is not an important figure in the Talmud, but there are a few scattered references to Jesus and to Christians.[2] In several instances, Jesus is not mentioned by name, yet the context indicates that the story is about Jesus. Most references to Jesus are to stories about his birth or to his death and resurrection.

Illegitimate Birth from a Roman Father

The birth narratives in the Gospels of Matthew and Luke tell that Jesus was conceived without a man, by the Holy Spirit, and that he was born to a virgin called Mary. The elaboration of this piece of memory about Jesus was expanded by the apocryphal gospels of Proto-James and Pseudo-Matthew. Through his social father, Joseph, Jesus was descended from the house of David, the old royal family. Thus, the birth story was one of the most significant pieces of memory that served to legitimate the claims that Jesus was both a Son of David and the Son of God. However, a few traces indicate that some aspects of these memories were questioned. Mark's Gospel relates

2. See a list in Schäfer, *Jesus in the Talmud*, 15–24.

that villagers in Jesus' hometown refer to him as "son of Mary" (Mark 6:3), a name that might indicate that his father was unknown. Moreover, Joseph's reaction when he learns that Mary is expecting a child who is not his may indicate that the author of Matthew's Gospel wants to counter rumors that Jesus was born out of wedlock.

It is this doubt that the counterhistory will fuel by its attempt to delegitimize the dominant Christ story. The Greek philosopher Celsus, in *The True Word* (*Alethes Logos*), circa 175 CE, voiced the first known criticism of the birth story about Jesus. Celsus actually reports a story by a Jew who accused Jesus of inventing the story of a birth by a virgin.[3] The Jew claimed that Jesus was born by a poor village woman who was sent away by her husband, a carpenter, to whom she had been engaged, because of adultery. In fact, a Roman soldier called Panthera fathered the child she bore. Since Jesus was poor, he had traveled to Egypt to find work. There he learned sorcery, and he returned home full of pride and made claims to be God. A similar story is told also in the Talmud, but without identifying the names of the persons involved.[4]

Obviously, this counterhistory was based on a certain knowledge of the Christian history of Jesus' parents. They were village people; Joseph was a carpenter, he was known not to be the real father of Jesus, and Jesus had been in Egypt in his childhood. The counterhistory does not mention descent from David or Bethlehem as the place of Jesus' birth. The most important claim in the counterhistory was that Jesus was born out of wedlock, and to further delegitimize Jesus, it named a Roman soldier as his father. The story of Joseph's flight to Egypt to bring Mary and the child to safety was used to associate Jesus with Egypt, known to be a center for magic and sorcery. In this way, the counterhistory fulfilled its purpose, viz. to undermine the trustworthiness of the original story.

Jesus Deserved to Be Executed

If the birth story was the first to be challenged, the execution of Jesus was the other most significant target for counterhistories. The Gospels told the story that the Jewish leaders in Jerusalem bore the main responsibility for the execution of the innocent man, Jesus. The Jewish response was a counterhistory to the effect that it was true that they had Jesus executed, but that he deserved it, since he was a sorcerer and a heretic.

We find the first mention of this counterhistory in a sermon by bishop Melito in Sardis, in Asia Minor. Sardis was a town with many Jews, and

3. Celsus's text is only known only through Origen's polemics against him in *Contra Celsum* I 28,32.

4. *B.Shab* 104b, *B.San* 67a.

with much contact between Christians and Jews. Melito was very much opposed to such contacts, and about 170 CE he gave an Easter homily where he accused the Jews of killing Jesus. In this sermon, he probably quotes the defense used by Jews in Sardis to this accusation: "Israel admits, I killed the Lord! Why? Because it was necessary for him to die."[5]

In the exchange it appears that the Jewish interlocutors accept the responsibility for the execution of Jesus; however, they claim that he was not innocent, and that therefore "it was necessary for him to die." Why was it necessary that Jesus died? We find one possible answer in the Jewish counterhistory in the Babylonian Talmud, which has a short story about the execution of Jesus:

> On the eve of the Passover Yeshu was hanged. For forty days
> before the execution took place, a herald went forth and cried,
> 'He is going forth to be stoned because he has practiced sorcery
> and enticed Israel to apostasy. Any one who can say anything
> in his favor, let him come forward and plead on his behalf.' But
> since nothing was brought forward in his favor he was hanged
> on the eve of the Passover.[6]

A later rabbi, Ulla, adds a further reason why Jesus was hanged: "he was near the authorities."[7] This story follows the rules for execution in rabbinic law; viz. that the convict was executed by stoning and when he was dead, he was hanged as an additional punishment (Deut 21:18–23). That Jesus was killed by being stoned differs from the story in the Gospels that Jesus was crucified, since crucifixion was the form of death penalty the Romans used for slaves and other low-status criminals. The accusation in the counterhistory that Jesus was a sorcerer parallels the accusation that Jesus was an illegitimate child, a counterhistory to the claim in the Gospels of Matthew and Luke that Jesus was miraculously born. It is not so simple to decipher the meaning or implications of the counterhistory's accusation that Jesus was near the authorities. One possible meaning is that it is a claim that the Romans protected Jesus. The Gospels report that during his interrogation of Jesus Pilate tried several times to set Jesus free, but that he was pressured by the Jewish leaders and their clients to sentence Jesus to death.

The story in the Talmud may convey the message that the Jews acted independently of the Romans when they executed Jesus after the manner of the Jewish law. The purpose of the story may have been to treat Jesus as a common criminal, and not as "the King of the Jews," which was the accusation cited by the Romans when they crucified Jesus. Thus, according to the

5. Melito of Sardis, *On the Passover*, 74.

6. b. Sanhedrin 43a.

7. b. Sanhedrin 43a.

story in the Talmud, it was necessary for Jesus to die. He was guilty of what he was accused of; the gospel story that proclaimed Jesus to be innocent, and therefore unjustly executed, was simply false.

But there was also another possible explanation of the claim that Jesus deserved to die, and this can be found in the dialogues between Christians and Jews. There is an early example of such a dialogue by the Christian philosopher Justin Martyr in the second century, in his *Dialogue with the Jew Trypho*. Justin is the author of the text, so he is the one who renders Trypho's turns in the dialogue. Thus, the dialogue does not present Trypho's views in a neutral way. Nevertheless, Justin may at the very least give us an impression of what he considered plausible Jewish arguments about Jesus. He ascribes to Trypho this statement: "If his Father wished him to suffer these things, in order that by His stripes the human race should be healed, we did no wrong."[8]

Trypho's response here seems to be a perfectly plausible theological argument, and it shows how Jews tried to adapt the Christian interpretation of Jesus' death. For the Christians, the death of Jesus was not only a judicial miscarriage; it was also understood as being in accordance with the will of God, since it was necessary for salvation of humankind. Therefore, Trypho seems to have a legitimate objection: if the suffering of Jesus was according to the will of God, why should the Jews be punished when they acted in such a way that God's purpose was fulfilled? However, Justin does not accept this (logical) argument. He responds that if the Jews had repented of their sins and believed in Jesus, their argument might have been valid, but not so long as they cursed Jesus and those who believed in him.

This argument, that Jesus' death was necessary for salvation, and that the Jews therefore helped bring about salvation, returned several times in Jewish handbooks for anti-Christian dialogue, from the Middle Ages. This was an argument in a polemical situation where the Jews tried to use Christian theological positions to defend themselves in these dialogues. In the Middle Ages, with an absolute Christian supremacy vis-à-vis the Jews, such dialogues were a means by Christian authorities to place Jewish scholars in an impossible situation. Against this supremacy it did not help to point out logical inconsistencies in Christian interpretations of why Jesus had to die.

Toledot Yeshu: A Popular Counterstory

The Talmud was an exposition of the Law, written by rabbis in a learned style. Its few references to Jesus followed this pattern. However, there is also a more popular and legendary Jewish story about Jesus, viz. *Toledot*

---

8 Justin, *Trypho* 95.3

Yeshu, The life Story of Jesus.[9] This story probably goes back to late antiquity or the early Middle Ages; it was transmitted orally for a long time before it was written down. This resulted in many different versions of it, and new stories were added as it was spread; it has come down in all languages that were used by Jews. Whereas the Talmud had only a few scattered references to Jesus, the *Toledot Yeshu* was fully focused on the story of Jesus as the founder of Christianity. The *Toledot Yeshu* delivers a vehement attack upon the Christian history of Jesus; it focuses especially on Jesus' birth and his death as the most central aspects of that story. Thus, the *Toledot Yeshu* is a typical example of a counterhistory.[10]

The earliest sources for the birth of Jesus in the *Toledot Yeshu* are some Aramaic fragments, probably from the sixth century.[11] They contain no new information beyond what we find in Celsus (second century) and the Talmud. It is only in Hebrew sources later than the thirteenth century that we find more information about Jesus' birth and childhood. After that time, right up until the nineteenth century, the story was expanded with new details. However, the core elements have been in place since the thirteenth century: Miriam (Mary) was engaged (or married) to a respected and pious man, Johanan, of the house of David. Miriam refuses to have intercourse with her husband because of her period of menstruation. However, their neighbor, Yosef, tricks her into sleeping with him. When Johanan realizes what has happened, and it becomes apparent that Miriam is pregnant, he seeks advice from the rabbi, Simon b. Shetab, and leaves his house and goes to Babylon. As a young boy, Jesus is taught the Torah, but he is rude toward his teachers and even ventures to teach the Torah in their presence. From Jesus' behavior, the rabbis draw the conclusion that Jesus is an illegitimate child and the son of a woman who had had intercourse during her period of menstruation. The rabbis interrogate Miriam; however, she is declared innocent, because she did not know that the man who came to her in the dark was not her husband, Yohanan, but Yosef. Jesus, on the other hand, deserves to die; however, he flees to Jerusalem.

The sources for this counterhistory are the Gospels and the Talmud. The main persons and place names are taken from the Gospels; other elements in the story, e.g., the laws of menstruation and the demand to show respect to a teacher, are part of rabbinic traditions. This narrative is clearly a counterstory to the birth narratives in the Gospels of Matthew and Luke, and to the idealized story of the twelve-year-old Jesus talking with the scribes in the temple. However, what is most surprising is the way Miriam is treated; in all the different versions of *Toledot Yeshu* she is declared innocent. In Christianity,

9 *Toledot Yeshu.*

10 Biale, "Counter-History."

11 Schäfer, "Jesus' origin."

the High Middle Ages was a period with a growing veneration of Mary as the mother of God and as an ideal of piety. Is it possible that since she was held in such high regard, Jews did not want to challenge her position? Instead, they put the blame on Jesus; not in fact because he was an illegitimate child, but because he was the ultimate example of a bad student of the Torah, since he was disrespectful to his teachers.

Counterhistories typically challenge the most central aspects of an established history. That is the case also with the story of the death of Jesus, which the *Toledot Yeshu* exposes to ridicule. Jesus and his disciples are accused of undermining the Jewish community by challenging the laws that ensure peace and stability in society. In the end, the members of the Sanhedrin are at a loss about what to do with Jesus, and they come up with the idea of having one of their members infiltrate this heretical group. The name of this volunteer is Judas Iscariot; in the *Toledot Yeshu,* he is not the betrayer of Jesus but a hero for the Jewish community. The description of the crucifixion verges on parody: Jesus is crucified not on a wooden cross but on a cabbage stalk. The reason for this is that Jesus had previously misused the name of God to make all trees swear that they would not carry him when he was hanged. However, Jesus had forgotten the cabbage stalk, since it was not counted among the trees.[12]

The *Toledot Yeshu* was a very popular legend that was spread throughout Jewish communities in the Middle Ages and afterwards. It may be compared to a sort of underground literature that poked fun of the majority culture. Most of the time, it could go under the radar of this culture and remain undetected since it was written in languages that were not easily accessible for most Christians. However, when Christians became aware of the stories in *Toledot Yeshu*, they caused strong reactions. The *Toledot Yeshu* is an example of how groups who experience their complete powerlessness in a society may react. They used ridicule as their weapon to undermine the dominant Christian story that served as the master narrative of society. Of course, this type of polemics was utterly unacceptable in dialogues and public discussions with Christians. When Jewish scholars were forced into such settings, they used philosophical arguments or rabbinic exegesis to confront Christian dogmas and stories about Jesus.

Both the Talmudic rabbis and the *Toledoth Yeshu* accepted the responsibility for the execution of Jesus since they claimed that he was an ordinary criminal. This approach was different from those found in more recent Jewish counterhistories. In the late nineteenth century, Jewish scholars did not accept the stories of Jewish responsibility for the death of Jesus that are found in the Gospels; they claimed that the narratives were historically false. These scholars claimed that the Romans, not the

12. Newman, "Death of Jesus."

Jewish authorities, were solely responsible for executions; and further, that the Gospels put the blame on Jewish leaders in order to secure good relations with Rome. This too was a counterhistory; however, it was based on historical discussions of the same sources. Moreover, in the end, the reconstruction by these Jewish scholars was generally accepted; the counterhistory became history.[13]

Rival Stories: Jesus in the Quran

The presentations of Jesus in the Quran are significantly different from those in Jewish sources. Their purpose was to undermine the Christian stories about Jesus; they had primarily a negative purpose. In the Quran, Jesus appears as a prophet; that is, in a positive role. However, the description of Jesus is placed within a conception of the world understood in terms of absolute monotheism. Therefore, stories about Jesus in the Quran could come into conflict with Christian stories; as a result, instead of counterstories we may characterize the relationship between Christian and Islamic stories of Jesus as one of rival stories.[14]

Christianity in Arabia

Before we discuss the picture of Jesus in the Quran, we should ask why Jesus is a figure in the Quran in the first place. Islam was the last of the three "religions of the Book" to emerge from the Middle East, in the seventh century. Judaism was the oldest of the three, and it had a large diaspora— that is, a large number of communities that lived outside Israel—spread over most of the Mediterranean area and the Middle East. In the Arabian Peninsula, there were groups of Jews in many towns; in some regions, such as Saba (present-day Yemen), they had at times a strong political influence. Muhammad and his followers had controversies and sometimes conflicts with Jewish groups. The relationship was thus characterized by both contacts and conflicts.

There were also Christians in many areas of Arabia, although few sources document their presence. There could be political reasons for Christian settlements. Two great powers in the area, the Byzantine Empire and the Persian, Sassanid Empire, were in competition, and Arabia was a buffer state between the two. The Byzantine emperors made agreements with client states to ward off attacks by Arab groups; they also tried to establish orthodox churches along the caravan routes. However, since

13. See below, 155–58.
14. Khalidi, *Muslim Jesus*; Leirvik, *Images of Jesus Christ*; Robinson, *Christ in Islam*.

orthodox Christianity was identified with the Byzantine Empire, these churches were unpopular with many Arabs.

The religion of the Sassanid Empire was Zoroastrianism, and it supported Christian groups and small states that had broken away from the Byzantine Empire over the conflicts about how to understand the nature of Christ. The Roman and later the Byzantine emperors were actively engaged in these controversies, because religious unity was important to secure the unity of the empire. What came to be known as the orthodox position was that Christ was both God and human ("man") at the same time; he had two natures in one person. The patriarch of Constantinople Nestorius (386–450) held a different position. He argued that one must distinguish between Jesus' two natures, the divine and the human. For this view he was condemned at the church council in Ephesus in 431 CE. It was this council that passed the resolution that Mary should be given the title "Mother of God" *(theotokos)*. Nestorius, however, argued that she should be called "mother of Christ" *(christotokos)* but not of God. This was a distinction that came to play an important role when the Quran described the relationship between Mary and Jesus. Since Nestorius and his position were condemned by the majority at the council in Ephesus, many of his followers left the Byzantine Empire for Arabia and the Sassanid Empire. The Christians who held Nestorius's position became the beginning of the so-called Oriental Orthodox Churches, which became widespread in Arabia, Persia, and even further east. There were also many other Christians who did not recognize the orthodox position on the two natures of Christ, but for a different reason. They were the so-called Monophysites, who claimed that Christ had only one nature, viz. a divine one.

In addition to the groups already mentioned, there were also groups of Jewish Christians.[15] Many were Jews who had continued their observance of Jewish law and rituals; they honored Jesus from Nazareth, but did not worship him as God. They had their own writings, some of which were condemned as heretical by orthodox bishops, and these groups gradually disappeared.

Even the Ethiopian church exerted influence in Arabia; it was close to Arabia, on the other side of the Red Sea. For a period, Ethiopian warfare established Christian rule over parts of southern Arabia. There must also have been contact with Syrian Christianity to the north of Arabia. From Damascus, caravan routes went south on the Arabian Peninsula, for instance to Mecca and Medina. It is also possible that Syrian Christianity had a direct influence on the Quran. Edessa was the most famous intellectual center for Syrian Christianity; much of the literature produced there had an ascetic character. Several of the apocryphal writings to the New

15. Ehrman, *Lost Christianities*, 95–103.

Testament originated as or were translated into Syriac—for instance the Gospel of Thomas, the Infancy Gospel of Thomas, and the Protevangelium of James. There was also a unique version of the Gospels in Syriac, Tatian's *Diatessaron* from circa 160 CE. It was based on John's Gospel and added sections from Mark, Matthew, and Luke, so that from four different gospels Tatian created one running narrative. The name, *Diatessaron*, explains the composition of the work; in Greek, it literally means: "through four." Several of these writings were probably known in Arabia when the Quran was written down; a number of Syriac loanwords appear in the Quran. Moreover, the Quran always speaks of "the gospel" in the singular; this may imply that it refers to Tatian's *Diatessaron*.

We may conclude that there were different groups of Christians, either within Arabia itself or in the neighboring areas. Most of them were outside the orbit of the orthodox church, which was the dominant church body within the Byzantine Empire. Strangely enough, at the time of Muhammad there were no translations of the Gospels into Arabic. Traditions about Jesus had probably reached Arabia via oral transmission or via apocryphal writings, perhaps arriving first even through oral tradition. We shall see that it is most likely these apocryphal writings that are reflected in the traditions about Jesus in the Quran.

This survey of Christian groups within or near Arabia shows that Christians were plentiful enough there for encounters with Christians to take place. Muhammad himself seems to have encountered Christians; several stories exist about such direct encounters. One story tells about a Christian monk, Bahira, who met Muhammad when he was a young man; his uncle had brought him along on a caravan trade journey. The monk immediately realized that Muhammad was a prophet and urged his uncle to protect him against enmity from Jews. This is most likely a legend; its purpose was to emphasize that if the Jews rejected Muhammad, Christians would recognize him.

Another tradition appears to be more trustworthy. Muhammad's wife, Khadija, had a relative who was a Christian; he supported Muhammad, who had begun to receive revelations, but who lacked self-confidence. In addition, there are stories about contact between followers of Muhammad and the Christian kingdom of Abyssinia (Ethiopia) across the Red Sea, when they sought refuge from persecution in Mecca. From the Medina period, there are stories about contacts between Muhammad and Christian groups in northern Arabia; in one case the Christian town of Najran paid taxes to Muhammad in return for protection from enemies.

Muhammad and the Quran

It is widely held that it was Muhammad himself who initiated the collection of texts that make up the Quran.[16] Muhammad appears to have been both a prophet and a poet; the Quran is based on his oral proclamations, perhaps in the form of recitations. In their written forms too are indications that the texts were performed orally; they have a rhythmic form and consist of repeated sayings, words, and themes. The style and form of the sayings in the Quran indicate that Muhammad's purpose was to convince his hearers that his message was true. When they were convinced, step 2 followed: it was their task to *repeat* what Muhammad had said.

Parts of the sayings in the Quran are known from Jewish and Christian sources, for instance the account of creation, and some stories about Jesus. However, we do not get the impression that the author of the Quran knew these stories as literary or written texts such as they are found in the Jewish Bible or in the New Testament. Rather, as they appear in the Quran, these stories give the impression that the author knew them as midrash, that is, as oral retellings of biblical stories, in which some points considered important are emphasized while others are left out.

We cannot say that Jesus plays an important part in the Quran; he is only one of many Jewish prophets who are included. Most of the sayings that are attributed to him do not distinguish him from other prophets. However, the Quran does include some stories exclusively about Jesus. Here I can only point out a few: the story of his birth, of his miracles, of his death and resurrection, and finally, of his "second coming."[17] We get the impression that the portrait of Jesus in the Quran has developed and changed over time. This is probably a result of changes in the situation for Muhammad and his followers. In Muhammad's period in Mecca, he was fighting polytheism; at that point, Jews and Christians were his allies. Stories about Jesus that may be assigned to that period show little that is polemical. However, when Muhammad had left Mecca and took refuge in Medina, his relationships to Jews and Christians became more problematic, and material about Jesus from this period has a polemical edge to it.

Mary and Jesus

In the Quran, Jesus is often spoken of as "Son of Mary." Mary plays an important role on the Quran, and therefore stories about Jesus are often linked to stories or sayings about Mary. There are especially two suras that

16. Peters, *Jesus and Muhammad*, 72–83.

17. For a full listing, see Leirvik, *Images of Jesus Christ*, 20–24; Peters, *Jesus and Muhammad*, 4–7.

combine stories about Mary, the birth of Jesus, and his later activities. Sura 19, which is actually called "Mary" (Maryam), originated in the early period in Mecca whereas sura 3 comes from the period in Medina.

The Virgin Mary and Jesus (old Persian miniature).
Historic Images / Alamy Stock Photo. Used by permission.

Sura 19 starts with the story of the priest Zachariah, whose son, John, was born in a miraculous way; it continues with the story of Mary, much in the same way as in chapter 1 in Luke's Gospel. The description of the annunciation to Mary and the birth of Jesus locates these events in Arabia. The Quran says that Mary "withdrew from her family to an eastern place" (19:16). The messenger from God is described as "a perfect man." When Mary is promised that she shall bear a son, and she objects that she is not "unchaste," the messenger says: "Thy Lord says, 'It is easy for Me'" (19:21) When Mary is about to give birth, she leaves for a lonely place and sits down under a palm tree, when the miracle happens: a well springs up under the tree, and ripe dates fall down from the palm tree (19:22–26). When she arrives home with the child, she is accused of being an unchaste woman (19:27). However, she encourages the baby to speak, and a new miracle happens: Jesus speaks, and he describes himself in a way that corresponds to the Quran's image of a prophet; "Truly I am a servant of God. He has given me the Book and made me a prophet" (19:30). Moreover, the call he has received from God consists in "prayer and almsgiving so long as I live" (19:31).

The accusation that Mary had led an "unchaste life," understated in Matthew's story, is brought out into the open in the Quran. The story of Mary under the palm tree probably derives from a similar story in Pseudo-Matthew 20. In Pseudo-Matthew, it is Jesus who makes the miracle happen when Mary and Joseph are about to succumb to thirst and hunger in the desert. Both Pseudo-Matthew and the Arabic Infancy Gospel describe how the infant Jesus speaks from the cradle. These stories of miracles in the desert bear the signs of oral retellings, maybe at night at a caravan stop. Mary and the birth of Jesus are moved to a place farther "East," and Jesus is portrayed as a Muslim prophet who declares that he is the servant of God. Moreover, by a life characterized by prayer and almsgiving, Jesus exhibits the most important Islamic virtues.

Some of the statements about Jesus may contain a polemical twist against the orthodox dogma of the two natures of Christ, human and divine. The Quran combines the saying "That is Jesus, son of Mary" (19:34) with the response from God's messenger: "It is not for God to take a child. Glory be to Him. When He decrees a thing, He only says to it, 'Be!' and it is" (19:35).[18] These sayings underline that as son of Mary, Jesus is not divine, but created by God. This seems to parallel the Nestorians' rejection of calling Mary the mother of God and suggests that there may have been contacts between Muhammad and his followers and nonorthodox Christians. Sura 4:171 is another text that univocally states that as son of Mary, Jesus was not divine, and the orthodox doctrine of the Trinity is totally rejected: "Messiah, Jesus, son of Mary, was only a messenger of God, and

---

18. Sura 3:39 draws a parallel between the creation of Adam and Jesus.

His Word, which he committed to Mary, and a Spirit from him. So believe in God and His messengers, and say not 'Three.'"

Jesus as an Islamic Prophet

Sura 3, which originated in the period of Muhammad in Medina, combines the promise to Mary with an extended description of the future of Jesus. God will teach him "the Book, Wisdom, the Torah, and the Gospel" (3:48). This list declares Jesus to be an Islamic prophet who knows the various sources of revelation; the last two refer to the law of Moses and the gospel of Jesus. The following verses describe what characterized Jesus' activity as a prophet:

> I will create for you out of clay the shape of a bird. Then I will breathe into it, and it will be a bird by God's leave. And I will heal the blind and the leper and give life to the dead by God's leave. And I will inform you about what you eat and what you store up in your houses . . . And I come confirming that which was before me, the Torah, and to make lawful unto you part of that which was forbidden unto you . . . Truly God is my Lord and your Lord. So reverence God and obey me. (3:49–51)

This list of Jesus' activities starts with a popular story from the Infancy Gospel of Thomas 2–4; it tells how Jesus as a young boy breathes life into birds he had made from mud. This story is combined with well-known miracles recorded in the Gospels: healings of the blind, of people suffering from leprosy, and the raising of the dead. Such lists were expanded and became an essential part of a Jesus piety in Sufism.[19] There may also be a criticism of Christian confessions to Jesus in the comment that Jesus makes these miracles "by God's leave." The comment may be directed at a Christian theology that used the miracles as a proof of Jesus' divinity. A parallel to this statement appears in 5:110, which emphasizes that Jesus did miracles with the consent of God. This sura quotes God, who repeatedly confirms that the miracle happened "by My Leave."

The last sections of the descriptions of Jesus' activities as a prophet are not direct quotations from the gospels, but they are adapted from statements by Jesus on purity and his relation to the Law. This portrait from Sura 3 corresponds fully to the responsibilities of a prophet in Islam. Thus, this image is applied in all the instances where Jesus describes his role in the Quran. That God is One is the main message of Jesus' teaching in the Quran; there

19. Leirvik, *Images of Jesus Christ*, 83–106.

is nothing in Jesus' teaching that goes beyond this monotheism. The Quran does not go into details about Jesus' teachings on special occasions; there are no specifics about Jesus' teaching to the crowds or to his disciples.

The most serious accusation against orthodox Christians was that they made Jesus and Mary into gods. This topic occurs several times when the Quran reveals conversations between God and Jesus:

> And when God said, "O Jesus son of Mary! Didst thou say unto mankind, 'Take me and my mother as gods apart from God?'" He said, "Glory be to Thee! It is not for me to utter that which I have no right. Had I said it, Thou wouldst surely have known it . . . I said naught to them save that which Thou didst command me: 'Worship God, my Lord and Your Lord.'" (5:116–17)

This criticism is clearly stated in 5:17: "They indeed have disbelieved who say, 'God is the Messiah, son of Mary.'" There are similarities to the criticism that Nestorians addressed to Orthodox Christians, that they turned Jesus and Mary into gods, in addition to God. However, we need not look for direct influence from the Nestorians; the Quran follows its own focus that God is only One.[20]

Jesus Was not Crucified

In several instances, the Quran describes the Jews as "infidels" in relation to Jesus, especially when it reports that they wanted to kill Jesus. Like the gospels, the Quran sees a parallel between their desire to kill Jesus and Israel's previous murders of prophets. With regard to the death of Jesus, however, it is difficult to get a clear sense of what their hatred actually implied. The Quran says that the Jews claimed, "We slew the Messiah, Jesus son of Mary, the messenger of God." However, the Quran gives its own comment on their claim: "though they did not slay him; nor did they crucify him, but it appeared so unto them. Those who differ concerning him are in doubt thereof. They have no knowledge of it, but follow only conjectures; they slew him not for certain. But God raised him up unto Himself, and God is Mighty, Wise" (4:157–58). This is a strange saying, which caused long discussions in early commentaries on the Quran.[21]

Most Quran scholars agree now that the Quran asserts that Jesus was not crucified, and that he was lifted directly up to God, in the same way as other prophets. The main issue that remains is therefore what is meant

---

20. Robinson, *Christ in Islam*, 20.

21. Robinson, *Christ in Islam*, 127–41.

with the statement "but it appeared so unto them." Most early commentators think that the Jews by mistake had crucified a man who looked like Jesus, but who was not Jesus himself. Behind this suggestion was the idea that Jesus' looks were transferred to another man, whom the Jews then considered to be Jesus. This idea may sound curious to modern minds; however, we find a similar suggestion in non-orthodox Christian groups. The *Apocryphal Acts of John*, from the late second century, stated that the crowds, who believed that they had crucified Jesus, were mistaken. They belonged to a lower nature and therefore they did not realize that the real Jesus, the Word, was not to be found in the person on the cross (see above; *Acts of John*, 97–102). Other non-orthodox (often spoken of as "Gnostic") texts also claim that Jesus only appeared to be hanging on the cross; in reality, he was not present in a body. Other Christian writings present theories similar to that of the Quran, that another man was crucified instead of Jesus; for instance, Simon of Cyrene, who carried the cross for Jesus.[22]

The Second Coming of Jesus

Part of Jesus' sayings about the future was that he would return in glory to judge the world. In the fifth century, this theme was included in the Apostolic Creed. Jesus Christ who was sitting at the right hand of the Father, would, in the words of the Creed, "come again to judge the quick and the dead." That Jesus would return was also part of the teaching about Jesus in the Quran, although the statements to this effect are not easy to interpret. The most important saying about Jesus' return follows the statement that Jesus was not crucified but was lifted directly up to God: "There is not one of the People of the Book, but will surely believe in him before the end, and on the Day of Resurrection he will be a witness against them" (4:159).[23] According to the earliest commentators, "he" who will be the witness against them is a reference to Jesus. However, there is uncertainty about whether "before the end" refers to the death of Jesus. That "the People of the Book" will "believe" in Jesus, should not be understood in a Christian, but in a Muslim sense; it implies believing that Jesus was a prophet and messenger from God. That he will be a witness against "the People of the Book" in the final Judgment gives him an eschatological role. However, this is not comparable to the unique role Jesus had in Christian faith; the Quran speaks of prophets whom God will send to all people, and who will serve as witnesses against them (4:41). Many early commentators think that sura 43:61 refers to Jesus, who

22. Robinson, *Christ in Islam*, 106–16.
23. Robinson, *Christ in Islam*, 78–89.

signals the end of time: "And he is indeed a portent of the Hour; so doubt not concerning it and follow me."[24] Later writings in the Islamic tradition, the Hadiths,[25] are more open to Christian eschatological images; however, they are placed within a Muslim world view. This reduces the importance of Jesus; his "coming again" is only one of several sign of the end of time, and he is not God's messenger at the final judgment.

A Polemical Portrait of Jesus

The earliest Christian reactions to the Quran treated it as a Christian heresy. They measured the presentations of Jesus by orthodox Christian dogmas and the images of Jesus in the gospels. In hindsight; however, we must say that this is not an adequate way to evaluate the images of Jesus in the Quran. Even if there is some common material, Islam quickly established itself as a separate religion, distinct from Christianity and Judaism, even if it recognized a familiarity expressed by the term "peoples of the Book," which included Jews and Christians. In consequence, the material that has been adopted from Christian traditions must be interpreted within the context of the theology of the Quran.[26] Although the presentations of Jesus in the gospels and in the Quran have much in common, it is more adequate to say that the Quran gives a rival story of Jesus to that of Christian orthodoxy in the seventh century.

In the Quran, Jesus is one among many prophets together with Abraham, Moses, and David. He is described with the characteristics of these prophets: they are carriers of the word of God and they are equipped with His spirit. The prophets are all sent by God to a "proud and recalcitrant people," who often reject their message; however, in the end, God will prove them right. Does Jesus represent something unique among the prophets in the Quran, in a similar way to the unique role he has in the gospels and Christian tradition? The answer, I think, is that these special aspects are toned down, and that Jesus is understood within a Muslim context.

This contextualization takes different forms; it can be more or less polemical, partly depending on the period of writing. Sura 19 from the Mecca period rewrites the birth narrative in a non-polemical way; it moves Mary and the birth of Jesus into a desert landscape in the East, and it has Jesus

24. Robinson, *Christ in Islam*, 90–105.

25 Hadith is a record of the traditions or sayings of the Prophet Muhammad, revered and received as a major source of religious law and moral guidance, and collected by the first generations of Islam.

26. Khalidi, *Muslim Jesus*, 9–17.

speak already as an infant. This is similar to apocryphal gospel stories. Suras 3 and 5 from the Medina period are much more polemical and emphasize that Jesus is merely human. He can perform miracles only by the consent of God; they cannot, as among many Christians, be used as proofs of Jesus' divinity. The most polemical issues concern the relationship between humanity and divinity not only in Jesus but also in Mary. In the seventh century, Mary was highly venerated; in orthodox Christianity, she had been granted the status of mother of God. In an exchange between God and Jesus, Jesus explicitly distances himself from the position that he and Mary should be called gods (5:17, 116–17). Thus, the Quran sets up a Christian orthodox position only to have Jesus distance himself from it. Similarly with regard to Jesus' crucifixion, the Quran sets up an alternative to the orthodox Christian position and places Jesus within the same pattern of ascension to God as other prophets in Islam. Several of these positions, which were critical of orthodox Christianity, showed similarities with nonorthodox Christian views, and this may explain why some orthodox Christian theologians regarded Islam as a heretical Christian group.

We have looked at some elements of similarity in the history of Jesus between the Gospels and the Quran. However, some of the most important elements in the teaching of Jesus in the Gospels are not included in the Quran: the Sermon of the Mount, Jesus' parables, his instructions to his disciples, and the predictions of his suffering and death. In the Quran, Jesus' teaching centers exclusively on God, and they often take the form of exhortations to follow Jesus himself in this belief. Thus, Jesus' teaching is more or less purged of specifically Christian positions. However, it is possible that Muhammad and his followers had only limited access to gospels, with their stories and teachings of Jesus. The later canonical Gospels may not have been available in Arabic translations at the time; therefore, it was the stories and teachings about Jesus from nonorthodox groups that influenced the Quran. However, it was above all the dominant theological position, that nothing must get in the way of monotheism, that formed the picture of Jesus in the Quran.

In this chapter, it has been possible only to give a sketch of the image of Jesus in the Quran, of the earliest period of Islam in the seventh century. However, this was only the beginning of broad and varied traditions about Jesus within Islam. They developed from the hadiths—the earliest normative traditions linked to Muhammad—into more specific and diverse traditions in Shia Islam and Sufism.[27]

---

27. For this development, see Khalidi, *Muslim Jesus*; Leirvik, *Images of Jesus Christ*; Peters, *Jesus and Muhammad*; and Robinson, *Christ in Islam*.

Part 2: Retellings

THE MEMORIES OF JESUS in the first section were oriented towards the past; Christians, Jews, and Muslims were concerned about the origins of the Jesus stories, and they told conflicting stories. In this section, we move into a different time and space. Christianity has moved toward Europe and the West, the churches have become powerful institutions, and that results in changes in the perspectives of memories. Attention is directed more towards the present, towards the importance of Jesus for the identity of believers and for society. In the High Middle Ages the human Jesus gets renewed attention; for instance the suffering, crucified Jesus becomes an object of identification for many in periods of crisis and suffering. Francis of Assisi is the main proponent of a spirituality that focuses on Jesus as poor, in an attempt to shape society in the image of Jesus. With enlightenment and the beginning of modernity comes criticism of the memory tradition that combined the human Jesus and the heavenly Christ in support of the authority of the Church and the princes. This criticism contrasts the human Jesus with Christ; it aims at establishing a memory of Jesus as a man and as a social critic called the historical Jesus. This reading of the Gospels had political repercussions: it undercuts the authority of the rulers, and at least initially, it fosters equality and democracy.

Memories are always part of the creation and development of identities. The memory of Jesus was retold to shape the identity of Europe. The central place that Jesus had in European Christianities means that he represented a collective memory that shaped common identities. However, group identities are often established in contrast to other group identities. From the Middle Ages down to the present, Jesus has often served as an identification figure for Christian Europe. He represents the European we, in contrast to "those we are not." Often, Muslims have served as the external "others." However, for most of history the Jews have been the "internal others," present within Europe but defined as "the others." It is very troubling that Jesus has been employed to divide Christians from Jews and to expose Jews to hatred. The retellings of narratives about Jesus' death in the Gospels carry a large responsibility for this situation; both the retellings and the situation they have led to have made necessary a critical-historical study of the Gospel memories of Jesus' crucifixion.

4

The Second Christ

*Saint Francis and the Human Jesus
in the Middle Ages*

IT WAS NOT A foregone conclusion that the narratives from Jesus' life
would play an important role for Christians and their faith and spirituality. The obvious example is Paul; in his letters, he almost never mentions
episodes from Jesus' life. He was exclusively concerned with the *meaning*
of Jesus the Christ, which Paul found in his death and resurrection. The
resurrection of Christ remained the most important aspect of faith for believers in the first centuries; the humanity of Jesus played a minor role. Of
course, this is not the full story; in particular, among monks the memories
of Jesus and his life were kept alive. Monastic rules emphasized that the
monks should follow the example of Jesus in a life of poverty, humility,
and obedience; moreover, in their prayers and meditation they held the
suffering of Jesus before their eyes.

As the High Middle Ages began, the humanity of Jesus gained greater
importance for Christian spirituality. One visual example can illustrate
this. In late antiquity and the early Middle Ages, crucifixes often portrayed
Christ as king; as a sign of victory, he was dressed in royal vestments and
was standing on the cross. However, in the twelfth and thirteenth centuries,
the presentation changes: Jesus is portrayed as a tormented figure, clearly
in a position of suffering, hanging on the cross. This artistic expression indicates a change in mentality; clearly Jesus is portrayed as identifying with
human suffering. We shall look into this development in more detail at the
end of the chapter; here I will mention how this turn toward Jesus' humanity
influenced Christian spirituality. Prayers and liturgies put more weight on
emotions, and on meditations on the life of Jesus, especially on his birth,

suffering, and death. This affected the very process of memory. The purpose of meditation was to bring forth in the mind central events in the life of Jesus and to try to create images of the events so that they became real to the person meditating. The last step in the process of meditation was to imagine oneself as actually participating in the event.

This model of meditation helped make memory of events in the life of Jesus come alive. Individual Christians, not just monks, could practice such meditation. We find a visual expression of this process of meditation in many paintings of scenes from the life of Jesus—for instance, nativity scenes where the patron of the painting is included as a participant in the adoration of the infant Jesus. Homilies and liturgies could have a similar function, and church buildings themselves, with stained-glass windows and sculptures, put memories of Jesus in front of people and invited them to participate in his life.

Francis of Assisi—A Living Memory of Jesus

Francis of Assisi (1182–1226) had a strong influence on this movement toward a Christian spirituality centered upon the humanity of Jesus. Francis was the son of a rich merchant in the city of Assisi, in Umbria in central Italy. In his youth he lived a life guided by ideals of troubadours and knights. In 1205, however, he experienced a sudden religious conversion and opted for a life of absolute poverty. He broke off all relations with his father and started to help the poor and to care for lepers. After some time, he also began to travel around in the nearest region to proclaim a discipleship of Jesus in poverty. Many started to follow him, and in 1209 he established an order of mendicants which received oral and provisional recognition by Pope Innocent III. However, in 1224, Francis retired from the leadership of the order; he had become disillusioned by what he saw as the brothers' betrayal of the ideal of poverty. At about this time, he received the stigmata, i.e. the bodily marks of Jesus' crucifixion on his own body. Francis died in 1226, and he was canonized only two years later, in 1228.

Most of the great theologians from the Middle Ages have left many books, sermons, or other writings. It was not so for Saint Francis: he was a layperson, and his life was a sermon. If he made a great impact in his own time and continues to do so, it is because he used his life as a model of how to follow Jesus through poverty; he shaped his life after Jesus' words in the Gospels.

Francis also used symbolic acts to great effect; we would say that he was a great communicator. A story that has become part of the legend surrounding Saint Francis tells how he created the first nativity scene, to re-create how Jesus was born into poverty. Thomas of Celano, the first biographer of Saint Francis, recounts how Francis asked a nobleman in the village of Greccio to prepare the midnight mass for Christmas: "For I wish to enact the memory of that babe who was born in Bethlehem: to see as much as is possible with my own bodily eyes the discomfort of his infant needs, how he lay in a manger, and how with an ox and an ass standing by, he rested on hay."[1] Celano continues by explaining that Francis with this symbolic act wanted to make those attending the mass participate in the event and to realize how it could become a model for their lives: "There simplicity is given a place of honor, poverty is exalted, humility is commended, and out of Greccio is made a new Bethlehem."[2]

This story illustrates the new importance of memory narratives. The starting point was the memory recorded in Luke's Gospel (whether historical or not) of Jesus' birth in Bethlehem where he was laid in a manger. Previously, Christians had been invited to make a mental image of the scene, helped by homilies or artistic representations. In Greccio, however, parishioners witnessed a live picture: a child in a manger, surrounded by animals. In this way, they became participants in an event that first happened in Bethlehem. Moreover, they were challenged to live according to the values that the scene of Jesus' birth made visible: simplicity, poverty, and humility.

To follow the Poor Jesus

The central point around which Francis formed his life, and the life of his companions, was to follow Jesus in radical poverty. Poverty as an ideal was not new in Christianity; however, Francis made this radical form of poverty his hallmark. In the Gospels we find words of Jesus about leaving house and property to follow him. These demands were expressions of the Jesus movement as a countercultural movement, a protest against the norms and values of the current society. However, these words of Jesus stand beside other, softer words that required followers to give alms to the poor and show hospitality to strangers.

The history of Christianity as a counterculture gradually came to an end: first with Constantine's decision to turn it into a recognized religion in the Roman Empire, and fundamentally when Theodosius I declared it to be the state religion of the empire in 380. Care for the poor and the sick continued to be part of the church's responsibility; however, the demand for a life in poverty was, so to speak, outsourced to the religious—to monks and nuns. The Rule of

1. Thomas of Celano, *Saint Francis*, 254.
2. Thomas of Celano, *Saint Francis*, 255.

Benedict of Nursia for monastic life from 586 became an important signpost; it emphasized that monastic life should be governed by the gospel of Jesus, and that poverty had an important place in this gospel. However, poverty was required from the individual monk, not from the monastery or the order. This may be the reason that Benedict in his rule does not refer to Jesus' words about poverty but instead refers to the story in Acts about the first disciples: "no one claimed private ownership of any possessions, but everything they owned was held in common" (Acts 4:32). As a result, the monasteries owned property and soon became rich; the monks could live comfortable lives, although they did not have individual property. This development of course resulted in criticism, both from within and from outside monastic orders. The history of monasticism is replete with repeated demands for reforms and attempts to bring back the ideal of poverty.

Francis entered into this history with his demand for absolute poverty, a demand that was directed not only to individual monks but also to the monasteries and the community of brethren. It seems that Francis was taken by surprise at the large number of men who wanted to join his fellowship. In his *Testament*, one of the few documents that he wrote himself, he says that he did not know what to do, but God revealed to him that he should "live according to the pattern of the Holy Gospel."[3] A legendary story says that Francis and two of his brethren went into a church in Assisi and three times opened the Bible, without any fixed plan. Every time their eyes fell on a word from Jesus to give all one's property to the poor, and to deny oneself (Matt 16:2, 4, 19:21; Luke 9:3).[4] This history confirms that it was the human Jesus and his words to renounce one's property that were at the center of Francis's life.

3. Armstrong et al., eds., *Francis of Assisi: Early Documents* 1:125.
4. Armstrong et al., eds., *Francis of Assisi: Early Documents* 2:85–86.

Giotto: *The Legend of Saint Francis; Renunciation of Worldly Goods*
(1297–1299). Wikimedia Commons.[5]

Francis lived during a period in Italy when his message was clearly controversial; however, in some ways several religious protest movements had paved the way for it. He had grown up in Assisi as the son of a rich merchant; that placed him in the middle of an ongoing conflict between the nobility and the merchants, who were literally fighting for power in many Italian cities. The church too was involved in this fight for power: bishops were also secular lords, with power and wealth. Moreover, popes were engaged in political struggles for power with princes of smaller states, and not least with the emperor of the Holy Roman Empire. The church was very rich, and many monasteries owned great estates. Thus many in religious

5. https://commons.wikimedia.org/wiki/File:Giotto_di_Bondone_-_Legend_of_St_Francis_-_5._Renunciation_of_Wordly_Goods_-_WGA09123.jpg.

orders who had made promises of personal poverty had the use of great wealth that belonged to churches and monasteries. As a reaction against this situation, a number of groups and movements arose to protest these excesses. Many, both women and men, chose to follow Jesus' message in the gospel; they left their homes and lived as itinerant beggars. Originally, Francis and his group had much in common with these other groups and movements. However, while many of these other groups were persecuted, ostracized, and accused of heresy, Francis managed to keep his movement within the church, and emphasized his loyalty to church authorities. He was successful, so much so that he had his movement recognized as an order by two successive popes. Moreover, after his death, he was quickly declared a saint, and his biography was redacted to make it conform to his image as a Christian who was loyal to the church.

With his representation of the poor Jesus, Francis established a picture unique in the Middle Ages. In antiquity and the early Middle Ages, the imitation of Jesus aimed at sharing in his resurrection and his divinity. In the High Middle Ages this shifted to an emphasis on imitating his human life. In periods of suffering and poverty, Christians needed a Jesus who could identify with them. Francis carried this identification with the humanity and poverty of Jesus almost (some would say certainly) to the extreme. One example is his *Testament*; in one place here, Francis explains how Jesus' call came directly to him. He felt abhorrence for lepers, but in the first paragraph of his Testament, he says that, "The Lord himself led me among them, and I showed mercy towards them."[6]

Since those who entered the order had to give away their property, they had to work in order to live. Like many other itinerants, they were allowed to beg if necessary. Moreover, they were not to be ashamed of begging since Jesus Christ himself had not been ashamed to beg. In the first rule for the community (the *Earlier Rule*), which was not accepted by the pope, Francis had made rather free use of the Gospels when he said: "Remember, moreover, that our Lord Jesus Christ, was poor and not ashamed. He was poor and a stranger and lived on alms—He, the Blessed Virgin, and His disciples."[7]

It was essential to Francis that those who wanted to follow Christ had to give up their property. Property, to Francis, represented an egocentric attitude to the world and interpersonal relationships; it was the root of all evil. To become a "follower of Christ" meant to become like him who had no part in this world, but who belonged to God, fully and exclusively. In

6. Armstrong et al., eds., *Francis of Assisi: Early Documents* 1:124.

7. Armstrong et al., eds., *Francis of Assisi: Early Documents* 1:70.

contrast to a world built on desire for property and wealth, Francis proposed a world built on the narrative of Christ and Mary, who lived from alms, and who trusted in the hospitality offered to them. Francis's vision was a world without money and property, and characterized by redistribution to people who had nothing. Alms was not a religious duty for Christians; it was "a legacy and a justice due to the poor that the Lord Jesus Christ acquired for us."[8] To be poor and to beg for alms was nothing to be ashamed of; in fact, it meant to be seated at table with Jesus.

Imitating the Sufferings of Christ

Francis's life had many facets. One important side of it was directed outward, journeying around central Italy, preaching and challenging people to lead a life of poverty. Another very important aspect was his withdrawal to live the life of a hermit, filled with meditation, prayer, and reflection on the crucified Christ. As Francis neared the end of his life, the importance of this inner work grew and took up more and more of his time. During this period Francis was afflicted by a number of illnesses and also endured many conflicts over the direction of the movement that he had started. It now numbered several thousand brothers and needed stronger leadership and organizational structure.

Francis had retired from his leadership position; however, he was worried that his brothers looked upon him as an obstacle to taking new directions as an order. It was at this specific moment, when he had retired to La Verna, an isolated place on Mount Penna, to pray together with a few trusted companions, that Francis's memory tradition offers us his extraordinary experience.[9] While praying, Francis had a vision of a man who looked like a seraph (Isa 6:1–7), and he noticed stigmata—that is, Christ's wounds from his cross—on his own body: two on his hands, two on his feet and one on his side. It was not until Francis was dead that others could see them; then they were immediately made known as a sign of his likeness to Christ, as a sign that he had shared Christ's sufferings.

The historical factuality of Francis's stigmata has of course been contested, and it is not possible to give undisputable proofs of them. However, the dramatic story of Francis's vision at La Verna corresponds to the intensity in Francis's veneration of Christ, well known from many sources. The memory and the meaning of the La Verna event and Francis's stigmata underwent

---

8. Armstrong et al., eds., *Francis of Assisi: Early Documents* 1:71.

9 Vauchez, *Francis of Assisi*, 127–31.

changes in various legends and biographies, and the stigmata received increasing weight as a sign of Francis's likeness to Christ.

Saint Francis as "the Other Christ"

Il Poverello di Cristo ("the little poor man of Christ") was a popular name for Saint Francis, and in many sources his life is modeled on the life of Jesus. There are parallels between the lives of Jesus and of Francis; in addition, there are also similarities between the written memories of their lives—that is, between the Gospels and the several Lives and legends about Saint Francis. In chapter 1, we observed how the four Gospels had quite different presentations of Jesus. Some of the differences may be a result of different opinions of what was most important in the memories of Jesus. In a similar way, differences between the various lives of St. Francis reflect long discussions and contestations about how his life should be portrayed. The main conflict was fought over what aspect of Francis's life should have most weight. One alternative was Francis as the radical follower of Jesus in a life of poverty, with strong criticism of the wealth in the city as well as in the church. The other alternative was Francis as a spiritual man with his stigmata as the exclusive signs that he bore the likeness of Jesus. The sources contain material for both sides of Francis's life; accordingly, his memories could be written in several ways.

There is no doubt that Francis's imitation of Christ as poor was a central key to understanding how Francis himself modeled his life on the life of Jesus Christ. However, this call to poverty became controversial, and many wanted to hide this part of his life. This started already when he was canonized only two years after his death, in 1228. Pope Gregory IX declared Francis a saint with two official papal documents in which he emphasized the main reasons for canonizing him: Francis had supported and preserved the church in a difficult period for the church. His life and message of poverty was not even mentioned. The Franciscan Thomas of Celano was charged with writing the first Life of the saint, the *Vita prima*, 1229.[10] Celano attempted to combine the radical renewal that Francis undertook with his message of poverty and obedience with Gregory's desire to integrate Francis into the official tradition of saints with the Catholic Church. At the same time, the Life was intended to portray Francis as an ideal for the Franciscans and their life in the order. For this purpose, Francis's stigmata played a central role. The stigmata showed God's confirmation of Francis's extraordinary holiness, and they also provided legitimacy

10. Thomas of Celano, *Life of Saint Francis*.

to the Franciscan order. This interpretation of the life of Saint Francis by Celano had a parallel in stone. The construction of the enormous basilica in Assisi started soon after the canonization of Saint Francis. The basilica reflects the growing status accorded to Saint Francis and the Franciscan order in the Church; however, many of the early brethren felt that it represented a total break with Francis's ideal of poverty.

Several writings about Saint Francis expressed their protest against this process of respectability; they wanted to preserve the picture of Francis and his vocation of absolute poverty. In light of these discussions, Bonaventure, the Minister General of the Franciscan order, found it necessary in 1263 to write a new presentation of Francis's life, the *Legenda major*,[11] to give the definitive version. This is an example of how a cultural memory is created; the "official" memories of Pope Gregory IX and Thomas de Celano had not succeeded in convincing all parties; and there were so many other memories. We may speak of these as "communicative memories" among different groups and individuals, of a nonofficial character.[12] The conflicts over the memories of Francis were so bitter because they carried his legacy for the identity of the members of the Franciscan order. This conflict was so strong that Bonaventure decided that his should be the only official memory of Francis; earlier works, such as that of Thomas Celano, should be destroyed.

Bonaventure structured his *Life* in three parts. The first and the last parts described Francis's life in a chronological order, while the central section portrayed Francis's virtues and, above all, his life in Christ. Bonaventure emphasized that Francis pursued Christ and identified with him, so that in the end Francis became a living image of Christ. The miraculous event when Francis received the stigmata played a central role in this process of "becoming Christ." Bonaventure says that Francis "was being transformed into Him Who chose to be crucified out of the excess of His love."[13] In Bonaventure's *Life*, Francis became the author of a mystic Christianity that made possible a new relationship between Christ and humanity. From this perspective, Francis's life of poverty in discipleship with Jesus lost much of its importance as a model for Franciscans. With Bonaventure, emphasis shifted away from poverty to spirituality; poverty was controversial because it was associated with heretical groups. The memories of Francis constructed by Bonaventure became the cultural memory of the Catholic Church. Within this cultural memory, Francis is recalled, above all, as a saint who embodied the spirituality of Christ. Within this

11. Bonaventure, *Major Legend.*
12. Assman, "Communicative and Cultural Memory."
13. Bonaventure, *Major Legend.*13.3, 632.

cultural memory, Francis is recalled, above all, as a saint who embodied the spirituality of Christ. Recently, Leonardo Boff, the Brazilian liberation theologian, brought back the radical image of Francis as a protagonist for poverty.[14] Moreover the first in history to choose Francis as his papal name indeed lives a lifestyle that calls the Church back to renew a commitment to Saint Francis's ideals of poverty and simplicity.

Bonaventure's selection of memories of Saint Francis met strong resistance from among the so-called Spirituals in the order. They wanted to hold on to the original ideal of poverty; however, they were persecuted by the leaders of the order and by several popes. Their memories of Francis are preserved in a group of early stories, the so-called *Assisi Compilation*.[15] They portray Francis as "a perfect mirror" of the poverty and sufferings of Christ. In this mirror, one could see "the poverty and weakness of our Lord Jesus Christ which he endured in His body for the salvation of the human race."[16] From 1330 onwards, the Spirituals were persecuted to such a degree that they disappeared completely; however, some of their writings were preserved and have continued to influence the memory of Francis in later generations.

Among these writings the best known is the *Fioretti*, "The little Flowers of St Francis."[17] It has some similarities to Bonaventure's *Major Legend* (for instance the portrait of Francis as the likeness of Christ). Francis is explicitly described as "in certain things like another Christ given to the world for the people's salvation."[18] *Fioretti* starts with a comparison between Francis and Christ: "how the glorious Sir Saint Francis was conformed to the blessed Christ in all the acts of his life."[19] Like Christ, Francis chose twelve disciples, who followed him in poverty. To speak of Francis as "the second Christ" was an ambiguous statement: it could be understood in more than one way. The simplest way was to say that Francis renewed a picture of Christ that had been hidden for a long time. Some of the Spirituals, however, wanted to draw the comparison further and considered Francis a reincarnation of Christ, a *Christus Redivivus*. At the end of the fourteenth century, the *Book of Conformities* presented an extreme version of this position. It lists no less than nine identical events in the life of Francis and that of Christ; Francis was even born in a stable and placed in a manger.[20]

14. Boff, *Saint Francis*.

15. Armstrong et al., eds., *Francis of Assisi: Early Documents* 2:113–231.

16. Armstrong et al., eds., *Francis of Assisi: Early Documents* 2:221.

17. Armstrong et al., eds., *Francis of Assisi: Early Documents* 3:566–659.

18. Armstrong et al., eds., *Francis of Assisi: Early Documents* 3:578.

19. Armstrong et al., eds.,*Francis of Assisi: Early Documents,* 3:566.

20. Vauchez, André, *Francis of Assisi*, 207–9.

The differences between the various legends about Saint Francis were also reflected in presentations of the saint in art. They came later than the legends, but from circa 1250 we can see the beginning of an iconographical tradition, starting with portraits.[21] Cimabue (1240–1302), who made several dramatic paintings of the crucifixion of Christ in the Upper Church in the Saint Francis basilica in Assisi, also painted an early portrait of St Francis, inserted in a painting of Mary and the Child, in the Lower Church. Francis appears as a man of small height, with a radiant, friendly face. In the Lower Church, there is also a series of paintings from the life of Francis in parallel with paintings of the suffering and death of Jesus, painted by an unknown "Master of Saint Francis," circa 1250–60. In this series is a scene where Francis parts with his father, handing his clothes back to him. The parallel from the life of Christ is an unusual scene where Christ himself divests before the crucifixion.[22] The message is unmistakably clear; Francis is portrayed as a second Christ.

The most complete cycle of pictures of Saint Francis is found in the Upper Church of the Saint Francis basilica. The motives in this cycle are taken from Bonaventure's *Major Legend*. There are twenty-eight frescoes in all; some of them show Francis's early life; the last ones cover the end of Francis's life, his death, the funeral, and the canonization by Pope Gregory IX. Most paintings show the miracles that Francis did and extraordinary experiences and visions; here Francis's receiving the stigmata holds a central place, with a total of three frescoes. However, apart from the scene in which Francis returns his clothes to his father, there are no scenes showing Francis's poverty or his contacts with poor people or lepers. The Upper Church cycle presents Saint Francis as a spiritual hero, a miracle worker, and a mystic, corresponding to the message of Bonaventure's *Major Legend*. Traditionally, this cycle of frescoes has been attributed to Giotto (1266–1337) and his school. However, this attribution is contested; some art historians think that the frescoes were painted in the period between 1291 and 1296, before it is known that Giotto worked in Assisi and painted several frescos in the Lower Church.[23]

21. Brooke, *Image of St Francis*.

22. In the gospels, the Roman soldiers undress Jesus, Brooke, *Image of St Francis*, 191–92.

23. Brooke, *Image of St Francis*, 415–53.

Jesus as Mother

The spirituality of the High Middle Ages focused on the human Jesus, with strong expressions of human emotions. The relationship between Jesus and ordinary humans was expressed in terms of typical human relationships and emotions rather than in dogmatic terms. Creation and incarnation were popular motifs since they described the proximity between the divine and the human. Incarnation was the guarantee that a human being, through Jesus, could be identified with God. Since it was Jesus in his humanity who was at the center of spirituality, the emotional relationship between Jesus and the believer was of the highest importance. Meditations on Jesus, especially on his sufferings, created a mental picture where the individual Christian could be present, almost physically, in the biblical story. Thus, the relation between Jesus and the *orans* could take on an almost physical relation. Francis's meditations on Jesus' sufferings on the cross led to an identification with Christ that resulted in stigmata as a bodily experience.

Another experience of being physically close to Jesus was associated with encountering Jesus as mother. This sounds like a form of "gender-bending." Jesus in the form of a woman is a part of medieval spirituality that we have been largely unaware of. It has been brought to attention through studies of women mystics; it was believed that descriptions of Jesus as mother expressed women's identification with him. However, it turns out that the picture is more complicated. The image of Jesus as mother was in fact more widespread in prayers and meditations by monks, especially in the Cistercian order. It is especially Caroline Walker Bynum, an expert on medieval piety, who has brought this phenomenon to broader attention.[24]

Images of women used of God and Jesus are well known from the Bible. In several passages within the Hebrew Bible God is identified with attributes of a woman or a mother. In prophetic sayings, God may compare himself with a mother who carries her child in her womb, who bears the child, or who suckles and comforts it (Isa 49:1, 15; 66:12–13).[25] Jesus speaks of himself as a hen who will gather her chicken under her wings (Matt 23:37). Early Christian authors use the metaphor "mother" about Jesus; for instance, Clement of Alexandria speaks of Jesus as a mother who cares for her child.[26] In the early Middle Ages, however, this motif does not play a significant role; in most images Jesus is masculine, for instance as Christ the King on the cross.

---

24. Bynum, *Jesus as Mother*.

25. Sebastian, *God as Feminine*, 216–27.

26. Clement of Alexandria, *Paidagogus* I, 6.

Jesus as mother appears—or reappears—as a new religious motive in the twelfth century, as part of the development of Christian piety that had a special focus on the human Jesus.[27] When relations between Christians and God or Jesus were to be expressed in terms of human relations, images from the family were close at hand: father, mother, and child. Therefore, images of Jesus as mother reflected contemporary ideas; we might say stereotypes, of what was typical of mothers: a mother gives life, and she does this through a painful sacrifice of her own life, through a painful childbirth. A mother shows tenderness and love towards her child. Finally, a mother nurtures her child through her own bodily fluid, her milk. Thus, the image of a mother was more suited to express the manifold roles of Jesus than that of a father.

We find one of the earliest expressions of Jesus as mother in a writing by the theologian Anselm of Canterbury (1033–1109):

> But you, Jesus, good Lord, are you not also a mother? Are you not that mother, who, like a hen, collects her chickens under her wings? Truly, master, you are a mother . . . For by your gentleness, those who are hurt are comforted; by your perfume, the despairing are reformed. Your warmth resuscitates the dead; your touch justifies sinners.[28]

The most extensive use of this metaphor, however, is in the writings of Bernard of Clairvaux (1090–1153), a very influential founder of monasteries and reformer of the Cistercian order. His widely read meditations focused on the human Jesus and especially his sufferings on the cross. However, Bernard used "mother" as a metaphor not only for Jesus but also for other biblical figures, including Moses and Peter, and even of abbots in monasteries.[29] For Bernard, it was not the image of a mother giving birth that was most important, but her life-giving function, especially in suckling an infant. Therefore, a mother's breasts were very important for him; they were symbols of emotions and love for others, but also of giving instructions and advice. It was as this latter aspect of the mother symbolism that Bernard applied to abbots and other leaders in monasteries.

It was primarily in his sermons on the Song of Songs that Bernard developed the symbolism of the mother. The Song of Songs was very popular in monasteries in the Middle Ages; it is said that more expositions were written on it than on the Gospels. The origin of the Song of Songs was a collection of love poems on the relationship between a man and his beloved. However, from an early time on, they were interpreted allegorically; Christian

27. Bynum, *Jesus as Mother*, 129–54.

28. Anselm, *Monologion*, 42; quoted from Bynum, *Jesus as Mother*, 114.

29. Bynum, *Jesus as Mother*, 115–18.

interpreters read it as an expression of the relations between God and the Church, or, in the exposition of Bernard of Clairvaux, as the relationship between Christ and the soul. The Latin text (Vulgate) of Song of Songs 1:1–2 reads, "thy breasts are better than wine."[30] In Bernard's exposition this refers to the soul that speaks to the bridegroom—that is, Christ. It is the breasts of the bridegroom that are praised as life-giving and nourishing, like the breasts of a woman. Bernard does not imply that there is an erotic meaning; the image refers to the spiritual nourishment that the breasts give. When a male monk who identifies with the female voice of the bride reads the text, the gender roles are turned around. To put men in the roles of women implies that men are dependent on Christ as much as women are.

Medieval conceptions of the human body and physiology continued the understandings from antiquity, that the bodies of men and women were similar; this may have contributed to imagining Jesus in a feminine body. Galen, a Greek doctor from the second century CE, developed theories that the menstruation blood from a woman was transformed to milk in her breasts. When these theories were transferred to Christ, a Christian could imagine being united with Christ in religious meditation; the Christian was nourished by the milk of Christ's breasts at the same time that the Christian was drinking the blood running from Christ's side at the crucifixion.[31]

Julian of Norwich and Her Visions of God's Love

An English woman mystic wrote some of the most famous visions of Jesus as mother in the Late Middle Ages.[32] We do not know her name; she lived as a hermit at a church in Norwich in Anglia: therefore, she is known by the name of the church: Julian of Norwich (1342–1416). She wrote down her visions in a book, *The Book of Showings*,[33] the first book written by an English woman.

Julian lays out her visions in the form of a theology of the Trinity. She describes the three persons in the Godhead by means of human roles and relations: "God rejoices that he is our father, and God rejoices that he is our mother, and God rejoices that he is our true spouse."[34] Julian assigns the three roles from a human family—father, mother, and spouse—to the three persons

30. Bernard used the Latin translation, the Vulgate, based on the Septuagint, which reads *ubera* ("breasts"). Modern Bible translations that are based on the Hebrew, Masoretic texts read "love." The Hebrew words for "breasts" and "love" are almost identical, *dodim* ("breasts") and *dadim* ("love"); see Fishbane, *Song of Songs*, 27, 226 n. 30

31. Bynum, *Jesus as Mother*, 132–33.

32. Reinhard, "Joy to the Father."

33. Julian of Norwich, *Revelations*.

34. Julian of Norwich, *Revelations*, 125.

in the Godhead. Consequently, Julian may have Christ in mind when she likens God to a mother. She continues the use of mother as a metaphor for Christ, but the metaphor receives a special meaning since she identifies it with a woman's bodily existence. The metaphor of mother may be used with two different meanings. It may mean that Christ is like a mother; that is, Christ cares for people and nourishes them as a mother cares for and nourishes her children. To nourish, to bring up, and to care for one's children are such tasks as a mother undertakes, and that Julian attributes to Christ.

However, Julian attributes more to this comparison. It is not enough for her to say that Christ acts like a mother; she says that he *is* a mother. She reaches this decision by contemplating the sufferings of Christ. Christ became our mother at the incarnation, when he assumed our body. Moreover, the incarnated Christ shows himself as a true mother by redeeming humanity and leading it into new life. This happens through Christ's suffering and death on the cross. Julian describes the pain that Christ suffered on the cross as birth pangs, and when they were completed, he had given us birth into new life. Julian meditates before Jesus on the cross; he suffered in his human body, and Julian perceives his pains as birth pangs, which biologically are women's pains. Therefore, Jesus really is a mother; there is a direct connection between the incarnated God and a woman's body. Julian follows up on this by using the image of Christ as a womb that holds and includes the fetus in her love. Through the wound in the side of Christ (at the crucifixion), Julian can look into his womb, and through this opening men and women may enter into his body. The opening has the form of a vagina; so there are sexual overtones in this image; men may enter into the feminine body of Jesus.

While Julian views the sufferings of Christ as those of a woman in childbirth, Christ remains the historical person Jesus. Even when she describes Jesus as mother, she uses the pronoun *he*. She does not attempt to turn Jesus into a woman; however, she wants to explicate how as a mother who gives birth, the body of Jesus shares the experiences of a woman's body. That Jesus Christ as a historical person was a man at the same time that God expressed himself through the bodily experiences of a woman was a dilemma that Julian solved through her theology of Mary. If the faithful were included in the womb of Christ, they were also included in Mary, who carried Jesus in her womb. In this way, Julian actually tells two stories of incarnation, one for each gender. Christ our mother was incarnated in a male body; however, he was also incarnated in a female body, in Mary.

With her image of Christ as Mother, Julian expands our understanding of the relationship between the Trinitarian persons and gender; she provides a supplement to the masculine image of God as Father. By speaking of Christ not only as *like a* mother, but also *as a* mother, Julian includes the specific bodily experiences of women in the incarnation.

To Meditate on Jesus on the Cross

The human Jesus in mediaeval spirituality was primarily the crucified Jesus. This Jesus was brought forth through prayers and meditations, so that the faithful could see the crucified Jesus with his /her inner eye. Furthermore, this was not only a mental picture; the crucifixion was by far the most popular motive in paintings and sculptures in churches and monasteries. I have already mentioned that the image of Christ on the cross changed with the deepening focus on the human person of Jesus as we approach the high middle ages. Jesus was increasingly portrayed as the suffering one, nailed to the cross. In the late middle ages, his body would become almost grotesque, especially in churches and monasteries dedicated to the care of people suffering from leprosy or with ulcers.

Mathias Grünewald: *Isenheim Altarpiece*
(around 1515, Unterlinden Museum, Colmar, France).
Wikimedia Commons.[35]

In homes and along roadsides during Julian's time crucifixes were set up for private devotions and prayers. The faithful had Jesus before their eyes and did not need to recall a mental picture but could establish immediate contact with Jesus. The faithful had the experience of being contemporaries of Jesus; they could enter directly into conversation with him. In monasteries and in monastic spirituality mediation on the crucifix held a central place. However, in what ways would the ordinary faithful interpret and attribute meaning to the crucifix, given that visual presentations and symbols were not always easy to understand?[36]

Many homilies and sermons from this period do help the faithful to "read" the crucifix. An unknown homilist who gave a sermon on Good Friday in 1272 or 1273 seems to presuppose that the congregation had before them a crucifix that showed Jesus turning his head to the side. Quoting from John 19:30 how Jesus died, "Then he bowed his head and gave up his spirit," the homilist continues, "Oh Christians, look, look! See how (Jesus) has his head leaning down to kiss you, his arms extended to embrace you!"[37] A literal reading might see that the crucifix shows Jesus at the moment of death; his head slumps to the side and his arms are stretched out because they are nailed to the cross. However, the homilist saw a greater meaning in the crucifix: it expressed how Jesus directs his love towards the faithful who have fixed their gaze upon him; he bends his head toward them to kiss them, and he stretches out his arms to embrace them.

There are many examples of homilies from the Middle Ages that emphasize the close emotional attachment between Jesus and the faithful. Experiences of human love are applied to the relationship between Jesus and the faithful. In a meditation on the head of the crucified Jesus, a young monk writes, "When I had most diligently gazed at it, I knew him to be the Lord Jesus himself, crucified and living, having his eyes open upon me."[38] For the medieval mind, visual expressions were very important in human relationships, and this was true of "seeing" Jesus with one's "inner eye," whether it was on a crucifix, in paintings, or in mental images. Therefore, it was important that this experience was confirmed and reciprocated by Jesus, that he also "saw" them.[39]

36. Lipton, "'Sweet Lean.'"

37. Lipton, "'Sweet Lean,'" 1175.

38. Lipton, "'Sweet Lean,'" 1175.

39. Cf. Orthodox icons: they also fix their gaze directly at the faithful who venerate them.

5

When Did Jesus Become "Historical"?

Jesus in the Enlightenment and Modernity

HOW DID THE MEMORY of Jesus become the "historical Jesus"?[1] In earlier historical periods, too, people were aware that Jesus had lived in the past; but how did it happen that the Jesus of historical research became *the* true Jesus? It did not happen suddenly; a long process led up to what we speak of as modernity. There have been attempts to divide it into three periods or phases;[2] modernity, however, represents more a way of thinking than a specific historical period. Therefore, a question arises: What were the reasons or changes that generated this new mode of thinking, this new mentality?

We must look at some of the changes that took place in Europe in relation to other parts of the world as well as at the rise of new sciences that introduced new ways of seeing the world. Explorations of unknown regions of the world and colonization of people and land in those regions expanded knowledge of the world. In a similar manner astronomy expanded the vision of the universe and showed that the earth was not the center of the universe. Advances in natural sciences produced knowledge about the world that questioned the biblical stories of creation. The net result was a growing confidence in empirical studies; only that which could be tested and proved was considered trustworthy. One of the results of the accumulation of all these new insights was that the Bible lost its hitherto uncontested role as a knowledge source not only about religion but also about the world and about history.

---

1. For the perspectives in this section I am indebted to Birch, *Jesus in an Age of Enlightenment*.

2. The three phases are these: early modernity, from circa 1500 until the French Revolution in 1789; classic modernity, from the French Revolution until circa 1900; and finally late modernity, until the fall of the Berlin Wall in 1989.

Moreover, the European wars of religion (1618–1648) furthered weakened the authority of the churches and Christianity.

Taken together, these changes introduced new ways of thinking about history; the new historical mentality established a sharp distinction between the past and the present, the now. Previous generations had attached great value to the preservation of traditions; now, a modern mentality wanted to distance itself from tradition and to establish independence from it. A growing individualism placed the individual at the center, with his/her common sense and free will to make independent decisions. Finally, in contrast to earlier beliefs in stability and continuity, there came a new and strong belief in progress. Of course, these developments did not happen at the same time and to the same degree; they were strongest among the groups that benefited most from them, especially the growing economic, social and intellectual elites.

In many ways, Europe continued to be a Christian culture. The doctrine of Christ as the heavenly king represented authority, which supported royal claims to power and traditional social structures that kept the lower classes in their place. Consequently, to question this dogmatic image of Christ was not just a religious or theological issue; it was directed toward the moral and political order of society. However, most of the critics preserved a belief in Jesus as a preacher of morals and as Savior of humanity. Discussions about the historical Jesus concerned ideals for humanity, goals for politics and for society as a community. Therefore, many engaged in discussion about Jesus, about who he was and what he represented. Theology and biblical studies had not separated into specialized subjects. Accordingly, people from many different backgrounds participated in discussions about Christian doctrine.

I can give only a few sketches of how these new, modern mentalities resulted in new images of Jesus as "the historical Jesus." However, there is a continuity between the earlier memories of Jesus and the quest for the historical Jesus. In both instances, listeners or readers were concerned with the meaning of the image of Jesus; he was associated with identities and societal and individual values. We shall first look back to the previous chapter as an example of a critical use of the human Jesus in a period of "premodernism." Then we shall look at the Enlightenment, to see how a mentality of rationalism criticized the Gospels, their images of Jesus, and the origin of Christianity. The main part of the chapter will deal with the nineteenth century. In this period, "the historical Jesus" was firmly established as a scholarly project. In conformity with popular literary genres, the project took the form of biographies, of Lives of Jesus.

The Human Jesus in Premodernity

In the High Middle Ages there was a new focus on the human Jesus, who identified with humans in their precarious lives, who was exposed to illness, poverty, and suffering. Francis of Assisi made the human Jesus visible in his own life; his main message to Christians was to follow his example. For Francis, and later for the radical branch of the Franciscans, this image of the poor Jesus amounted to a strong criticism of the wealthy aristocracy and the merchants, and not least of the rich church. For many people, the brilliant detective novel and church history narrative *The Name of the Rose* by Umberto Eco,[3] has served as an introduction to this period in medieval life. Eco brings to life how the Franciscan Spirituals and other radical groups were condemned as heretics and finally crushed by the powerful church. These radical groups invoked the poor, human Jesus in their criticism of the church and its tradition of a powerful Christ. This criticism in the name of Jesus was a precursor to later criticism of the church in the name of the historical Jesus. Thus, Francis's human Jesus was an early stage on the road to modern presentations of the historical Jesus.[4]

Jesus—An Advocate for Reason

The *Enlightenment* has become a catchall term for the mentalities that resulted from social, scientific, and political changes that happened in the sixteenth and seventeenth centuries. Reason became the measure of all things, trumping tradition and authority. Critics of religion questioned that it proclaimed revealed truths, truths not arrived at through rational means. To Bible critics, the historical Jesus represented rational religion, which had been distorted by later superstitions and dogmas.

The English Rationalists

The Bible remained a central source of knowledge in this period, so it is no wonder that some of the leading philosophers in Europe engaged in Bible criticism, especially Thomas Hobbes (1588–1679) and Baruch Spinoza (1632–1677). However, I will introduce some critics who were among the earliest to discuss the historical Jesus: the Irishman John Toland (1670–1722), the Englishman Thomas Chubb (1679–1747), and the German philosopher

3. Eco, *Name of the Rose*.

4. Meeks, *Christ Is the Question*, 9–10.

Herman Samuel Reimarus (1694–1768). The English critics preceded the German; they are often called the English deists. They belonged to a rationalist group and claimed that a monotheistic faith must be built on reason. Most of them rejected a divine revelation in the form of the Bible or a divine Jesus Christ. They claimed that there was no connection between the teaching of Jesus and Christian doctrine, which came later. Their main interest was to establish the original teaching of Jesus; however, they conducted a rather simplistic reading of the Gospels, read in translation.

John Toland was one of these deists. His best-known work is *Christianity not Mysterious* (1696). Here, he claims that Jesus did not create a new religion, and that he did not revoke the law of Moses. This point was held by most of the early critics, and it was shared among Christian and Jewish critics. They held that Jesus continued a Jewish tradition, and they emphasized that the first Christians were Jews. However, later Christian communities had primarily Gentile members, and with their dogmas and their discontinuation of Jewish practices, they had betrayed Jesus. For the deists, Judaism emerged as the rational belief in God.

Thomas Chubb had no formal theological training; he was a self-taught writer. In 1738, he published *The true Gospel of Jesus Christ asserted*. The purpose of the book, he said, was to show the true purpose of the gospel, and how that purpose had been challenged. According to Chubb, the truth of the gospel was that Jesus wanted to call people to conversion and salvation. He directed his teaching to audiences who were free to follow his message, and who adhered to no authorities other than Jesus. However, when this message was later used to promote worldly powers, the words and revelation of Jesus were misused, Chubb held that the message of Jesus conformed fully to reason; however, the apostles had distorted the gospel, especially its teaching about salvation, which they had based on the teaching of the apostle Paul.

Reimarus—The Hidden Critic

Herman Samuel Reimarus (1694–1768) is the best-known critic of the church's doctrine of Christ from this early period. This is partly because Albert Schweitzer gave him a prominent position in his famous book on the quest for the historical Jesus,[5] but also because of the dramatic history around the publication of his writings. Or one might rather say, the drama of the nonpublication of his studies. Reimarus allowed only a very few close friends to read the manuscript of his "An apology for, or some

5. Schweitzer, *Quest of the Historical Jesus*, 14–26.

words in defense of, reasoning worshipers of God." After his death, his friend, the philosopher H. E. Lessing, published parts of the manuscript as "Fragments by an Anonymous Writer" (1774–1778).[6] Not until forty years later did it become known that the author was the highly respected classicist and philosopher Reimarus. He had publicly defended the view that Christianity and natural religion, based on human reason, were not in conflict. In the Apology, his positions were quite different from and radically critical of the Christian doctrine of Christ. In this light, it is easy to understand that his name was withheld at the time of writing; authors of books that voiced criticism of the Bible and of Christianity risked arrest and imprisonment. This was a risk not only in the seventeenth century; a century later, David Friedrich Strauss and Ernest Renan lost their academic positions over their books on Jesus.

Reimarus built his arguments on a thorough reading of the Gospels; his criteria for the locating the authentic words of Jesus were consistency and an absence of contradictions. He found, like Chubb, that Jesus had two goals with his teaching: the kingdom of God and conversion of people. Jesus did not intend to reveal any mysteries; he did not want to establish a new religion or abolish Judaism. Jesus merely set up moral responsibilities: to love God and one's neighbor. Jesus' teaching on faith and the gospel did not include the doctrines of the churches; for Reimarus and other critics, it was especially important that Jesus' teaching did not include the doctrine of the Trinity. On that point, the later followers of Jesus had abandoned his teaching. Similarly, Jesus had kept the law of Moses, including the ritual laws regulating the Sabbath, religious feasts, and ceremonies. Here too the disciples eventually broke away from the legacy of Jesus, although they themselves were Jews. Jesus had merely preached to the Jews that they must be converted and act righteously, better than the hypocritical Pharisees.

Besides a moral life, the kingdom of God was the main point in Jesus' teaching. Since Jesus did not explain the term "kingdom of God," but proclaimed it as something that was well known, he must have shared a Jewish understanding of the kingdom. It was a future realm in this world, with the Messiah as a political figure. It was this kingdom that the disciples preached; and which they were expecting. It was only after Jesus had died, when this hope had proved false, that the disciples came upon the idea that Jesus was a suffering savior for humanity. Therefore, they changed Jesus' sayings and wrote them down so that they should support this new teaching, and they left out everything that could reveal the original meaning of Jesus' words.

6. Reimarus, *Fragments.*

Reimarus draws a negative conclusion about the trustworthiness of the disciples and their message. Their teaching was not supported by historical facts; instead, doctrine determined history. The "facts" to which the doctrine referred were simply false and fabricated. When he seeks to explain how this could happen, Reimarus finds an explanation in the disciples' psychology. The disciples belonged to the lower classes; they were, for instance, fishermen. When they left work to follow Jesus; they were motivated by his promise of power, honor, and wealth. The death of Jesus meant a total disappointment of their hopes to rule a kingdom in this world. They reacted by turning the kingdom of God into a spiritual realm; however, their ambitions to have wealth and power were the same. Stories in the Acts of the Apostles and references in the letters in the New Testament give clear evidence of how they gained power over the Christian communities. They forced people to sell their property and to give it to the apostles; they cheated people into believing in the gospel by promising them a return when Jesus returned in glory.

The purpose for some of the English deists in finding the original message of Jesus was to reform Christianity. Reimarus was more radical. He found that much in the teaching of Jesus corresponded to natural religion, which he viewed positively; the Christ cult, on the other side, was a fraud, which he detested.

Thomas Jefferson and Jesus as Teacher of "Common Sense"[7]

Theologians were not the only ones who had a great interest in the historical Jesus during the Enlightenment. Like many prominent American politicians of his time, Thomas Jefferson (1743–1826), American president from 1801 to 1809, was strongly influenced by rationalistic deism.[8] However, this deism represented a moderate Enlightenment, not like the radical, anti-Christian Enlightenment in France. His political opponents denounced Jefferson as an atheist. He did not defend himself publicly, but he described his religious beliefs in letters to friends.[9] He declared himself a "true Christian," that is, a disciple of the teaching of Jesus, in contradistinction to those who proclaimed a dogmatism that Jesus never preached. Jefferson admired the ethics of Jesus and held this to be the most advanced moral teaching that ever existed. Jefferson was uninterested in questions of Jesus' divinity or his communication with God; he was concerned with the inner quality of Jesus' teaching. On that

7. This expression is borrowed from Pelikan, *Jesus through the Centuries*, 189–91.

8. Fox, *Jesus in America*, 159–72; Prothero, *American Jesus*, 19–28.

9. Jefferson, "Syllabus of an estimate of the doctrines of Jesus."

basis, he undertook an analysis of the presentations of the life and teaching of Jesus in the Gospels. Jefferson had no direct information about the European discussion of Jesus; however, he had an indirect contact via Joseph Priestley (1733–1804), an English philosopher, chemist, and theologian who visited America. Priestley's main interest was to distinguish between the original words of Jesus and later teachings of the apostles.

Jefferson did not actually write an exposition of the teaching of Jesus; however, he produced a "purified" edition of the Gospels. He included everything that corresponded to Jesus' moral teaching but excluded all references to the divinity of Jesus. Jefferson started this work in 1804, spending many late nights at the White House when he was president but without completing his work, "The Philosophy of Jesus of Nazareth."[10] He resumed work on the manuscript after his presidential period, and in 1819 he completed a work with the title "The Life and Morals of Jesus of Nazareth." However, it was never published. After his death, his family kept it, until it was finally published in 1902.[11]

Jefferson's work has some similarities with Tatian's *Diatessaron* (second century CE), a gospel based on a harmonization of the four Gospels. Jefferson's harmonization is organized partly chronologically, partly thematically. It is obvious that Jefferson had read the Gospels very carefully. For instance, he gives extended versions of the Sermon on the Mount and the parable of the sower, combining sayings from various gospels into a thematic unity.[12] Jefferson also makes a unity of stories by combining opposites; for instance, by combining stories of those who did not follow the call of Jesus with stories of sinners and tax collectors who followed him.[13] Jefferson gives central space to Jesus' criticism of the Pharisees and the scribes, and to sayings against hypocrisy and external moralism. When his book is read as a whole, we see that Jefferson succeeded in giving Jesus a clear moral voice, which he found more perfect than Jewish or Christian ethics. The morality of Jesus included not only relatives, friends, neighbors, and countrymen, but all of humanity. It was an ethic that united everybody into one family; it was bound together by love, peace, and charity.

When he distinguished the words of Jesus from later additions in the Gospels, Jefferson's reasoning was quite similar to that of Reimarus. The sayings of Jesus were written down long after the events themselves; the people

10. Adams, ed., *Jefferson's Extracts*.

11. Jefferson, *Life and Morals of Jesus*.

12. Matt 5:1–12: Luke 6:24–26; Matt 5:13–47; Luke 6:34–36; Matt 6:1–34, 7:1–2; Luke 6:38.

13. Luke 9:57–62; 5:27–29; Mark 2:15–17.

who wrote them down were uneducated and had little knowledge. Thus, what was written down were only fragments of the original. According to Jefferson, untrustworthy people who were set on creating dissent had situated the teaching of Jesus in a mystical context, and that made "good people" reject it. Jefferson's criterion for evaluating the moral teaching of Jesus was his own conception of good morals, which he considered self-evident. Jefferson was the main author of the Declaration of Independence in 1776, and there too he declared values "self-evident."

This conviction that his morality was self-evident made it possible for Jefferson to undertake this evaluation of the Gospels without knowledge of source- and tradition criticism of the gospels. Accordingly, Jefferson could exclude all statements that described Jesus as divine, for instance sayings that he was the Son of God. Jefferson shared the views of Jesus' moral sayings, but he eliminated all references to Jesus as the Son of Man or belief in the divinity of Jesus.[14] In Luke's birth narrative, Jefferson excluded the annunciation and the message from the angels to the shepherds. There are no traces of the nativity story in Matthew's Gospel with its many prophecies about Jesus from the Old Testament. Likewise, there were no traces of Jesus as the divine Word in the Prologue in John's Gospel. The most significant exclusion, however, was that the gospel ends with Jesus crucifixion and burial; there are no traces of the story of the empty tomb or the visions of the risen Jesus.

The *Life and Morals of Jesus of Nazareth* is an interesting illustration of views that many of the political and cultural elite in Europe and North America in the eighteenth and nineteenth centuries shared. Jesus was an uncontested teacher of morals that were not restricted to one group or one religion only. Jesus' teaching was considered universal, although it is now easy to see that it corresponded primarily to the views of the educated elite. After this criticism of the Bible and the Gospels, what was left was the moral teaching of Jesus and a deistic God.

The Historical Jesus as a Nineteenth-Century Ideal

The question, Who was Jesus? was an important question, not only within the Christian churches, but also within culture and politics in Europe in the nineteenth century. To question doctrine about Jesus threatened the very system of authority in this period.[15] The French Revolution is the most

14. For instance, in Matt 7:3–29 he removed vv 21–23; in Luke 12:1–15 he removed vv 8–12; and in Matt 18:1–35 he removed vv 5–6, 10–11 and 18–20.

15. Moxnes, *Jesus and the Rise of Nationalism.*

significant case in point. It started a process of transferring authority and power from kings and princes to the people, a process that eventually was to affect many European countries. The authority of kings and princes was associated with divine authority, and rulers legitimated their power "by the grace of God." Studying the historical Jesus went hand in hand with offering higher criticism of the Bible: both seriously questioned the continuity of Jesus on the one hand and the dogma of Christ, the heavenly King, on the other. This criticism was perceived as directly affecting Christ in his role as political protector, and this is why some of the first Bible critics suffered persecution and imprisonment.

In the seventeenth and eighteenth centuries, the Bible critics in Europe had been few, and mostly situated at the margins of academic society. However, in the first part of the nineteenth century, a number of new developments created a new situation for biblical criticism and critical studies of the historical Jesus.

First, study of the historical Jesus was professionalized. In many European countries, the university system was renewed; new universities were established with structures that classified scholarly disciplines, in much the same way that modern universities do. This affected, for instance, the study of history and put it on a more scholarly basis. Biblical studies were divided into two areas. The study of the New Testament became a separate discipline, with the study of the historical Jesus as a recognized subject. Thus, from being almost a subversive activity by independent critics, studies of the historical Jesus became a recognized university realm of study.

Second, studies including the Life of Jesus (that is, of the human Jesus) were inspired by the growing importance of biographies of "great men" who shaped history.

Third, explorations and colonization of the so-called Orient (referring especially to what is now called the Middle East) led to a growing interest in the history, geography, and archaeology of that region. Given the Western exposure to this area, the historical context of Palestine became a new, important field in the study of the historical Jesus.

These three factors shaped the modern study of the historical Jesus, and nineteenth-century studies prepared the ground for further developments in the twentieth century. I will present three scholars who had a significant impact on recent trends in historical Jesus studies: Friedrich Schleiermacher (1768–1834), David Friedrich Strauss (1808–1874), and Ernest Renan (1823–1892).[16]

---

16 This section draws on Moxnes, *Jesus and the Rise of Nationalism*, 61–148.

Friedrich Schleiermacher: What Is It to Write a Biography of Jesus?

Friedrich Schleiermacher has been called the father of modern Protestant-ism, and he has had a far-reaching influence on Protestant theology for almost two centuries. He played a central role in the establishment of the University of Berlin (later Humboldt University) in 1810. Schleiermacher was a Renaissance man of a scholar; he worked in all areas of theology as well as in philosophy and classical philology.

His book *On Religion; Speeches to its Cultural Despisers*, from 1799, established the foundation for a new way of understanding religion, based not on supernatural revelation but on the human experience of absolute dependence on the divine. This focus on a person's absolute dependence on God moved the emphasis in religion from the church's authority to one's own religious experience. Schleiermacher was also central in the development of hermeneutics.[17] With regard to interpretation of biblical texts, he insisted that the Bible should be read in the same way as other texts.

This position influenced the lectures on the Life of Jesus that Schleier-macher gave in Berlin between 1819 and 1832.[18] He started with the ques-tion, what do we "actually mean by biography"? "For that is what we wish to provide for the person of Christ."[19] When Schleiermacher chose to write about Jesus in the genre of biography, this meant treating Jesus in the same way as other subjects of biographies. This was obviously a controversial decision; it signaled a shift from the tradition of writing about the divine Christ in terms of a dogmatic treatise.

A biography is a history based on a human life, and the first question concerns the issue of available sources. For a life of Jesus, the Gospels were the obvious answer. However, biblical scholars were aware of the difference between the Synoptic Gospels and John's Gospel. At the beginning of the nineteenth century, there was a broad agreement that John's Gospel was the most trustworthy historical source. Schleiermacher shared this view. His reading of John's Gospel as history was influenced by his engagement for the unification of the many German states into one nation. In John's Gospel he found a portrayal of a Jesus who was concerned with the Jewish people in its totality, not only with Galilee, as in the Synoptic Gospels. John's Gospel describes how Jesus traveled all around the country, so that Jesus' travels re-flected his concern that his mission was directed to all of the Jewish people.

---

17. Hermeneutics deals with the theory and methodology of interpretation. See the classic study: Jeanrond, *Theological Hermeneutics*.

18. Schleiermacher, *Life of Jesus*; Moxnes, *Jesus and the Rise of Nationalism*, 61–93.

19. Schleiermacher *Life of Jesus*, 3.

Another issue was whether a biographer should focus on a person as a separate individual or as part of a community. Schleiermacher argued for the latter alternative, that Jesus belonged to his own time and to his own people. Thus, Jesus was not totally independent; he was influenced by others; for instance, his message was shaped by the language that he shared with his people. However, this position met with criticism, and Schleiermacher was accused of posing a threat to the divinity of Jesus. Schleiermacher defended his position and raised the question whether it was possible to speak of Jesus as "a unique person."

The term "unique person" reflected the circumstance that in the nineteenth century, biography was a literary genre not concerned with "common" people. Biographies were reserved for men of the bourgeoisie and the academic elite. Biographies were also associated with the idea of "the great men" who shaped history.[20] The concept of the great man was part of the heritage from antiquity—philosophers such as Socrates and Plato, leaders and military commanders such as Alexander the Great and Julius Caesar. They were regarded as moral ideals and initiators of social and political change, and Jesus was seen to belonging to this group of "great men."

However, Schleiermacher introduced an alternative to this one-sided focus on the "great man" who shaped history. Instead, he emphasized that leader and people were dependent on one another. There are parallels between the way he describes Jesus and his portrayal of Frederick the Great (1722–86), who was greatly admired by the Prussians as their ideal king.[21] In eulogies presented at the annual remembrance of Frederick the Great, Schleiermacher describes the relationship between the king and his people in terms of fellowship and mutuality. Thus, Schleiermacher departs from the traditional picture of the absolute monarch. Similarly, his Jesus was no longer the distant Christ, elevated above his subjects; rather Schleiermacher's was a Jesus in a reciprocal relationship with people.

Most Jesus scholars have now abandoned Schleiermacher's view that John's Gospel is the best historical source for a Life of Jesus. Moreover, especially David Friedrich Strauss and Albert Schweitzer criticized him for not being a true historian, since there were faith elements in his picture of Jesus.[22] However, the most important heritage from Schleiermacher's lectures on Jesus is the questions he raises about the presuppositions for writing a Life of Jesus. What does it mean to write a biography of someone? Should the emphasis be on the person as a separate individual, or as

20. Moxnes, *Jesus and the Rise of Nationalism*, 27–28.
21. Moxnes, *Jesus and the Rise of Nationalism*, 69–71.
22. Moxnes, *Jesus and the Rise of Nationalism*, 24–25.

part of a community? What are our ideas of an ideal person, which shape the way we look upon Jesus? These are questions that will influence the way we see Jesus, and they should be discussed before starting to write about him. However, modern Jesus scholars appear to overlook this heritage from Schleiermacher. Most of them start writing without explaining their ideas about what a human being is, or what constitutes a society, or finally, what sources move history. Since the underlying presuppositions are not discussed, it is not surprising that the modern pictures of "the historical Jesus" are so diverse.

A biography from another part of life may illustrate how various presuppositions result in different portraits of the same person. The psychologist Barry Schwarz has studied how the life of Abraham Lincoln was told differently in various periods according to the political purpose that shaped the biographies.[23] The historical "facts" did not change, however, and different positions on what aspects of the life of Lincoln should serve as ideals for the American people determined what memories were given preference. That changed from a culture of hierarchy in the nineteenth century to a time of equality in the twentieth century, especially in the period of the civil rights movement in the 1960s. The situation with regard to writings about the historical Jesus is similar; different historical situations and different social contexts influence the way the memories are shaped.

David Friedrich Strauss: Life of Jesus as Myth

David Friedrich Strauss was a young teacher of theology and philosophy in Tübingen when he published *The Life of Jesus Critically Examined* (1835–36), a voluminous work of 1,400 pages.[24] It turned out that after Strauss had conducted his critical examination of the Gospels, there was almost no Life of Jesus left. Strauss concluded that most of the stories about Jesus were myths. His books drew enormous attention, not only in churches and theological circles, but also within culture and politics. Within only a short period there appeared many pamphlets and books that wanted to refute Strauss's position. The books were quickly translated into English and stirred a heated debate in England as well. Strauss's *Life of Jesus* was the most influential critical work on the historical Jesus in the nineteenth century, and it had great importance well into the twentieth century.

Strauss's examination had the usual structure of a Life of Jesus study, with three parts: Jesus' birth and childhood; his public life; and his suffering,

23. Schwartz, *Abraham Lincoln*.
24. For this section, I draw on Moxnes, *Jesus and the Rise of Nationalism*, 95–120.

death, and resurrection. However, unlike other historical presentations of
the Life of Jesus, the book starts with a long chapter on *myths* that influence
Strauss's examination of the individual gospel narratives. Strauss considered
the Gospels not as historical sources for the Life of Jesus but as myths shaped
by early Christian groups. This was especially the case with all stories about
the miracles Jesus performed. These stories have a central place in Strauss's
discussions of the Gospels as historical sources. In Strauss's day two opposing positions were staked out: the supernaturalists claimed that Jesus' miracle stories are historically trustworthy, and rationalists held that the stories
are not historical. However, rationalists accepted that there might be natural
explanations for Jesus' miracles. Strauss shared the historical skepticism of
the rationalists; however, he found that attempts to find natural explanations
for the miracles rendered the stories meaningless and ridiculous. His position was that the miracle stories were myths that had important religious
meanings, even if they were not historical.

Strauss's method was to examine each story individually, to see whether
there was a logical coherence to it, and especially whether it was credible according to natural laws. According to these criteria, Strauss classified as myths
stories that were not credible. His main hypothesis was that the miracle stories about Jesus were based on narratives in the Old Testament of how God
intervened in history. For instance, stories of Jesus feeding many thousands
in the wilderness were based on the narratives of how God provided for the
Israelites in the desert during their flight from Egypt (Exod 16). Behind the
story of Jesus opening the eyes of the blind was a similar story in 2 Kings 6.
Likewise, there was a precedent for Jesus' raising of the dead in a story of the
prophet Elijah in 1 Kings 17. From this evidence of parallel narratives, Strauss
concluded that the miracle stories in the Gospels did not have a historical
basis but were created by groups of Jesus' followers.

Not surprisingly, many theologians, pastors, and ordinary Church
members, even many who sympathized with his position, met Strauss' studies with strong criticism. His older colleague, Ferdinand Christian Baur
(1792–1860), who was one of the most influential biblical scholars of his
time, did not want to support Strauss. Strauss had been offered a professor's
chair in Zurich; however, after the publication of his book, the offer was
withdrawn, and he never got a permanent university position.

Strauss's criticism of the Gospels' trustworthiness was regarded as a
general criticism of authorities, and he was therefore regarded as a threat
to the political authorities in Germany. His book challenged the proclamation of Christ as a divine figure who legitimated the authority of the mon-
archy. However, he received support from unexpected quarters, namely
the democratic, nationalist movement that worked for the unification of

Germany, and that was very critical of the power of the German princes. They regarded Strauss's suggestion that the stories of Jesus were myths created by early Christian groups as a criticism of authorities and a support for the activities of common people.

Thus, Strauss presented a Jesus who could be understood as a democratic and radical figure. However, this was probably not the intention of Strauss himself. He was initially influenced by the philosopher Georg Friedrich Wilhelm Hegel and was politically liberal; however, he became more and more conservative. Strauss revised his *Life of Jesus* several times. He first moderated his positions to comply with the criticism of the first version of the book. However, in the next edition he returned to his original radical position. Thirty years after the publication of his first book, he published a book called *Life of Jesus for the German People*.[25] This was a much more conventional Life of Jesus, and politically conservative.

The political criticism that Strauss encountered has not received much attention in the evaluation of Strauss' contribution to New Testament scholarship. I suggest that this is a result of the marginal role of theology in modern societies. In the nineteenth century, Bible and theology played a central role within European politics and culture. Since that is not the case today, the history of New Testament scholarship is no longer part of a cultural-political history but has been placed within a small niche of academic history.

Within the history of theological studies, Strauss's work is recognized as initiating the study of myths in the interpretation of the life and message of Jesus. Rudolf Bultmann (1884–1976), the most influential New Testament scholar and theologian in the twentieth century, continued this approach. He created the term *demythologizing* and argued that the message of the New Testament had to be liberated from the mythological worldview of its time. Instead, scholars must find expressions that recognize a modern worldview and a self-understanding based on existentialist philosophy.

Strauss also participated in the discussion of which Gospel was the most trustworthy source for the history of Jesus. He regarded all the Gospels as mythical, but especially John's Gospel, which he wrote off as a historical source. This debate continued throughout most of the nineteenth century; in the end, the proponents of John's Gospel lost their case. Some scholars supported Matthew's Gospel as the oldest among the Synoptic Gospels; they regarded Mark's gospel as an abridged version of Matthew. However, after decades of discussion, several historical studies in the 1860's resulted in a general acceptance of Mark's Gospel as the oldest, so that Matthew and Luke were based on Mark. In addition, most scholars accepted

---

25 Strauss, *Das Leben Jesu für das deutsch Volk.*

the hypothesis that the common material of Jesus' sayings in Matthew and Luke came from an earlier source, called Q.

Acceptance of the Synoptic Gospels as the best historical sources had important consequences for locating Jesus in space and time. John's Gospel describes how Jesus traveled over many parts of Judea and Galilee, and how Jesus visited Jerusalem at more than one Passover celebration. In the Synoptic Gospels, on the other hand, all Jesus' activities take place in Galilee, and they report only one visit to Jerusalem at Passover, namely, when he suffered execution. Thus, following the Synoptic Gospels, we may imagine that Jesus' public activity take place within the time frame of one year. Most presentations of the life of Jesus presuppose this structure. Thus, the research on the Gospels in the 1860s has had an extraordinarily great influence on generations of historical Jesus scholarship.

Ernest Renan: The Landscape of Jesus as "the Fifth Gospel"

German scholars like Schleiermacher and Strauss searched for the historical Jesus in the biblical writings. At the same time, other scholars engaged in a search for Jesus in the biblical geography. The nineteenth century was a period when the interest for the Holy Land and the geographical home of Jesus grew to an extent unknown earlier.[26] This was part of the great interest in the history, geography, and archeology in the eastern Mediterranean in at that time. Napoleon's military expedition to Egypt and Syria (1798–1801) opened up what today is called the Middle East to a wide range of European interests: imperialism, scholarly studies and popular travels. Napoleon brought along many scholars to investigate the culture and history of that region. This was also a search for the roots of Europe in the ancient cultures around the Mediterranean (the region today called the Middle East). The large national museums of Europe (e.g., the Louvre and the British Museum) wanted to collect cultural artifacts from the area in order to strengthen their own national identities. Historians, archeologists, mapmakers, biblical scholars, pilgrims, and tourists all traveled through what today we know as the Middle East, and their travel books became immensely popular with a growing number of armchair travelers.

The French philologist and scholar of religion Ernest Renan was part was one of the actual travelers to the region in the middle of the nineteenth century.[27] He was on an expedition to Syria to search for archeological artifacts for the Louvre, protected by French warships. Renan

26. Moxnes, *Jesus and the Rise of Nationalism*, 19–60.

27. This section draws on Moxnes, *Jesus and the Rise of Nationalism*, 121–47.

also went to Palestine, and while he was there he wrote his *Life of Jesus* (*Vie de Jésus*, 1863). The book became a sensational success; it was both the most popular and the most criticized Life of Jesus in the nineteenth century, and it is still reprinted today. The book came under fire from the Catholic Church, and faced criticism even from Emperor Napoleon III, that Renan had portrayed Jesus as a mere human being. Criticism had started already before he published the *Life of Jesus*. In 1862, Renan held his opening lecture as professor of Hebrew at the prestigious Collège de France, and in that lecture he described Jesus as "an incomparable man whom some call God."[28] The emperor himself suspended his lectures, and in 1864, Renan was dismissed from his chair.

Renan based his *Life of Jesus* on contemporary Gospel research; however, in terms of literary genre, it combined elements of a psychological biography of Jesus and a travel narrative where the landscape itself played a prominent role. Renan said that he had received a totally new impression of Jesus when he traveled in the areas where Jesus himself had walked, and he described the landscape as "the fifth gospel." In the nineteenth century, it was a commonly accepted idea that there was an interdependence between nature and landscape and human character and forms of social life. Renan envisaged that in antiquity, Galilee, with its nature and landscape was an "earthly paradise."[29] Galilee's natural environment helped form Jesus' positive attitude toward God and toward people. In stark contrast to sunny Galilee, the mountainous landscape of Judea and Jerusalem was dark and foreboding. Moreover, the people in these areas shared the character of the landscape; they were fanatical and full of strife. Renan describes the area and the people in historical categories, based on the authority of his scholarly studies. However, from his private letters we learn that these negative characterizations were shaped by his encounters with Arabs he met in his travels. He compares the Pharisees during the time of Jesus with Muslim teachers and their "barren doctrine," and he suggests that discussions among the scribes in the temple in Jesus' day were similar to those Renan himself had encountered in a mosque.

Renan claims that the main conflict between Jesus and the Jewish scribes concerned the very understanding of religion itself. For Renan, Jesus transcended the boundaries of Judaism: "He proclaimed the rights of man, not the rights of the Jew; the religion of man, not the religion of the Jew; the deliverance of man, not the deliverance of the Jew."[30] This statement

---

28 Renan, *Inaugural Lecture*, 135–36.

29 Renan, *Life of Jesus*, 86.

30. Renan, *Life of Jesus*, 226.

was acceptable to many in Europe at the time; today, of course, it leads to accusations of anti-Semitism, and in the next chapter we shall look into that discussion. Here we shall explore how Renan participated in shaping patterns of thought among European scholars when they described the relationship between Jesus and his Jewish context. Renan's negative opinions of Jews and Muslim reflected political and cultural attitudes in Europe at the time. They belong within a larger framework of thought that now goes by the name *orientalism*, which describes how the West viewed the so-called Orient, including today's Middle Eastern regions.

The term *orientalism* and accompanying concept first appeared in a book by the same name by the Palestinian American literary critic Edward Said.[31] In this book Said describes how Western, mostly European writers and scholars created a picture of the Orient as the "others," very different from "us." The "others" were more primitive, not as developed as "we" Europeans, who represented progress and evolution. However, in Orientalism there was an ambiguity in the view of the "others."[32] Social anthropologists have identified a similar ambiguity in the concept of "primitive." To be "primitive" had partly positive connotations: it signaled a life in agreement with nature, and therefore it was regarded as an ideal for many people who regarded modern civilization as alienating. On the other hand, "primitive" could also have a negative connotation, for instance as dangerous and threatening to "our" civilization. We find a similar ambiguity in Renan's presentation. The "other" had both a positive and a negative meaning, and these were represented by different geographical locations: Galilee was the positive location; Judea and Jerusalem were the negative ones. Jews—and for Renan also the Muslims— were negative "others," foreign to Europe and its values. Jesus from Galilee, however, represented a positive ideal for Europe.

Compared to earlier scholarship on the historical Jesus, Renan introduced new material. In addition to the biblical texts, he worked with Jesus' landscape, both as nature and culture. This approach was only in its beginning in the nineteenth century; by Renan's time, it had become fully integrated into historical Jesus scholarship, primarily through studies of archaeology, geography, and social anthropology in the land of Jesus and his first followers. The orientalism of Renan has also influenced the patterns of how the historical Jesus has been presented. Consciously or unconsciously, the history of Jesus has been built over a dichotomy between we and they, between Jesus and the Jews.[33]

31. Said, *Orientalism*.

32. Moxnes, *Jesus and the Rise of Nationalism*, 127–28.

33. Moxnes, "Jesus in Discourses of Dichotomies."

This dichotomy is so ingrained in our mode of thinking about Jesus, above all because it corresponds so well with the way the Gospels describe relations between Jesus and the Jewish leaders. Biblical scholars face a critical question here: are we willing to challenge the gospel narratives as historical sources on this fundamental issue? In the next chapter, we shall see that this has actually happened in recent biblical scholarship on the question of who is responsible for the execution of Jesus.

Albert Schweitzer and the End of the First Quest for the Historical Jesus

In this chapter, I have emphasized how historical Jesus scholars in the nineteenth century raised questions that pointed towards the discussions in the next century. Thus, I have looked more for continuities than for differences. This is in contrast to the famous classic review of the historical Jesus research before the twentieth century, Albert Schweitzer's *The Quest of the Historical Jesus* (1906/1913). Schweitzer reviewed almost all, mostly German, contributions to historical Jesus studies in the nineteenth century. His main criticism was that they portrayed Jesus so that he looked like their own religious ideals, so that the kingdom of God was described as a moral world order. In contrast, Schweitzer claimed that Jesus was an eschatological prophet who must be understood against the background of Jewish apocalypticism. Apocalypticism represents a worldview that the end of the world is imminent, and that it will come about through a tumultuous catastrophe. Schweitzer's position was extremely influential; it became the premise for most studies of the historical Jesus in the twentieth century. In consequence, his *Quest of the Historical Jesus* has been regarded as the most important book on religion in the twentieth century.

There is, however, something strange and unsatisfactory about Schweitzer's concept of the apocalyptic Jesus as the true historical Jesus. According to Schweitzer, Jesus shared the expectation of Jewish apocalypticism that the kingdom of God would soon arrive, that God's intervention in history was imminent. However, that worldview simply could not be transferred to the modern, present-day world. A historical Jesus who shared Jewish apocalyptic ideas of the kingdom of God belongs indubitably to the past. Schweitzer said:

> The study of the Life of Jesus has had a curious history. It set out in quest of the historical Jesus, believing that when it had found him it could bring him straight into our time as a teacher and saviour. It loosened the bands by which for centuries he had been riveted to the stony rocks of ecclesiastical doctrine, and rejoiced

to see life and movement coming into the figure once more, and the historical Jesus advancing, as it seemed, to meet it. But he did not stay; he passed by our time and returned to his own.[34]

Schweitzer found a possibility for a direct contact with Jesus, however, not through history but through a mystical unity with him. In this way, it was also possible to share the ethical commitment of Jesus. Schweitzer was concerned that the modern world was in the process of collapsing as a moral culture. This is a concern that Schweitzer voiced in many books where he criticized modern culture. His criticism was explicitly directed at nationalist ideologies in Germany in the period between the two world wars. Schweitzer emphasized that moral awareness depended on sharing the moral will of Jesus. This was possible only by means of a mystical unity with Jesus; only in this way could Jesus create a fellowship between those who put the kingdom of God above everything else. Schweitzer concludes his large historical work with a portrait of this mystical Jesus:

> He comes to us as one unknown, without a name, as of old, by the lakeside; he came to those men who did not know who he was. He says the same words, "Follow me!" and sets us to those tasks, which he must fulfil in our time. He commands. And to those who hearken to him, whether wise or unwise, he will reveal himself in the peace, in the labours, the conflicts and the suffering that they may experience in his fellowship, and as an ineffable mystery they will learn who he is.[35]

Schweitzer will not claim that this is a picture of the historical Jesus; however, those who read this conclusion will recognize it as a memory of Jesus in the Gospels. It brings to life the narratives of Jesus at the Sea of Galilee when he called disciples to follow him and to take up tasks that would bring conflicts and suffering. In contrast to many mystics and their abstract impressions of Jesus, Schweitzer's picture brings up, almost intuitively, memories of Jesus from the Gospels.

Schweitzer's theories of the eschatological Jesus influenced much of the research on the historical Jesus in the twentieth century. However, his postulate of a total break between the historical Jesus and the present was not accepted. Most historical Jesus scholars from the so-called second quest in the mid-twentieth century were concerned that their research should influence the images of Jesus in their own time. In the period before the 1950s, it was not the history but the words of Jesus that were in the focus of biblical studies.

34. Schweitzer, *Quest of the Historical Jesus,* 478.
35. Schweitzer, *Quest of the Historical Jesus,* 487.

The interest shifted toward the transmission of Jesus' words in groups of early followers of Jesus. This brought also modern followers into contact with the retelling and adaptation of the memories of Jesus' sayings.

6

Histories of Hate Speech

*Jesus and the Jews before and
after the Holocaust*

"Was Jesus a Jew?" This seems a superfluous question. There can be no doubt that the stories of Jesus' birth and childhood in the Gospels of Matthew and Luke describe Jesus' parents as Jews. Moreover, Luke tells that Jesus was circumcised and brought up as a Jew. However, the reason this question is raised at all is that the two words *Jesus* and *Jew* have had totally different meanings in European history and in Western history and culture generally. Jesus has been a positive symbol for Western identity, as an expression of who we (Westerners) are. Jews, on the other hand, have had a very different history. Over a very long time in European history and in Western history and culture generally, Jews have been perceived as others, as those who did not belong to the great We. This perception has had direct social and political implications: for instance, when Jews were expelled from Spain in 1492 (the same year that Columbus came to the Americas). Underlying such events were stories and myths that attributed to Jews all sorts of negative attitudes and deeds. More recently, the Holocaust showed how strong the animosity toward Jews was in the very center of so-called Christian Europe.

Thus, was Jesus a Jew? is not an innocent question. It links Jesus—possibly the most important symbol of identification in European and Western history—with Jews, who were, for a long time, not regarded as part of European and Western identity. The goal of this chapter is to explore how this disconnect between Jesus and Jews has played out across history. It is the negative side of this history that made me choose "Histories of Hate Speech" as the title for this chapter.

The website *Oxford Constitutional Law* gives a definition of hate speech: "'Hate speech' consists of verbal or non-verbal communication that involves hostility directed towards particular social groups, most often on the grounds of race and ethnicity, gender, sexual orientation, age, disability, etc."[1]

Several European countries have adopted special legislation against hate speech. However, in its legislation and in court practice the United States has adopted a less restrictive approach to hate speech. My native Norway is one of many countries that have established strategies to combat hate speech. A Norwegian governmental strategy points out that minority groups are more often exposed to hate and discriminatory speech than the population at large.[2] Differences in ethnicity, religion, gender, and sexual orientation are among the most common causes for hate speech. Studies have shown that hate speech is not necessarily based on strong feelings of hatred from the speaker; more often it is caused by prejudices, stereotypes, and perceptions of differences between groups.[3] Strong protection of free speech in many legal systems means that not all forms of hate speech are punishable by criminal law. Nevertheless, such speech may cause great harm. International studies have shown that there is a clear relationship between the amount of hate speech and violence and discrimination. Among the consequences of discriminatory speech may be that exposed groups withdraw from public life and internalize negative stereotypes. At a general level within society, hate speech may serve to normalize discrimination. Taken together, these effects may restrict democracy and impair citizens' rights. Anti-Semitism is a clear example of hate speech and violence against a group on the basis of race and religion. The European Commission has launched a policy to promote participation in an inclusive society, tackling all forms of discrimination and anti-Semitism.[4]

These studies of hate speech that I have mentioned reflect the situation in modern societies. However, they may help us to understand the serious effects of sayings about and characterizations of Jews during earlier periods of European history. I use the term "hate speech" in order to establish a critical perspective on the language that the Christian majority in Europe used when speaking about Jews and their relationship to Jesus. The most obvious case is that throughout history Jews were accused of killing Jesus; another example is how Christian historians have described Jesus and his relationship to Jewish faith and praxis. To confront this Christian

---

1. *Oxford Constitutional Law* (website), "Hate Speech."

2 Norwegian Government, Strategy against hate speech 2016–2020.

3. See Fladmoe and Nadim, "Silenced by Hate?"

4. European Commission," Combatting Antisemitism."

storytelling, I will introduce Jewish Jesus scholars and their views of these issues. It is a promising sign that their explanations have now been largely accepted by Christian scholars too.

"The Jews Killed Christ" in Christian Tradition

Already in the second century, most Christians were non-Jews (i.e., Gentiles). Christians took possession of the Jewish scriptures, the Bible, and claimed that the prophecies and promises about the Messiah had been fulfilled in Christ. Jews did not accept that Jesus was the Messiah, and this nonacceptance of Jesus became the most serious criticism against them, expressed in the charge that "the Jews were Christ-killers." This accusation was first voiced in antiquity, and it became stronger throughout the Middle Ages.

This accusation linked to a trend that became visible in the images of Jesus in paintings and sculptures during the Middle Ages. From the eleventh century onwards, images increasingly depicted a human Jesus and consequently focused on the strongest proofs of his humanity, viz. his suffering and death. Jesus' suffering became a focus of adoration and meditation for Christians. Increased attention on Jesus' suffering led to more focus on those held responsible for that suffering. Soon a common accusation had become that "the Jews killed the Christ," that Jews were "Christ killers."[5] This was not a simple historical statement; so far, there was no serious historical discussion of what had happened in the process against Jesus, or about who were responsible for his execution. The accusation against Jews lumped together past, present, and future and made all Jews throughout history responsible for and guilty of Jesus' death.

5. Cohen, *Christ Killers.*

Hieronimus Bosch or a follower of Bosch: *Christ Carrying the Cross*
(circa 1510–1535). Wikimedia Commons.[6]

Such hate speech was voiced in sermons as well as in pamphlets. Caricatures where Jews took part in whipping and crucifying Jesus were popular; Jews were easily recognizable by their dress and hats.[7] Martin Luther (1483–1546), the leading figure of the Protestant Reformation in Germany, is notoriously known for his strong anti-Jewish statements. Offering rather conciliatory statements at the beginning of his career, he grew increasingly critical, ending up with what must be called hate speech in *On the Jews and Their Lies* (1543). Luther was influenced by the anti-Jewish attitudes of his time; however, his position was also directly a result of his studies of the Bible and thus an integral part of his theology. Initially he had hoped that his preaching would bring the Jews to convert to Christianity; when this did not happen, Luther grew increasingly bitter. Toward the end of his life, he proposed that Jews should be expelled from the German states, and that

6. https://commons.wikimedia.org/wiki/File:Jheronimus_Bosch_or_follower_001.jpg

7 Schreckenberg, *Jews in Christian Art*, 157–96.

their synagogues should be burned.[8] In Luther's polemics, Jews, Papists (i.e. Roman Catholics), and (Muslim) Turks are united as enemies of the gospel. And in some of his sermons he accuses the Jews of handing Jesus over to pagans to be executed.

Jesus and Judaism in Nineteenth Century Jesus Research

Early critics like Toland and Reimarus in the eighteenth century emphasized the similarities between Jesus and Judaism. According to them, Jesus did not bring a new religion; he observed the law of Moses and urged an observance that went deeper than the superficial obedience of the Pharisees. These critics drew a distinction between the teaching of Jesus himself and later interpretations by his disciples. Toland and Reimarus were very critical of these interpretations that morphed into Christian doctrine.

In the nineteenth century, when historical Jesus studies found a place at universities, the picture changed. History was viewed in light of the present: the fact that Jesus was the founder of Christianity meant that he was the beginning of European civilization. Schleiermacher emphasized the continuity between the teaching of Jesus and Christianity. Consequently, he focused on Jesus' conflicts with Judaism. For Schleiermacher, the kingdom of God was the central aspect in Jesus' teaching; however, this kingdom was very different from the concepts of the kingdom of God in the Old Testament. In the Old Testament the kingdom of God had been an expression of theocratic, authoritarian rule. That was a model based on the state; in contrast, in Jesus' teaching the family and household formed the models for the kingdom of God.

Schleiermacher built his presentation of the historical Jesus on the Gospel of John. Later in the nineteenth century, most scholars reckoned that the Synoptic Gospels were better sources for the history of Jesus. This decision was important for the presentation of Jesus' relations to his fellow Jews and to Jewish faith and practice. The Synoptic Gospels place most of Jesus' activities in Galilee; it is here that he recruits his followers. In Jerusalem, on the other hand, Jesus is rejected and executed. This picture became influential; it was accepted as historical truth, and consequently it influenced the general conception of Jesus' relation to Judaism.[9]

When Jesus went on his walks in Galilee, the open and fertile landscape revealed truths that otherwise would not have become visible. Thus,

8. Kaufmann, *Luther's Jews*, 94–124.

9 This terminology reflects the tendency both among scholars and among general readers in the nineteenth century to think of Jesus and Judaism as two separate entities.

the landscape itself contributed to Jesus' proclamation of God as friendly and generous. Renan said that the landscape of Galilee provided Jesus' education. David Friedrich Strauss likewise found that Galilee played an important role in shaping Jesus' teaching. However, he argued that it was Jesus' education, not the landscape, that gave his speech an originality and freshness. According to Strauss, Jesus' originality was very different from the dogmatism that the Pharisees, Sadducees, and Essenes taught in their schools.

Many scholars tried to find reasons for the support that Jesus received from Galileans. Strauss characterizes Jesus as a typical Galilean, and posits a contrast between Galilee on the one hand and Jerusalem and Judea on the other. He describes this as a result of history; the population of Jerusalem practices a formalistic religion with superficial rituals. Here Strauss makes a comparison with what he regards as Germany's formalistic religious practice at his time. With regard to the reasons that Galileans had a more open attitude towards Jesus, Strauss suggests that a condescending attitude from Jerusalemites toward Galileans played a role, also the fact that Galilee was a distant region. Even more important, the population in Galilee consisted not only of Jews; it was mixed with non-Jews. Thus, Strauss suggests that Jesus must have had contact with this mixed population.

"Galilee of the Gentiles"

This mixed population turned out to become very important in future discussions of Galilee. In Jewish tradition, Galilee was characterized as "Galilee of the Gentiles" (Isa 9:1, quoted in Matt 4:15). Among nineteenth-century historians it was a generally accepted theory that Galilee had a mixed population. This hypothesis was based on discussions of the results of the Assyrian occupation of the Northern Kingdom of Israel in 733–732, when large parts of the Israelite population were moved to Babylon. One theory was that the Assyrians moved other ethnic groups into the empty areas, so that the result was a mixed population in Galilee. Most Assyriologists accepted this theory; they were recognized as experts on this issue, and thus Jesus scholars accepted their theory as a historical fact.

The theory of a mixed population in Galilee was more than a historical statement about Galilee. It was also an implicit reference to Europe and the discussions of the advantage of mixed populations. During and after the decline and fall of the Roman Empire, tribes from the east migrated into western Europe. As a result, modern states such as England, France, and Germany had racially mixed populations. This led scholars in those countries to look for similarities between Galilee at the time of Jesus and their own home countries. They could identify with Jesus, who grew up in an area with a mixed population, in contrast to in Jerusalem, which had a "pure" Jewish population. For these scholars, racial purity seemed old-fashioned and backwards.

Ernest Renan appears to share this opinion. He claims that the population of Galilee was mixed, including non-Jewish groups such as Phoenicians, Syrians, Arabs, and even Greeks. On the basis of this observation, Renan draws the following conclusion concerning Jesus: "It is therefore impossible to raise here any question of race, and to seek to ascertain what blood flowed in the veins of him who contributed most to efface the distinction of blood in humanity."[10] There is something strange about this statement. Renan rejects "race" and "blood" as valid categories to describe the identity of Jesus. But why does he introduce them, only to reject them? Renan's position seems to respond to an ongoing discussion in which race played a central role.

Renan was negative about basing identity on race. This becomes obvious when he describes how Jesus broke with Judaism and posits a contrast between Jews and Jesus, who represents "humanity": "He proclaimed the rights of man, not the rights of the Jew; the religion of man, not the religion of the Jew: the deliverance of man, not the deliverance of the Jew." Renan drew the conclusion that, with Jesus, "the religion of humanity, established, not upon blood, but upon the heart, was founded."[11] Here Renan speaks of "man" (i.e., the human being) and "humanity" that represents the totality, which was not limited to a specific religion or race. Renan regards this development as a sign of progress; Jesus represents a universal religion superior to less developed religions. Renan considers race something that belongs to the past, and which characterized Judaism as a particularistic religion.

Renan distances himself from the tendency to identify nations with races, which he considers a dangerous proposition. This he found in Germany, even in the positions of David Friedrich Strauss, whom he admires as a historical Jesus scholar. In an exchange of letters with Strauss, Renan tries to establish a common understanding of nation in the war between France and Prussia in 1870; however, he is unsuccessful. He accuses the Germans of conducting a politics of races that will lead to the end of a "fruitful mixture, composed of numerous and quite necessary elements that is called humanity."[12] Renan argues that the division into races is also scientifically false; only a few countries have so-called pure races; moreover, such

10. Renan, *Life of Jesus,* 90.

11. Renan, *Life of Jesus,* 226.

12. Renan, "Nouvelle lettre," 456.

divisions will result in war and extermination. When Renan outlines the differences between the German concept of nation and the French concept that he presents, we can see in the contrast between two concepts of nation similarities to his contrasts between Jews and Jesus. In both cases, Renan posits a contrast between race and humanity.

Recently there has been a return to a mentality based on race, now under the category of ethnicity, combined with nationalism. In some instances, this ideology has resulted in violence against minorities. In this situation, it is easy to feel sympathy with Renan and his arguments about race. However, Renan's position also raises problems. When he accuses Jews of a racial thinking in contrast with the inclusion of all humanity, he in fact characterizes Jews as others, as those who do not belong to Europe. This way of categorizing groups runs parallel to his classification of languages. Renan distinguished between living and dead languages. Indo-European and Aryan languages belonged to the first group, Semitic languages to the second. The problem with this classification of languages was that it was transferred to the speakers of these languages. As a result, speakers of Semitic languages (that is, Jews and Arabs) were put in the dead category; they were seen as backwards in terms of culture and civilization. Since Renan's philological and religious studies were highly regarded, he enjoyed a unique authority when he participated in the discussion of languages and races. However, Renan is also an example of how research is influenced by underlying attitudes and ideologies, even straightforward prejudices and stereotypes. In consequence, Renan has been charged with being one of the founders of European anti-Semitism.[13]

Jesus Was Galilean, Not Jewish

That Galilee had a mixed population was a commonly accepted theory among historians in the nineteenth century. However, in discussion of Jesus' identity, this theory was used for ideological purposes to distance Jesus from his Jewish environment. This was the case especially within so-called cultural Protestantism in Germany. This was a movement within the liberal bourgeoisie that wanted to bring Christianity into modernity. One aspect of this modernization was the suggestion to leave the (Jewish) Old Testament out of the biblical canon of the church. That Jesus was Jewish was a problem for many who emphasized that Christianity was an integral part of German culture and identity.

---

13. Heschel, *Aryan Jesus*, 33–38.

Paul de Lagarde (1827–1891) was a well-known Orientalist and biblical scholar who wanted to create a Christianity adapted to German culture.[14] He wanted to remove Jewish elements, which according to Lagarde had been introduced by the apostle Paul. Instead, he wanted to return to the original message of Jesus. That meant distancing Jesus as much as possible from his Jewish environment. Lagarde therefore emphasized that Jesus was formed by his upbringing in Galilee, and that Galilee was very different religiously from Jerusalem and Judea.

The next step was to separate Jesus from his Jewish ancestry. In order to accomplish this, Lagarde resorted to the theories that the population of Galilee was of mixed origin. He developed intricate hypotheses about the possibility that Aryan tribes had immigrated into Galilee, and that Jesus was descended from these tribes. Consequently, Jesus was no longer Jewish in terms of biological ancestry. These ideas were expanded and widely spread by the historian Houston S. Chamberlain (1855–1927). Originally English, he married the daughter of the composer Richard Wagner, whose anti-Semitic opinions were well known. Chamberlain emphasized the biological aspect of race, which had become popular in the last part of the nineteenth century. According to Chamberlain, biological race, not religious practice, defined identity. Thus, even if Jesus had received a Jewish upbringing and education, he was not racially Jewish. Chamberlain advocated his position in a large monograph on Europe in the nineteenth century, which received much attention.[15]

The Aryan Jesus

Lagarde and Chamberlain espoused a nationalism that wanted to make Christianity into a German religion, free from Jewish influence. In *The Aryan Jesus*, the American professor Susannah Heschel has documented the history that prepared the way for Nazism in Germany.[16] We all know the result: a regime that killed six million Jews and several hundred thousand other "inferior" people (e.g. gypsies, homosexuals, and people with mental or physical disabilities). Nazi ideology regarded the Jews as an "interior enemy," and its anti-Semitism was based on biological race theories. This was the official policy of Nazi Germany. When Hitler gained power in Germany and established his Nazi regime, there were two organized reactions within the Evangelical (Protestant) Church in Germany.

14. Lagarde, *Deutsche Schriften.*
15. Chamberlain, *Foundations of the Nineteenth Century.*
16 Heschel, *Aryan Jesus.*

The "German Christians" (*Die deutsche Christen*) supported Hitler's rule, while the "Confessing Church" (*Die bekennende Kirche*) rejected a collaboration with the totalitarian regime. The German Christians supported an anti-Semitic ideology and wanted to separate Christianity from Judaism: this included distancing Jesus from any possible Jewish ancestry. The Confessing Church also saw Judaism as a negative influence upon Christianity. The conflict with the Nazi regime was over its desire to gain control of the church, not specifically over its persecution of the Jews,[17] and the Confessing Church as an institution did not assist Jews under persecution, although some individuals and groups got involved.

The Nazi regime had an ambiguous relationship with Christianity. On the one hand, it exploited Christian anti-Semitism to make the German population accept its racial ideology towards the Jews. On the other hand, it wanted to eradicate Christianity and to replace it with Nazi ideology; for instance, replacing the Bible with Hitler's *Mein Kampf* (*My Struggle*). Given their their support for Nazi ideology, the German Christians may have served as "useful idiots."

Some theologians and pastors attempted to construct a scholarly justification for a non-Jewish Jesus, and for that purpose they established "The Institute for the Study and Eradication of Jewish Influence on German Church Life."[18] The initiator and chair of the institute was a respected New Testament professor, Walter Grundmann (1906–1976). He argued that Jesus was no Jew; rather, Jesus combatted Judaism. Initially, Grundmann claimed that Jesus could not be identified by human categories like race; he could not be classified as a Jew or as Aryan. The main point was that his teachings were totally opposed to Judaism. However, for Grundmann too, Galilee was the key to the identity of Jesus, and his *Jesus der Galiläer und das Judentum* signaled a shift of opinion when it came to the importance of race. Now, biological race had become important for him, and *Galilean* became a code word for Aryan. Together with many other German scholars, Grundmann claimed that if Jesus was a Galilean, this meant that he was not a Jew. Grundmann even resorted to the old Jewish accusation, known from the Talmud, that the real father of Jesus was a Roman soldier (see chapter 3, above). Grundmann maintained that Galilee was home to a non-Jewish religion that was opposed to Judaism. Eschatology was one example: Jesus did not speak of himself as the Messiah, which was a Jewish term. Instead, he used the Hellenistic term" Son of Man." In this way Jesus represented a new

---

17. Heschel, *Aryan Jesus*, 4–5.
18. Heschel, *Aryan Jesus*, 67–164.

religion and a new concept of God that had no relation to Judaism. Many German theologians and pastors shared these views.

Grundmann and other members of the Institute for the Study and Eradication of Jewish Influence on German Church Life went beyond a theological anti-Semitism; they supported the racial anti-Semitism that led to mass killings of Jews. Many of the members of the Institute had, like Grundmann, joined the Nazi Party, some of them before 1933, when the party gained political power in Germany. After 1945, many theologians and pastors who had been members of the party and had voiced anti-Semitic views, retained their positions and were even appointed to new, important positions. At a distance of more than seventy-five years, it is difficult to understand this policy on the part of the German churches to collaborate with the Nazi Party. Those who had been party members excused themselves by saying that they had assumed only theological, not political, responsibilities, and that their position on Jesus' relations to Judaism was within a commonly accepted view in the Protestant churches.

Jesus in Jewish Research—A Neglected Chapter[19]

In the nineteenth century, Christian scholars largely neglected the viewpoints of Jewish scholars in their studies of the historical Jesus. In *Abraham Geiger and the Jewish Jesus*,[20] Susannah Heschel shows how Jewish scholars represented a critical alternative to the Lives of Jesus by Christian scholars, and challenged the Christian view of Judaism at the time of Jesus. The German rabbi and scholar Abraham Geiger (1810–1874) played a central role. He was the founder of Reform Judaism, a liberal branch of Judaism, which accepted historical criticism of the Scriptures. He considered the Pharisees a reform movement within the Judaism of their time. Geiger saw Jesus as a Pharisee, and he claimed that in the original words of Jesus there was nothing new compared to the teachings of the Pharisees. However, some parts of the teaching of Jesus did not correspond to that of the Pharisees. Typical examples were his positive teaching about poverty, his rejection of the present world and his focus on the coming world. Geiger held that these positions were characteristic of the Galileans; accordingly, he characterized Jesus as a Pharisee with Galilean viewpoints.

---

19. For a thorough presentation and discussion of Jewish research on Jesus, from the beginning in the nineteenth century up to the twenty-first century, see Jaffé, *Jésus* (unfortunately only in French); Susannah Heschel provides a concise and rich summary in "Jesus in modern Jewish thought."

20. Heschel, *Abraham Geiger.*

The Prussian historian Heinrich Graetz (1817–1891) was the first to write a comprehensive history of the Jews from a Jewish perspective, *Geschichte der Juden* (*History of the Jews*) in eleven volumes. Here he described Jesus as an Essene.[21] At the time, a popular theory affirmed that Jesus was a member of the Essene fellowship (now considered to have been located at Qumran near the Dead Sea). According to Graetz, Jesus' mission was to bring people back to a true Jewish life. Jesus directed his attention to a specific group of people: those who were excluded from the Jewish fellowship and who did not know the Jewish law. They were the so-called *am-ha-aretz* (people of the land). Graetz's suggestion corresponded to the picture that he drew of Galilee as a backward part of the land.

For Geiger and Graetz, it was important to place Jesus within Judaism of his time, and they rejected the attempts by Christian scholars to distance Jesus from Judaism. However, at the same time that they claimed Jesus was a Jew, they also admitted that some parts of his teaching did not fit into a Pharisaic system. They solved this problem by ascribing Jesus' teaching on these points to his position as a Galilean or an Essene.

Jesus within Jewish Zionism

Many Jewish intellectuals were influenced by the growing nationalism in Europe in the nineteenth century. The most prominent example is Theodore Herzl (1860–1904). In reaction to the anti-Semitism in eastern Europe, he proposed that Jews should establish their own land where they could be safe from persecution. In 1896 he published the pamphlet *The Jewish State*, and he became the leading figure of the Zionist movement. Many Jewish scholars referred to Judaism as *a nation*, both with regard to ancient Judaism in Palestine in the first century and in their own time. This terminology was especially popular with Jews who were Zionists and who wanted to establish a Jewish homeland in Palestine.

Among them was Joseph Klausner (1874–1958), who emigrated from Ukraine to Palestine in 1920. In 1922 he wrote *Jesus of Nazareth: His Life, Times and Teaching* from a Zionist perspective.[22] This Zionist viewpoint brought ambiguity to his portrait of Jesus. Klausner's primary concern was to portray Jesus fully as a Jew; together with Geiger and Graetz, he concluded that Jesus was close to the Pharisees. At the same time, however, he accused Jesus of being an individualist and thus

---

21. Graetz, *Geschichte der Juden*, 3:216–29.

22. Klausner, *Jesus*.

breaking away from the collectivistic, Zionist perspective that saw Judaism as a religion for a people, for a nation.

Klausner rejected the position of Christian scholars that the Jewish *nation* was guilty of the death of Jesus. He acquitted the Pharisees; they considered Jesus one of their own, and they did not find that his teachings made him guilty of death. On the other hand, Klausner found that the Great Sanhedrin (the supreme council) carried a heavy responsibility for Jesus' death. The Sadducees made up the dominant group in the council; and they could not accept that a Galilean proclaimed himself the Messiah, created disturbances in the temple area, and challenged leaders of the Jewish nation. Moreover, the Sadducees carried the responsibility before the Romans to preserve peace and calm in the city. The Sadducees were responsible for the preliminary interrogations of Jesus. According to Klausner, the authors of the Gospels chose to introduce them as representatives of the Jewish people, and thereby to the blame the people as a whole. However, this was an apologetic strategy. The Gospels were written down long after the death of Jesus, during a period when Christians depended on good relations with the powerful Romans. Klausner emphasizes that after the preliminary investigation, no Jews participated in the process; Pilate, the Roman governor, was responsible for the execution of Jesus.

Even if a small group of priests carried the responsibility for Jesus' death, Klausner asserted that the Jews "as a nation" were much less guilty for the death of Jesus than the Greeks were for the death of Socrates.[23] Nevertheless, for 1,900 years the world had continued to avenge the death of Jesus by punishing the Jews. In Klausner's conclusion, we find two perspectives that were accepted by many history-of-Jesus scholars in the twentieth century.

The first concerns the historical evidence for the responsibility for the death of Jesus. The Jewish people were not self-governing; its leadership ruled at the mercy of the Romans and depended upon Roman power. The recognition of the supremacy of Roman power became important in evaluating historically the responsibility of the Jewish authorities for the guilty verdict against Jesus.

The second aspect was hermeneutical. How was the guilty verdict against Jesus that precipitated his execution interpreted and used in contemporary debates? Klausner accused Christians of using Jewish responsibility for the death of Jesus to punish Jews for 1,900 years. When Klausner claimed that the Jews had paid with their own blood for the death of Jesus,

---

23. Klausner, *Jesus*, 348.

who was himself a Jew, the suffering of Jesus was juxtaposed with the suffering of the Jews across the centuries.

Marc Chagall: *White Crucifixion* (1938).
Peter Barritt / Alamy Stock Photo. Used by permission.

This parallel found a visible expression in Marc Chagall's pictures of Jesus in an eastern European village, crucified as a Jew with a *tallith* (prayer shawl) as a loincloth, while in the background Jews are persecuted by communists. By depicting Jesus as a Jewish martyr in a series of paintings of the crucifixion, Chagall drew attention to the suffering and persecutions of the Jews in Europe in the 1930s.[24]

24. Chagall, *White Crucifixion*.

Historical Jesus Research after World War II

Klausner—and Chagall—strongly indicated a link between the suffering of Jesus and suffering of the Jews. We might have expected that the Holocaust would have brought greater awareness of these parallels to Christian scholars, and new perspective on the relationship between Jesus and his Jewish environment. However, it took a long time before this happened. Christian theologians continued to speak of Jesus as representing something new and different from the Judaism of his day.

From the 1950s, there was a new beginning of research on the historical Jesus; this went by the name "a new quest for the Historical Jesus."[25] The German professor Rudolf Bultmann (1884–1976) was a dominant figure in Protestant theology in the twentieth century. He emphasized that Christian faith was based on the proclamation of Christ, not on the historical Jesus. However, in 1954 Ernst Käsemann (1906–1998), who had been one of Bultmann's students, advocated for the importance of Jesus as the historical starting point for Christianity.[26] Since the Gospels are the result of a long history of transmission of sayings and narratives about Jesus, it is difficult to go back to Jesus himself. This requires a critical reading of the Gospels, and Käsemann established *dissimilarity* as a criterion to evaluate which sayings or narratives might be ascribed to Jesus. When a saying could not be ascribed to a Jewish tradition or to primitive Christianity, one could be reasonably certain that it went back to Jesus. The picture of Jesus that emerged from this discussion was one that distanced him both from the Judaism of his time and from the disciple movement that Jesus initiated.

What would an image of Jesus based on these principles look like? Käsemann himself did not write a book on the historical Jesus, but another student of Bultmann, Günther Bornkamm (1905–1990), wrote *Jesus of Nazareth*.[27] In this book, Bornkamm preserves the traditional, negative picture of Judaism. To give one example, he says that Jewish belief existed in a tension between the past and the future, while the present was an empty void. It was into this void that Jesus entered with his "difference." Jesus appears as "the other," in contrast to Judaism. According to Bornkamm, Judaism was a religion that belonged to the past.[28] However, Christian scholars did not universally recognize this standpoint. Already in 1953, the

---

25. The term "new quest" refers to the English title of Albert Schweitzer's famous book on the historical Jesus research in the nineteenth century, *The Quest of the Historical Jesus*.

26. Käsemann, "Problem."

27. Bornkamm, *Jesus of Nazareth*.

28. Bornkamm, *Jesus of Nazareth*, 55–56.

Norwegian New Testament scholar Nils Alstrup Dahl (1911–2001) emphasized that Jesus must be studied *within*, not in contrast to, Judaism. Dahl
claimed that there were more continuities between Jesus and his Jewish
environment than Käsemann allowed for.[29]

Jesus Within, Not Outside Judaism

The suggestion that Jesus must be studied within his Jewish environment was
followed up in the historical Jesus research in the 1970s. This was a result,
inter alia, of a growing interest in the historical Jesus among Jewish scholars,
and of a growing recognition of their research among Christian scholars. This
was very different from the situation in the nineteenth century, when leading
scholars like Renan and Strauss paid little attention to the views of scholars
like Geiger and Graetz. A hundred years later, Jewish scholars were more
widely read, and they were part of the debate on the Historical Jesus with
scholars from different—or no—religious confessions.

Paul Winter's *On the Trial of Jesus*[30] was among the earliest Jewish contributions. Winter continues Klausner's perspectives on the Jewish authorities and their responsibility for the execution of Jesus, viz. that they were
under pressure from the Roman authorities to preserve peace and order in
Jerusalem. Jesus' entry into Jerusalem with his disciples created expectations that he was a messiah who would liberate the people, and this created
unrest in the city. Thus, both Jewish and Roman authorities would have had
reason to prevent Jesus from fomenting tumult. Jewish leaders, not ordinary
people, carried some of the responsibility for the death of Jesus; however,
this was a result of their dependence on the Romans.

David Flusser (1917–2000), a professor at Hebrew University in
Jerusalem, and Geza Vermes (1924–2013), a professor at Oxford University, were among the most prolific and influential Jesus scholars of their
generation. They shared Klausner's interest in placing Jesus with Judaism
of his day; however, they did not share Klausner's Zionist perspectives.
Consequently, they were not so critical of Jesus for parting company with
a collectivistic basis for Jewish morals. Flusser argued that Jesus' focus on
love of neighbor, which many considered distinguished him from Judaism,
was in fact part of a development within Judaism at the time. However,
Flusser found that Jesus was unique in that he expanded love of neighbor
to include even love of enemy.[31]

29. Dahl, "Historical Jesus."
30. Winter, *On the Trial of Jesus.*
31. Flusser, *Jesus.*

Vermes's earliest and still best known book on the historical Jesus is *Jesus the Jew*.[32] In this book, Vermes describes Jesus as a charismatic prophet and miracle worker of a type that was well known from Galilee at the time. The two best known from tradition were Honi the Circle Drawer and Hanina ben Dosa, and Vermes suggests that they represented a distinctive trend of charismatic Judaism that existed in the last period of the Second Temple. Vermes continues the description of Jesus as a Jew; however, he portrays Judaism as less monolithic than in Klausner's construction. Vermes was also an expert on the Qumran community, so he viewed Jesus in relation to many different groups and trends within Judaism. According to Vermes, Jesus showed similarities with an eschatological tendency; however, Jesus understood eschatology primarily as a break with the past and a challenge from the future. This made Vermes's Jesus a representative of a more individualistically oriented Judaism.

Many Jewish scholars share a picture of the historical Jesus in which he has a place within a pluralistic Judaism; however, most see him as particularly close to the Pharisees. It is possible that popular expectations that he was the Messiah created fear of unrest and made Jewish leaders collaborate with the Romans, who carried the responsibility for Jesus' execution. Paula Fredriksen, in *Jesus of Nazareth, King of the Jews*, has convincingly argued this viewpoint.[33] This has now largely become a shared position among Jesus scholars, regardless of their background. However, it represents a dramatic shift from the way earlier Christian scholars anchored their historical reconstructions based on the passion narratives in the Gospels. In the passion story, including in the accusations from Jewish leaders, Jesus' teaching was presented as in conflict with Jewish belief and praxis. It was Jesus' blasphemous sayings that made the Jewish leaders react angrily and pressure the reluctant Pilate to have Jesus executed.

It was not easy for Christian scholars to let this traditional interpretation go. There had been earlier protests against this paradigm;[34] however, it was a North American scholar, E. P. Sanders, who first successfully challenged it. The change did not come about with individual research results, but rather by shifts in the mental concept of Jewish religion held by Christian scholars. Both Bible readers and scholars had largely accepted the picture that the Gospels presented of a Jesus in conflict with a Judaism that emphasized a rigid observance of the law. One reason that this paradigm held sway was that it could be made useful in a contemporary situation. The conflict between the

32. Vermes, *Jesus the Jew*.
33. Fredriksen, *Jesus of Nazareth*.
34. Montefiore, *Synoptic Gospels*.

freedom of the gospel of Jesus versus a legalistic religion was applied to the conflict between Luther and the Roman Church at the time of the Reformation. Moreover, it is not that long ago when words like *Pharisaic* and *legalistic* were used in church debates to characterize opponents.

E. P. Sanders rejected this paradigm. Starting with a reading of Jewish texts from antiquity, he found that Paul's negative characterizations of the law were expressions of polemical rhetoric, and not historically trustworthy.[35] Sanders continued these studies in *Jesus and Judaism*[36] and claimed that Jesus wished to reestablish Israel and the Jerusalem temple. Sanders builds his result on studies not only of Jesus' words, but also on Jesus' praxis, which was more directed at the people as a collective. Even Jesus' proclamation of the kingdom of God, combined with miracles and meals, showed a positive attitude to Judaism.

Sanders claims that Jesus did not break with the law;[37] his interpretations were all within the plurality of views that characterized the many varieties of Judaism. A renewed look at Jesus' relations to the law shows the same. According to Sanders, Jesus' criticism of the law of Moses should be considered part of an inter-Jewish discussion, not a break with the law. Many Jesus scholars have now accept this position. We cannot enter into this development in detail; the purpose of this section has been to point out the remarkable transition from neglect to recognition of Jewish scholarship in Jesus studies. However, I will point out one significant aspect of recent Jewish studies of Jesus. Historical Jesus studies were for a very long time a male domain. Jewish studies represent a break with this trend, especially in the United States, where many women scholars are engaged in the study of the historical figure of Jesus and of the reception history of Jesus. Significant contributions have been made especially Paula Fredriksen, Susannah Heschel, and Amy Jill Levine.[38]

At the end of this brief historical survey, it is useful to reflect on the different contexts of Christian and Jewish Jesus studies. Nineteenth-century Jesus scholars saw him as the founder of Christian Europe. Consequently, they focused on those words and acts that pointed to a specific Christian tradition. Jewish scholars understandably were concerned to study Jesus within the Jewish context of his time, and to show the importance of Judaism for the development of European culture. The present

35. Sanders, *Paul.*

36. Sanders, *Jesus.*

37. Sanders, *Jesus*, 245–69.

38. Fredriksen, *From Jesus to Christ;* Fredriksen, *Jesus of Nazareth;* Heschel, *Abraham Geiger;* Heschel, *Aryan Jesus;* Heschel, "Jesus"; Levine, *Misunderstood Jew;* Levine et al., eds., *Historical Jesus in Context.*

stage of historical Jesus studies is concerned to place Jesus within his first-century context, not so much explicitly asking for the meaning of Jesus for the present. However, there are still different presuppositions and points of view, not only between Christian and Jewish scholars, but also within each group, as we will see in the following chapters.

How to Put an End to Hate Speech?

Many historical Jesus scholars have changed their descriptions of the relations between Jesus and Jews. However, as Amy Jill Levine has pointed out in *The Misunderstood Jew*,[39] it takes long time before these changes are reflected in popular presentations, in preaching and teaching in Christian churches. The launching of the second volume of *Jesus of Nazareth* by Joseph Ratzinger (then Pope Benedict XVI)[40] provides a good example. The Vatican Press office presented it as revolutionary news that the pope had declared that the Jews had no collective guilt for the death of Jesus. However, this was really no news at all. Already the Second Vatican Council in 1965 had said that the Jews bore no collective responsibility. That it was presented as revolutionary news in 2011 suggests how widespread this misconception is. The Catholic Church has worked systematically to remove this basis for hate speech. In the declaration *Nostra Aetate: The Relation of the Church to Non-Christian Religions* (1965), the council warned against drawing inferences for the present from a historical situation. It said, "True, the Jewish authorities and those who followed their lead pressed for the death of Christ; still, what happened in His passion cannot be charged against all the Jews, without distinction, then alive, nor against the Jews of today."[41] The Roman Catholic Church has followed up this declaration with many statements and regulations—for instance about how the passion of Jesus should be interpreted, preached, and represented (e.g., in passion plays).[42]

Among Protestants, Lutherans have found themselves in a particularly difficult position because of the role of Martin Luther (1483–1546), the founder of Lutheranism, and his increasingly hateful speeches against the Jews. From the end of the nineteenth century onward, Luther's position on the Jews was used to support anti-Semitism, especially in the Nazi period in Germany. At the five-hundredth anniversary of Luther's birth, in 1983, the

---

39. Levine, *Misunderstood Jew*.

40. Pope Benedict XVI, *Jesus of Nazareth. 2*.

41. Vatican II, *Nostra Aetate*.

42. Bishops' Committee for Ecumenical and Interreligious Affairs, *Bible, the Jews, and the Death of Jesus*.

Lutheran World Federation issued a self-critical declaration that denounced Luther's views.[43] Most other Protestant denominations have issued statements or introduced policies denouncing anti-Semitism. Thus, I think it is fair to say that Christian historical Jesus scholars and Christian churches in general have tried to turn around their long history of anti-Judaism. However, that does not mean that they have succeeded; hate speech has many sources outside a specifically Christian context.

This chapter started by pointing out how Jews throughout the history of Europe and eventually of the United States were regarded as the "other" compared to "we." For the longest part of that history, Christian churches played a central role in defining European identity. This is no longer the case in the same way as in the past. However, in recent years there has been a rise in hate crimes, both of physical violence and of hate speech, toward Jews in most European countries and in the US. Many Jews report that this intensification makes them feel that they "do not belong" in the societies where they live. The feeling among Jews of belonging or not depends on several factors, not least the politics and attitudes of the majority population.[44] Groups on the extreme Right, which have been on the rise recently, represent a polarized world view of "we" versus "them." They exploit an ethnonationalism that has also been on the rise in mainline parties. For ethnonationalism, a shared heritage is important; it usually includes a common language, a common faith, and a common ethnic ancestry. In Europe such ethnonationalism has been directed mostly against Muslim refugees, but it also targets Jews as internal strangers. In both cases, the churches could do more to protest hate speech and hate crimes. Many churches in Europe have had a long history as state churches, that is, as privileged by the state and identified with the nation. Now they need to turn around and not continue to defend an outdated version of the nation-state. Instead, they need to support the development within nations to accept differences—different ethnicities, faiths, and cultures, for example.

43. Lutheran World Federation and the International Jewish Committee for Interreligious Consultation, *Luther, Lutheranism, and the Jews.*

44. A survey of several European countries shows that Hungary and Sweden represent two very different positions (Dencik and Marosi, "Different Antisemitisms"). In Hungary, 95 percent of the Jews were born in the country, but only 70 percent feel that they belong. This corresponds to the fact that two-thirds of the population at large considered Jews as "strangers." In Sweden, on the other hand, only two-thirds of the Jews were born in the country, but 85 percent said that they felt a strong sense of belonging. Only a quarter of the population at large considered Jews a strange element in society. The investigators attribute the situation of Swedish Jews to the fact that many of them came from Eastern Europe and experienced that they were welcomed by the Swedish welfare state.

Against anti-Semitism, the churches ought to bring together what was for so long separated: Jesus and Jew. Now is the time to say that hate speech and violence against Jews is directed against Jesus. This should not prevent churches from saying that excluding refugees because they are Muslims is excluding Jesus.

Part 3: Challenges

In the last three chapters, we move into modernity and the present. In this period North America takes a prominent position in studies of Jesus, both in terms of the historical Jesus and of memories of Jesus. Memories of Jesus were traditionally part of established cultures and their values. These social and political cultures have been challenged by many conflicts related to issues of gender, class and race. In the first chapter I focused on three examples of conflicts that have affected national identities and cohesion, and where memories of Jesus have played a part: early modernity in Norway, postwar politics in Italy, and the civil rights movement in the United States.

The following chapter introduces challenges to the hegemonic, status-quo memories of Jesus as a white heterosexual and privileged man. These challenges come from groups that previously have been excluded from conversations about Jesus; however, in the last part of the twentieth century they claimed their own voices and told their own memories, identifying with Jesus from the margins. The result is a multiplicity of voices and images of Jesus.

This broad range of memories raises the question of the relationship between many memories and the one historical person of Jesus. I suggest that the quest for a historical Jesus is a modern way of raising the same question as the memories do, and the question is, what is the meaning of Jesus? In modernity, history is believed to provide meaning and identity. Therefore, the final chapter explores the possibility of establishing a historically based memory.

7

Jesus and Gender, Class, and Race

Memories of Jesus in Modern Conflicts

MEMORIES OF JESUS HAVE shaped the identity of the present—particularly the present of the Western world. We saw in a previous chapter how the image of Jesus in conflict with the Jewish people became the image of a Christian Europe. The new image of Jesus in the nineteenth century, with its focus on the human Jesus, not the heavenly Christ, continued to shape the identity of Europe and to a large degree the USA. The human Jesus became a paradigm for Western identity, which contrasted with an Oriental (Eastern) identity. Jesus represented progress and the future of society whereas Judaism and Islam represented the past, what was backward. As we moved into the modern world, memories of Jesus still today play a role in our discerning identities and in discussing our national heritage.

In this chapter, we shall especially look out for representations of Jesus in times of changes and crises. There are so many examples that I cannot claim to give even a partial overview, so that this chapter reflects some of my own experiences and interests. I have chosen examples that deal with identity formation in modern societies, in terms of gender, class, and race.

I start with my own country, Norway, at the brink of modernity in the late nineteenth century. Together with many other countries, Norway experienced changes with regard to industrialization and new forms of work. A split between work life and family life in the home represented challenges to men's roles and identities. Moreover, this was also a period when women started to challenge the taken-for-granted superiority of men. I explore how pastors and theologians responded to these challenges by rethinking the masculinity of Jesus. Thus, Jesus became "the modern man," representing a revised form of masculinity and a reformulation of gender.

Class was for a very long time a nonissue in presentations of Jesus. Obviously, this was so when Jesus was presented as the heavenly King, or solely in religious categories as savior, helper, or suffering for our sins. Thus, it was a dramatic moment when an institution on the left wing of the Roman Catholic Church in Italy in the early 1950s launched a project that challenged artists to create images of "Jesus as worker." The project drew many well-known modernist artists in Italy over a period of more than ten years. It ended in the early 1960s, and is documented in the art collection of the academy Pro Civitate Christiana in Assisi. Moreover, the same group that was behind the "Jesus as worker" project also inspired one of the most challenging Jesus films ever made, *Il Vangelo secondo Matteo* by Pier Paolo Pasolini. Pasolini's Jesus was an unsparing critic of the wealthy who destroyed the ideals for human life found in the Gospels.

The question of race represents a third challenge to presentations of Jesus. When the center of Christianity moved to Europe from the East in the High Middle Ages, Jesus became white. From artistic representations in medieval paintings onward to modern Jesus films, there was no doubt that Jesus was white. Moreover, white was not an innocent color. Through European (and later US) colonization, the message and image of Jesus were spread all over the world. There was no doubt that a white Jesus was identified with power and might that controlled and subjected nonwhites to an inferior status. The civil rights movement in the US in the 1960s is one example of how the whiteness of Jesus was questioned.

Jesus' Masculinity and the Rise of Modernity in Norway

In the nineteenth century, Norway was a poor country in the northern part of Europe. A country with a long history back to the Viking period, it had been a province under Denmark for four hundred years. At the end of the Napoleonic wars Norway declared independence from Denmark. However, the great powers of Europe forced it to enter into union with Sweden, although as separate countries with a common Swedish king. Its history illustrated the political and ideological structures that changed Europe in the nineteenth century, especially the rise of nationalism. The nineteenth century was a period of nation building, in terms of economics and social and political structures, but also through art, literature, music, and religion. Norway was a Lutheran country with a strong pietistic lay movement. Jesus held an important place in social life and religious culture. For instance, Christmas hymns placed Jesus in a Norwegian landscape at wintertime; this was very far from

Bethlehem, but close to Norwegian identity. Moreover, Jesus came to play a role in the social changes that happened also in Norway.

Poverty led young men and families from Norway to immigrate to the USA to find work and better opportunities than in their homeland. However, it shared with the rest of western Europe the transformation from a rural to a more industrialized society. Norwegian society was in a process of transition from traditional patriarchal authority structures to a society based on the individual. There were changes in family structures, with women claiming their rights. This situation has been described as the crisis of "the Modern breakthrough," named after an influential book by the Danish cultural critic George Brandes.[1] However, it is often overlooked that the full title of the book is *The* Men *of the Modern Breakthrough*. The title suggests that we should look at how these changes were initiated by men, and how they affected their self-understanding. Brandes frequently used the term "manly" (*mandig*) to characterize modernity. However, this modern breakthrough did not only affect individual men; also at stake was the identity of society and of the nation. National identity was expressed in terms of masculinity so that changes in conceptions of masculinity were indications of national self-understanding.

This concern that institutions and citizens project a masculine identity emerged as a response to the rise of feminist movements. Churches too and their teaching on patriarchy and the submission of women represented a strong ideological support for social structures. Theologians and church authorities were slow to respond to criticisms of excessive masculinity, and they were even slower to change their teachings. However, we may see a partial reaction in the ways that theologians and pastors (who, of course, were all men) gradually changed their positions on Christian masculinity.

These changes took the form of discussions of the masculinity of Jesus. To even raise the question of the masculinity of Jesus was a result of studies of the historical Jesus, which made it possible to discuss Jesus and his social relations. At that time many theologians were concerned that Christianity was losing its grip on men, especially on young workers. In Norway, one of the most influential pastors around the turn of the twentieth century, Christopher Bruun, argued that a renewal of Christianity must happen through young men. He shared a concern raised in many societies undergoing industrialization, and which resulted *inter alia* in the birth of organizations such as the Young Men's Christian Association (YMCA). Many theologians and pastors feared that Christianity had become too feminized and attempted to reach out to young men by presenting Jesus

1. Brandes, *Det Moderne Gjennembruds Mænd*.

as a (young) worker. In a small book on *Jesus as a Man* (or human being),[2] Christopher Bruun warned against "soft images" of Jesus and emphasized that he was a "real man." Bruun criticized the social and cultural situation in Europe, which he accused of decadence and "softness." In contrast, Jesus represented the ideal of a simple life. In social conflicts between workers and owners, Bruun argued that Jesus was not on the side of the capitalists; rather, he was "a worker and a friend of workers." Jesus did not support the destructive rule of capitalism in the world; instead, he would secure a better place for his old comrades and force the rich to accept a more modest place. Bruun was not alone in presenting Jesus as a worker. In England, a group of Christian socialists under the leadership of Charles Kingsley portrayed Jesus as a worker. Moreover, they emphasized the masculinity of Jesus so much that they were accused of presenting a "muscular Christianity."[3] Both Bruun and Kingsley represented a robust masculinity, not attempting to integrate emotions into the picture. Their image of Jesus was a protest against not only feminine aspects of Christianity; the words *feminine* and *soft* were used to criticize bourgeois society as well. Portrayed as a worker, Jesus could serve to integrate the working classes into the nation during a period when they were new groups with little power.

Christopher Bruun presented Jesus as an ideal worker, although he himself, as a Lutheran pastor, belonged to the social elite. Some of his younger colleagues, however, wrote books about Jesus, but they had other ideals. A New Testament professor, Lyder Brun, wrote a portrait of Jesus[4] that did not include a class perspective. Instead, he lifted up the question of the *character* of the individual, with a combination of feminine and masculine traits. This focus on character was common among men from the middle classes; good character was important for men who aspired to positions of power and responsibility. This focus on character was not only a Nordic preoccupation; in particular, in Victorian Britain it was an important issue. The educational system with public schools for the upper classes put great emphasis on building a "manly character," which was necessary for Britain's *national* character as an empire and a colonial power. Among the Victorian Lives of Jesus, the work by the Scottish biblical scholar George Adam Smith portrayed Jesus as a young man in Galilee, as an ideal for young men in Britain, to help build a national character.[5]

2. Bruun, *Om Jesus som menneske.*

3. Hall, ed., *Muscular Christianity.*

4. Brun, *Jesu billede.*

5. Moxnes, *Jesus and the Rise of Nationalism,* 169–73.

Members of the bourgeoisie wrote books on Jesus, and for the most part they were addressed to men of the same class. That was the case with *The Man Jesus*,[6] which started as a lecture series for university students, mostly men, in Oslo around 1920. Again, its focus was not on social class but on the individual. The author was Eivind Berggrav, a scholar of the psychology of religion. He later became the leading bishop of the Church of Norway, and spokesman for the Christian churches in Norway during the Nazi occupation. The book was not a historical study of Jesus; with the help of the psychology of religion, Berggrav wrote a portrait that modern readers could identify with. In a central chapter of the book, Berggrav discusses "manliness." He rejects the notion that manliness was the opposite of femininity, and he distinguished manliness from extreme positions on both sides. On the one side, Berggrav claims, is an exclusive emphasis on strength and power; in contrast, true manliness actually includes emotions. On the other side is sentimentality, which expresses itself in self-centeredness and the desire to be admired by others. Jesus represents true manliness; he is not sentimental, he did not crave the admiration of the masses. He was able to stand by himself, almost like a character in some of Ibsen's plays. Furthermore, Jesus showed the importance of holding on to one's goals and putting one's ideas into practice. Thus, in Jesus Berggrav found a man who steered a middle course between the temptations experienced in his life. The portrait of Jesus reflected the dilemmas of creating a Christian masculinity in encountering modernity.

The book was first published in 1921 with a second edition in 1941, during the German occupation of Norway. The Nazi authorities censored all publicity about the book, but it sold in large numbers. Obviously, this portrait of Jesus as "a true man" served as an inspiration for Norwegians during the hard times of occupation.

Moreover, the most iconic painting of a Nordic Jesus originated as a reaction to Nazi politics and threats against Europe before World War II. The artist was Henrik Sørensen (1882–1962), one of the most influential Norwegian painters in the first part of the twentieth century. His paintings of Norwegian landscapes re-created their mystical, magic nature. Many of his paintings reflected and were responses to political events—for example, the apocalyptic triptych *Getsemane, Golgata og Pietà* [1921–1925] and the monumental *Dream of Peace* in the Palace of Nations in Geneva from 1939,[7] when the war in Europe was about to break out. Sørensen was one of the first Norwegians to realize the danger of Nazi Germany,

6. Berggrav, *Mannen Jesus*.

7. http://www.ikff.no/the-dream-of-peace.

and it was as a reaction to this danger that he painted a large triptych in the Cathedral of Linkjøping in Sweden with the risen Christ at the center. He describes the Christ figure in this way: "The Savior appears as walking from a blue background—from these dark colors Christ emerges as representing the light."[8] This Nordic Jesus appears as if in protest against totalitarian forces in Europe. In another version of this theme, a triptych in the Cathedral at Hamar in Norway, this becomes even more obvious. Jesus in the central panel comes as a liberator for the suffering women under the cross, representing the misery of the world.[9]

Against this historical background, the accusations that Sørensen's Christ typifies a prototype of an Aryan are unfounded. However, the model for the original sketch was a young Norwegian, so Christ comes across as a Nordic Jesus. Sørensen painted many different versions of the young, risen Christ in many churches in Norway. The image was also spread as prints, so that in Norway it had an iconic status like Werner Sallman's *Head of Christ* (1940) for Americans.

Before Sørensen, most representations of Jesus in Norwegian churches were very traditional, often figuring Jesus in first-century dress and landscape. In contrast, Sørensen's Jesus appears as contemporary and young. An art historian gives this description: "Sørensen has portrayed the mild, life-giving Christ who encounters the whole of humanity with open arms. His Christ is Nordic, tall, with a light complexion and without a beard, very different from traditional presentations of Christ."[10] Sørensen's Christ shares similarities with the images of him in the Gospels. This is the human Jesus as a young man; however, he is at the same time the risen and living Christ. The human and the divine are woven together. This Jesus/Christ has Nordic features; at the same time, he opens his arms toward all humanity. There need not be a contradiction between what is local and specific to one region, and what is universal and open to all.

Jesus as Worker: Communism and Christianity in Postwar Italy

Postwar Europe was characterized by conflicts between Christian churches and laborers, labor unions and Marxist and socialist political parties. In this context, there were also various efforts to bridge this gap. Among them was

8 Sørensen, *Søren*, 397, n. 32.

9. https://digitaltmuseum.no/011012931296/altertavlen-i-hamar-domkirke-utfort-av-henrik-sorensen-midtbilde-den-seirende/.

10. Hoff et al., *Henrik Sørensen*, 199.

the worker-priest movement in France, where several priests worked in industrial plants to identify with the workers. Although they were few, they had an important function by contributing to a shift in attitudes among the French Left towards more tolerance toward the Catholic Church and toward priests. However, the worker-priest movement was an initiative of local priests, and it was controversial within the church hierarchy.

In Italy, there were diverse initiatives to improve relations between the Roman Catholic Church and workers and their unions. Some initiatives were launched by the Vatican and some by lower-level actors. In a move to counter the Marxist influence in Italian society and in celebration of international workers' day, in 1955 Pope Pius XII declared May 1st as a feast day for Saint Joseph "the Worker."[11] Furthermore, in the same year the Vatican dedicated a church in Rome to *Gesù Divino Laboratore* (Jesus the Divine Worker). In line with several papal encyclicals on social issues, the Church wanted to show its concern for the situation of workers from a Christian, non-Marxist position. Postwar Italy presented many changes for Italian workers. Increasing industrialization and urbanization and the mechanization of work represented a serious challenge to traditional lifestyles and social cohesion in society. Politically and ideologically Italian society was divided. The Christian Democrats and the Communist Party, the largest in western Europe, were the main contenders for power. The powerful Catholic Church supported the Christian Democrats and wanted to use its power to influence politics.[12]

It was in this context that the Catholic lay organization Pro Civitate Christiana (PCC) in 1939 launched an initiative to engage artists to create images of Jesus as worker. This meant adding to the Christian iconography of Jesus a completely new set of images of him outside the traditional religious context. PCC is a lay Catholic organization engaged in cultural and societal issues, on the left side of the Catholic Church in Italy. It has its center in Assisi, with a library, an art collection, and spaces for seminars, workshops, and meetings. The founder of the PCC was a visionary priest, Don Giovanni Rossi, who also had the idea of the project Jesus as Worker. Thanks to support from a wealthy industrialist, PCC was able to engage some of the best modernist Italian artists to display their works at annual exhibitions between 1951 and 1962. The exhibitions included paintings,

11. Kosloski, "St Joseph the Worker."
12. Carillo, "Italian Catholic Church."

sculptures, reliefs, and ceramics.[13] Many of the artworks are now collected in the Galleria d'Arte Contemporanea in Assisi.[14]

With the project Jesus as Worker, the PCC wanted to present Jesus as a religious and cultural ideal specifically for workers. The purpose was to support Italian workers, to give them self-respect and recognition. In order to reach that goal, it was necessary to develop a new iconography that expressed the identity of the human Jesus. Traditional iconography focused on the events in the life of Jesus that were most important for faith: his birth, baptism, miracles, suffering, death, resurrection and ascension. Although Jesus was presented as a human being, the divine aspects predominated.

An image of Jesus as a worker did not have the same basis in the Gospels as other, traditional images. Therefore, a new iconography had to be based on the "hidden years" of the life of Jesus, a time when he identified with the life of ordinary people and their occupation. Thus, this perspective showed similarities to the interests behind the apocryphal infancy gospels: What did Jesus do before he became a prophet? The project was challenging, both artistically and theologically. For artists, a project like "Jesus as worker" was difficult, since it was almost unknown in art history.[15] Moreover, there was the problem of how a presentation of Jesus as a humble worker might reflect his divinity. Another issue was whether pictures of Jesus as a worker could evoke an emotional response from viewers. Traditional presentations of Jesus often portrayed him in situations with strong emotional appeal. For instance, Jesus' death and resurrection engaged people emotionally; they were personally affected by these events, which were directly related to their own lives. A presentation of Jesus performing an act of ordinary work would hardly engage in the same way. Moreover, there was also a tension between Jesus identifying with ordinary workers and at the same time having a sublime character. These were some of the issues discussed by art critics, and the artists themselves found individual solutions to these dilemmas.

The Vatican also made demands on the artists and their choice of themes and modes of representation. They demanded that the PCC change the name of the project from Jesus as Worker to Jesus as Divine Worker, and that the artists made the traditional image of the holy family, with Mary, Joseph, and the infant Jesus their starting point. A historical precedent was set by a group of artists in England at the end of the nineteenth century called the Pre-Raphaelites; several of them painted Jesus as a child or a

13. Bignami et al., eds., *Galleria*.

14. I am grateful to Anna Nabot, director of the Galleria d'Arte Contemporanea, for her generous assistance in making the collection available to me, and to the previous director, Tony Bernardini, for illuminating conversations.

15. But see Ansaldi, "Cristo e Lavoratori."

young man in an ordinary setting. One example is *Christ in the House of His Parents*, painted in 1849–1850 by John Millais (1829–1896), which shows Jesus in Joseph's workshop. This painting became very controversial because it differed from the pious portraits of the holy family and showed them as ordinary people in an untidy and dirty workshop.[16]

Jesus as Carpenter

Georgio de Chirico: *Gesù Divino Lavoratore* (1951).
Used by permission of the Galleria d›Arte Contemporanea
della Pro Civitate Christiana in Assisi, Italy.

16. Sullivan, *Pre-Raphaelites*, 23–25.

Among the artworks in the PCC exhibitions, some followed the tradition that showed Jesus as a child in his father's workshop. However, already in the first exhibition in 1951, Giorgio de Chirico (1888–1978) presented a new version of this theme. De Chirico was one of the most influential Italian painters in the first part of the twentieth century, known especially for creating metaphysical art and influencing surrealism. Later, however, he developed his works into a more naturalist style, inspired by Baroque paintings; his *Jesus as Divine Worker* represents this trend.[17] He transformed the image of Jesus as a boy in Joseph's workshop. The setting is still a workshop; however, now Jesus is the carpenter. He is presented as a strong and masculine man. The image of the child Jesus is still present, but now he is a small boy who watches the adult Jesus. His mother, Mary, is also present; strangely, she appears to be the same age as the adult Jesus. As is common in medieval paintings, de Chirico has placed himself in the painting, as a man with a bare torso in the back of the workshop. Although the picture looks very naturalistic, Jesus has a halo. Other elements point to the death of Jesus. On the work desk are the instruments used to affix Jesus to the cross. Moreover, a man in the back, with strokes on his back, brings to mind one of the bandits crucified with Jesus in de Chirico's 1947 painting *Salita al calvario* (*The Ascent to Golgotha*).

De Chirico was a well-established artist when he participated in the Assisi exhibition. A younger painter, Dilvo Lotti (1914–2009) also reworked the Nazareth home scene, in his Jesus the Divine Worker from 1954.[18] His picture is an expressionist explosion of colors: it no longer presents a carpenter's workshop but that of a wheelmaker. The background with pine trees and fields identifies the place as Tuscany, where carriage making was a typical industry. Because of new technology, in the 1950s the carriage industry was on its last legs. Jesus is a young, strong worker while an elderly man, probably Joseph, is assisting; Mary, in a devout position, is placed in the back. Thus, Lotti has created a scene where he has moved *la sacra famiglia* into a setting with a local, contemporary atmosphere. However, Lotti has preserved an element of tradition in that Jesus, Joseph, and Mary all wear haloes.

New Occupations

When artists no longer felt obliged to portray Jesus as part of the holy family, they were free to place him in other occupations besides woodworking. However, with this new freedom it became more difficult to maintain the

17. Bignami et al., eds., *Galleria*, 103–5.
18. Bignami et al., eds., *Galleria*, 128–30.

religious interpretation associated with Jesus in the setting of his family. These presentations were criticized for making Jesus too human, with few references to his sublime character.

At the first exhibition of *Gesù divino lavoratore* in 1951, a sculpture by Pericle Fazzini (1913–1987) caught public attention. It shows an unexpected motif: Jesus as a railroad worker, fastening railroad ties with a drill.[19] The movements of the human body fascinated Fazzini; drilling required much strength, so the sculpture showed Jesus' strength as well as his fatigue. One art critic was very positive about the sculpture, and judged that it maintained a noble character, and that it could teach its viewers how hard work entails pain.[20]

A similar combination of strength and fatigue characterizes Gesù divino lavoratore by Felice Carena (1879–1966), from 1953, which gives the impression of being an autobiographical work.[21] At the time, Carena was seventy-four years old, and he portrayed Jesus as an old worker in a vineyard, fatigued after his day's work. Carena was a highly recognized artist who had been a prominent member of the Novecento movement, a group that supported Mussolini and was very critical of European avant-garde in painting. In the 1950s, religious motifs became more dominant in his work. In a long letter, Carena describes his intentions. He said that he worked on this painting in an atmosphere of humility and love. As a practicing Catholic, Carena wanted to portray Jesus in his essential character, as a noble person.

Critics who agreed that Carena had succeeded in combining humanity and divinity in his painting of Jesus found this lacking in the depiction *Gesù divino lavoratore* by Aldo Carpi (1886–1973).[22] This was not because of the depiction of Jesus as a carpenter working to put a new mast on a ship. Rather, the figure of Jesus posed a problem. One critic said that although Jesus was surrounded by a halo, Carpi had not paid attention to this being a sacred motif. Jesus was almost nude, his body was all red and very thin, and his eyes were not downcast, the ideal position, but penetrating. Carpi, who himself had a Christian identity, explained that the figure and the color of Jesus were not naturalistic. The color red had a symbolic value; it signaled that the fire of the Spirit carried Jesus.

Gesù divino lavoratore from 1956 by Domenico Purificato (1915–1985) has few obvious religious aspects.[23] In appearance and dress, Jesus

19. Bignami et al., eds., *Galleria*, 108–9.

20. Nicodemi, "La figura di Gesú divino lavoratore," 11.

21. Bignami et al., eds., *Galleria*, 69–71.

22. Bignami et al., eds., *Galleria*, 71.

23. Bignami et al., eds., *Galleria*, 183.

looks like a typical agricultural worker in the south of Italy. With his open shirt, he has a masculine, erotic look; at the same time as he is caught in a moment of rest and reflection. Beside him are a hammer and a pair of pincers, used for work, but also symbols of Jesus' crucifixion. Purificato was a member of the Italian Communist Party, and he identified with the southern, poor and agricultural part of Italy. He painted many scenes of workers and peasants from this region, so his *Gesù divino lavoratore* is in character with many of his other paintings.

The Challenge of Jesus as Worker

At a distance of sixty years, the project of Jesus as Worker is still challenging. It took seriously a central aspect of Christian belief, viz. that God became a human being. Throughout history, Christian art has concentrated on presenting Jesus as divine. The project Jesus as Worker turned this predominance upside down. Almost as a counterhistory, a group of Italian artists portrayed a Jesus who identified with those at the lowest level of society. It was obviously challenging for those who viewed the paintings. We know little of how workers actually responded to these expeditions. The Pro Civitate Christiana organized seminars for workers during the exhibitions; however, I have found no reports about the reactions of workers themselves. Art critics came from inside the art world; they judged the exhibitions from a traditional perspective of religious art. They measured the pictures by how the divinity of Jesus was expressed: e.g., if his face had a sublime expression or a trace of divine light, or if the picture followed the conventions of sacred art. There was little discussion of the meaning of works as expressions of divine presence. From a middle-class background, it appeared that work does not belong to the emotionally significant world of people. Is this a middle-class perspective that views self-identification with work as a limited experience? Moreover, would a worker think that his or her relation to work was not emotionally significant? Several of the pictures showed Jesus as a worker experiencing fatigue. Was that not an experience that touched his emotions?

Comments from art critics reflect that the main difficulty was how the presentation of Jesus as a humble worker might reflect his divinity. But perhaps another question is more important: how did the work of art show Jesus sharing the humanity of workers? How does it point to his life among them? Purificato's Jesus as a worker from the poor south may be an example of such a sharing of human life in a specific situation.

This is also a question for Christian art today: Does it portray Jesus in such a way that not only the distance between Jesus and human beings becomes visible, but also his identification with human life in all its diversity, with people from all ethnicities, classes and genders?

The Gospel according to Pasolini: Jesus as a Social Critic

Pro Civitate Christiana not only launched the project Jesus as Worker, but it also played an important role in initiating what many consider the best Jesus film of all times, *The Gospel according to St. Matthew*, by Pier Paolo Pasolini. In the 1960s in Italy, Pasolini was a communist and controversial writer; he was accused of blasphemy and of homosexual transgressions. So, what made him create this unique film that has continued to engage and challenge viewers around the world? To understand this, we must look both at Pasolini's life and at the situation in Italy.[24] Pasolini's father was an officer and a fascist; his mother was from a peasant background. Pasolini rejected his bourgeois origin as well as his father's fascism and chose to lead a life at the margins of society. He was a communist, but without following the party line. The fascists tried to make him an object of scandal because of his homosexual lifestyle. However, Pasolini was recognized as an author, and in the beginning of the 1960s he started making films.

In 1962, he was invited to the annual film seminar organized by Pro Civitate Christiana in Assisi. There was a Bible in his hotel room, and Pasolini read the Gospel of Matthew and was fascinated by its description of Jesus. Don Rossi and other leaders encouraged him to make a film about Jesus; a suggestion that he first rejected but eventually accepted. However, he had little economic and social credit, since he had been sentenced for blasphemy and was well known as a homosexual and a communist. Then Don Rossi made a bold move. The political situation was changing, and the new pope, John XXIII, wanted to improve relations between the Catholic Church and communism.[25] Don Rossi was a friend of John XXIII and was encouraged by him to support Pasolini's film project. The PCC also agreed to assist Pasolini with their biblical expertise. As a result of this unlikely alliance, Pasolini dedicated the film to Pope John XXIII, who died before the film was released.

There was a continuity between the "Jesus as worker" project and Pasolini's portrait of Jesus in the film. Both friends and critics found it strange that Pasolini would make a film about Jesus. However, Pasolini saw similarities between Christianity and Marxism, both of which opposed neocapitalism and its values. He chose the Gospel of Matthew as his manuscript, and

24. Greene, *Pier Paulo Pasolini*.
25. Carrillo, "Italian Catholic Church," 653–57.

wanted to keep strictly to the text of the Gospel, since he considered it an epic of a national character.

Pasolini had initially planned to film at a location in Palestine. However, he became disappointed with a modern, industrialized Israel. Instead, he decided upon a location in southern Italy—the town of Matera with its ancient cave dwellings in the Sassi district. The landscape was similar to Palestine; moreover, socially and politically the situation for the poor village population was similar to that of the people in Galilee at the time of Jesus. Arrogant leaders who misused their power ruled over them. For Pasolini, the selection of the location implied a conscious choice of perspective. He wanted to "see Christ, the Son of God, through the eyes of an ordinary, simple Italian." Here, the Italian Marxist philosopher Antonio Gramsci and his ideas about the intellectuals who identified with the working classes inspired Pasolini.

From the beginning of the film, Pasolini introduces Jesus as a social critic. He changes the order of events in the gospel and starts with a sermon in which Jesus introduces himself by saying: "Do not think that I have come to bring peace to the earth; I have not come to bring peace, but a sword" (Matt 10:34). For Pasolini, this becomes the key to understanding Jesus and his protest against modern life, which is characterized by cynicism, brutality and conformity. Pasolini directs his criticism against the upper classes who bear the responsibility for the destruction of a human life shaped by religious and classical ideals. The contrast between the wealthy and the poor becomes visible in their bodies: the poor have under-nourished, suffering bodies, whereas the wealthy look well fed and satisfied.

Pasolini decided to present a Jesus who was very different from the mild, blond Christ who had dominated the picture since the Renaissance. Therefore, he chose a young radical Spanish student with piercing eyes and a dark, lean body. He directed his speech explicitly to the viewers rather than to the disciples and the crowds. This proved very effective in the Sermon on the Mount, which Pasolini divided into short passages; the disciples are absent, Jesus addresses us, the viewers of the film, directly. In this way, Pasolini breaks up well-known structures, and Jesus' words take on new and unexpected meanings.

The Gospel according to St. Matthew is a very personal work by Pasolini.[26] His Jesus is not merely a social critic of bourgeois society; he is also a person with whom Pasolini can identify. The crucifixion scene is a case in point. In this scene, Pasolini diverges from the Gospel of Matthew. He includes Mary, the mother of Jesus, among the women at the foot of the

---

26. Chiesi, ed., *Cristo mi chiama.*

cross, despite the fact that she is mentioned only in John's Gospel (19:25–27). However, in this way Pasolini is able to include his own mother in the role of the mother of Jesus, who shared his suffering. Was it a result of Pasolini's homosexuality that Jesus' relationships with women are asexual so that in the end Jesus' mother is the only woman left, the one to take part in the intense mother-son relationship typical in Italian society? Moreover, was casting his own mother as Mary a way for Pasolini to identify with the crucified Christ? At the time of making this film, Pasolini faced libel charges and was accused of blasphemy for producing his previous film, *Mamma Roma*.

Pasolini faced the challenge of translating the text of the Gospel of Matthew into a film. Pasolini decided not to use professional artists, and therefore his friends and family, mainly local residents from Matera, played most of the central roles. He told them not to worry about acting; they should behave normally and photography would do the rest. His goal was to catch the actors in decisive moments. Since Pasolini did not want to include anything beyond the text of Matthew, the actors were for the most part silent. However, Pasolini made their faces speak the language of physical presence. The film starts with such a moment of silence that speaks more than many words. In the opening scene, Joseph encounters Mary and realizes that she is expecting a child—which is not his. No words are exchanged, but their faces and bodies speak.

The Gospel according to St Matthew was Pasolini's definitive breakthrough as a filmmaker. It represents his reading and his pictorial representation of Matthew's Gospel, so we may be justified in speaking of it as the Gospel according to Pasolini. The strength of the film, which continues to draw new viewers, is that Pasolini did not attempt to create an illusion of Jesus in the Holy land. Rather, Jesus appeared in situations that were recognizable in Pasolini's own time. That raises the question of the picture the film gives of Jesus. Some critics found that it made Jesus so human that his divinity disappeared. Pasolini said that although he was not himself a believer, he did believe that Christ was divine, in the sense that his humanity was so severe, so exalted, that it transcended our common ideas of humanity. Thus, the film transcends simple distinctions between what is human and what is divine. Pasolini's image of Jesus is not one-dimensional; rather, it makes possible new interpretations and understandings.

What Color Was Jesus?
The Invisible Whiteness of the American Jesus

"I see color," an American colleague of mine said, "and I am White." When I came to the USA as a PhD student in the early 1970s, I only slowly learned to see color, and I do not know if I realized that I was white. That is, I do not know when I understood what color meant: the color black carried with it a history of discrimination, of poverty and inferiority, of experiences of being shamed, of sitting at the lower end of the table, if at the table at all. It was only much later that I read the famous words by James Baldwin from *The Fire Next Time*: "Color is not a human or a personal reality; it is a political reality."[27] The early 1970s were just a short time after the civil rights movement. Coming from Norway, I had heard and read about these events, but I had not understood what they actually meant for American society, and how they had dramatically raised the question of American identity. What was it to be American? Or, who was an American? Only much later did I begin to understand how the events of the civil rights movement affected the color of Jesus.

In 1963, the White Jesus was killed together with four Black schoolgirls. This is the only way I can describe what happened one Sunday morning in September 1963 in Sixteenth Street Baptist Church in Birmingham, Alabama. White racists exploded a dynamite bomb outside this Black church; it killed four girls and blew out the face of Jesus in a stained-glass window. The Jesus who had lost his face was white; so what did that say about the white churches and their place in the campaign to end racial segregation? A White theologian said that White Christians had lost face together with their white Jesus. The author James Baldwin struck another note, from an Afro-American perspective: "If Christ has no face, we must give him a new face. Give him a new consciousness. And make the whole ideal, the whole hope of Christian love a reality."[28]

---

27. Baldwin, *Fire Next Time*, 110.
28. Blum and Harvey, *Color of Christ*, 4.

John Petts: *A Black Christ* (2011).
Sixteenth Street Baptist Church,
Birmingham, Alabama. Wikimedia Commons.[29]

Martin Luther King Jr. and the White Jesus

This horrendous story illustrates how the image of Jesus was linked to
the politics of race in American society. Jesus has always been an iconic
figure in America. This means that he has been linked to the hopes and

---

29. https://commons.wikimedia.org/wiki/File:Stained_glass_window_at_
the_16th_Street_Baptist_Church_in_Birmingham.jpg.

aspirations of many Americans, but also to the oppression and White supremacy that so many have experienced throughout American history. This story from the beginning of the civil rights movement in the US is the prologue to a book that traces the history of Christ in relation to race in the US—*The Color of Christ: The Son of God and the Saga of Race in America*, by Edward J. Blum and Paul Harvey.

According to Blum and Harvey, the bombing at Sixteenth Street Baptist Church represented a challenge to Martin Luther King Jr. and his attempt to present Jesus as an end to racism. King once received a letter that posed the question: "Why did God make Jesus white, when the majority of peoples in the world are non-white?" In his response King said, "The color of Jesus' skin is of little or no consequence," because skin color "is a biological quality which has nothing to do with the intrinsic value of the personality."[30] King's position was that Jesus transcended race; it was not his external color that mattered, but his internal spiritual commitment to God.

Both the question and King's answer took for granted that Jesus was White. The assumption of Jesus' whiteness was so ingrained in American culture that the majority of the population, regardless of their color, did not question it. Blum and Harvey suggest that Martin Luther King Jr. and the civil rights movement, which included many Whites, presented Christ as a "universal savior." It was his actions and words that mattered, not the color of his skin. Martin Luther King Jr.'s vision and the vision of the civil rights movement was a world where righteousness and equal opportunity were more important than racial categories. King's great contribution was that he brought Jesus into this vision, and into a liberal public discourse which previously had had little place for Jesus. It was probably only King, coming out of the African American tradition, who could bring about this change.[31] Thus, Jesus became a "civil rights crusader whose skin color was irrelevant."[32]

This position was supported by scientists and anthropologists, who wanted to do away with the category of race. However, it failed to convince those who were not White. Moreover, White supremacists used the whiteness of Christ to defend the justness of segregation. Jesus was not an abstract idea or principle, but an individual human body; therefore, it was impossible not to imagine his race. King's proclamation of a universal Jesus without a skin color failed to address the racial problems that exploded in this period. The Black Power movement rejected both King's strategy and

30. Quoted from King, "Advice for Living," *Ebony* 12/12 (1957) 53, in Blum and Harvey, *Color of Christ*, 205.

31. Fox, *Jesus in America*, 358–59.

32. Blum and Harvey, *Color of Christ*, 207.

his aim of integration. Moreover, those in the Black Power movement absolutely rejected the notion of a White Christ. Vincent Harding, one of King's followers, tried to explain to White Christians what African Americans felt over against a White Jesus. A White Jesus "signified a gospel of shame." A White Jesus put to shame everything that Black people represented: their Blackness, their hair, and their ways of expressing emotion in singing and shouting and dancing. This White Jesus they rejected.[33]

Black Power and Black Theology

Reading about the position of Black Power and their rejection of integration into a faith in a White Jesus brought back memories from Yale Divinity School when I was an international student in the early 1970s. I had many friends among other overseas students, especially from Africa; they easily mixed with the crowd of White students. African American students, however, did not interact with White students; they kept to themselves and sat at separate tables in the dining room. In hindsight this is easy to understand; it was a result of their need to keep a distance from the predominant Whiteness of the school and to explore their own identity and Black theology.

Albert Cleage (1911–2000), who wrote *The Black Messiah* (1968), was the best-known representative of a militant Black Power theology.[34] A review said of the book that "The style, from generations of black preachers, will remind readers of Martin Luther King; the content will not."[35] This comment was on point: Cleage argued against racial integration and presented a Black Jesus for Black people. Cleage started out by saying that "Jesus was the non-white leader of a non-white people struggling for national liberation against the rule of a white nation, Rome."[36] Israel was a non-White people because it was a mixture of many different Eastern and African peoples, "all of whom were already mixed with the black people of Central Africa." Liberation, not racial integration was the goal. For Cleage, this meant that "Black people cannot build dignity on their knees worshipping a white Christ. We must put down this white Jesus which the white man gave us in slavery and which has been tearing us to pieces."[37]

Black Power also made it into the universities. The most influential Black theologian was James H. Cone (1938–2018), a professor at Union

33. Blum and Harvey, *Color of Christ*, 218–19.

34. Prothero, *American Jesus*, 200–205.

35. *Library Journal* review, quoted in Cleage, *Black Messiah*, back cover.

36. Cleage, *Black Messiah*, 3.

37. Cleage, *Black Messiah*, 3.

Theological Seminary in New York.[38] In an early work, *Black Theology and Black Power*, he explained Black Power to White readers and established a Black theology of liberation. He spoke of Christ "who meets the blacks where they are and becomes one of them,"[39] and he explicitly countered the objection, "Oh, but surely Christ is above race." Cone's response was, "But society is not raceless, any more than when God became a despised Jew." It was incarnation, that Christ was where the oppressed were, that required him to be Black, for in America, "blacks are oppressed because of their blackness." Therefore, Cone must draw this conclusion: "Thinking of Christ as nonblack in the twentieth century is as theologically impossible as thinking of him as non-Jewish in the first century." Thus, Cone also went beyond Martin Luther King Jr. and his White Jesus; however, like King, Cone saw Jesus as absolutely dedicated to justice and righteousness.

In contrast to Cleage, Cone saw a possibility, if not of integration, then at least of reconciliation between Whites and Blacks. However, reconciliation could not build on the White values that had created slavery and Black ghettos. Therefore, Cone argued, "God's Word of reconciliation means that we can only be justified by becoming black. Reconciliation makes us all black!"[40] In response to objections from White people that they could not become Black, Cone presented an argument that went beyond color in itself: "Being black in America has very little to do with skin color. To be black means that your heart, your soul, your mind, and your body are where the dispossessed are." In addition, he concluded, "The real questions are: Where is your identity? Where is your being? Does it lie with the oppressed blacks or with the white oppressors?" Like Cleage, Cone held that Jesus was/is Black. However, Cleage argued from a historical reconstruction of the Jewish people as Black; based on such a reconstruction, Jesus must also be Black. For Cone, by contrast, Jesus' Blackness was a theological conclusion. It was incarnation, that Christ became human in order to identify with the oppressed, that made it necessary for him to be Black, since Blacks are oppressed.

My American colleague who said, "I see color, and I am White," had realized that color was, in Baldwin's words, "a political reality." Moreover, my colleague differed from many of us who, being White, see neither our own color nor our privileged place within the political reality. In his book, *After Whiteness: Unmaking an American Majority*, Mike Hill deconstructs this position and points to the "absence of whiteness from discussions of race,

---

38. Prothero, *American Jesus*, 205–8.

39. This and the following quotations come from Cone, *Black Theology*, 68–69.

40. This and the following quotations come from Cone, *Black Theology*, 151–52.

its pretense to unmarkedness or purity."[41] This is a form of blindness caused by the hegemonic position of whiteness, and that allows Whites to position ourselves outside the discussion of race.

Colorblind Evangelical Christianity

Two recent collections of studies explore how christological discourse and racial discourse are still entangled in American Christianity, especially in Evangelical Christianity. The titles of both volumes highlight the issue of color: *Christians and the Color Line*,[42] and *Christology and Whiteness*.[43] What is it that makes Christianity so ingrained in, or even an initiator of, racial thinking? How did it happen that Jesus "has been deracialized from a dark-skinned Mediterranean to a light-skinned Euro-American"? "Jesus is made white."[44] As a result Jesus is associated with Whiteness, and in many instances identified with racism. Shawn Kelley has explored the roots of racism in biblical scholarship in Europe, which was transplanted to the USA.[45] The studies we are discussing here look at contemporary Christianity in America. Especially among evangelical Christians, who make up the largest group of the White Christian population in the US, there is a strong correlation between christological discourse and racism. This trend has a long history, going back to the civil war period in the nineteenth century. White evangelical Protestants were also largely opposed to racial integration efforts and the civil rights movement discussed above.[46] Contributors to *Christians and the Color Line* found that White Christian Americans associated Christian identity with national identity, and that they were both linked to Whiteness. Thus, there was a theological rationale behind the lack of racial integration among evangelical Christians.

Furthermore, these scholars found an additional factor in an important difference between the theologies of White and Black evangelicals. White evangelicals tend toward an individualistic approach to faith, belief, and spirituality, emphasizing spiritual matters like being born again. Black evangelicals, on the other hand, tend toward a theology that is more communal and social in character and therefore will confront matters such as race. For White evangelicals, social matters like race are not as important as spiritual

41. Hill, *After Whiteness*, 7.
42. Hawkins and Sinitiere, eds, *Christians and the Color Line*.
43. Yancy, *Christology and Whiteness*.
44. Park, "Christological Discourse," 215.
45. Kelley, *Racializing Jesus*.
46. Evans, "Protestant Responses."

issues such as conversion. As a result of Whiteness, says one scholar, they see their own emphasis on spiritual topics as superior to other emphases. Thus, "whiteness is much more than a skin color, but a political idea that maintains structural forms and privilege over and against non-white others."[47] Another scholar, George Yancy, focuses on the problem of Whiteness that is so difficult to recognize; he defines Whiteness as a structural system of power and privilege that "functions, paradoxically, as that which signifies the 'superior' race while precisely obfuscating its status as raced."[48]

Thus, Yancy makes explicit the convergence of White identity with Christian identity. Together with the subtitle of the book, *Christology and Whiteness*, Yancy challenges White Christians to rethink *what would Jesus do*. "Christology becomes a deep existential prism through which to think about what ought to be done about one's whiteness and the problem of whiteness in our contemporary moment."[49]

The books that I have referred to here were published before Trump became president, but their observations explain why such a large percentage of White evangelicals (81 percent) voted for him in 2016, as well as in the 2020 election (76–82 percent).[50] However, the challenge to those of us who are White—to realize the structural and political reality we are part of, and to act upon that insight—is not limited to Trump supporters.

47. Darryl Scriven, quoted in Park, "Christological Discourse," 220.

48. George Yancy, quoted in Park, "Christological Discourse," 223.

49. Yancy, quoted in Park, "Christological Discourse," 223.

50. Martínez and Smith, "How the faithful voted"; Religion News Service, "Exit polls show few changes."

8

Jesus from the Margins

The Power of "Dangerous Memories"

IN THE STUDY OF the historical Jesus, the hegemony has been in the West, exercised by a White male elite. It started in Europe in a period that was dominated by the rise of nationalism and even more by colonialism, the European quest for new territories and new groups of people to conquer and to dominate. Viewed from the perspective of those who were conquered, studies of Jesus were part of a political, Western system dominated by patriarchy, colonialism, and empire.[1] However, although this system persists thanks to globalization and worldwide capitalism, these forces are being challenged, both within Western societies, and in previously colonized countries. Over the last generation, there has been an enormous growth in presentations of Jesus from various perspectives, including from marginalized groups who will no longer accept being silenced. These include groups marginalized within a society or a country, or voices that speak for oppressed peoples in Africa, Asia, and Latin America. Moreover, they include women facing discrimination resulting from sexism, classism, poverty, or ethnicity—or from any combination of these.

In a short chapter, it is of course impossible to present even an overview of the literature about Jesus from nonhegemonic positions. I have chosen to focus on presentations of Jesus that have arisen within or close to a Western hegemonic tradition, especially in the Americas.[2] This chapter is written in a different genre from the other chapters, which attempt a broad presentation of sources and literature on a particular period. Instead, I have chosen a few

1. Kwok, "Jesus/the Native."

2. It has not been possible to include the broad range of studies in Africa and Asia; see Stinton, *Jesus of Africa*, and Sugirtharajah, *Jesus in Asia*.

185

works by the founding figures within a number of separate groups. My primary interest has been to explore what joins them together in a shared project of identification with the historical figure of Jesus. People on the margins feel that they have been excluded from full access to Jesus and from the possibility of identifying fully with him. This is why they present discourses that focus on the relationship between Jesus and themselves. These stories from people in socially subordinate positions represent "dangerous memories." They represent protests against the dominant discourse of the meaning of Jesus, which in theological parlance is termed *Christology*, that is, faith in Jesus Christ as risen and living today. As part of the hegemonic discourse of the churches, this Christology has been presented as universal, as theological ideas that belong to a sphere above any separate contexts in which Christians may find themselves. These ideas are based on a reading of the Gospels and other New Testament writings that focuses almost exclusively on a (pretended) religious meaning of Jesus' sayings and actions.

Those who speak from the margins challenge these readings. They argue that Jesus must be understood from his relationship to specific people and groups, in particular those who in his own time lived at the margins of society. Thus, those who today speak from the margins look for other memories than those applied by the hegemonic powers. The leading feminist scholar of New Testament studies to-day, Elisabeth Schüssler Fiorenza, says that when the Gospels center on the life-praxis of Jesus and the movement following him, they preserve it as either a "dangerous" or a "status quo" memory.[3] Sharon Welch explains the different characters of these two types of memory: "Dangerous memories are a people's history of resistance and struggle, of dignity and transcendence in the face of oppression."[4] Memories of the dominant groups, on the other hand, are not dangerous: "they tend rather, to reinforce the defense of privilege and often evoke despair or cynicism in the face of oppression."[5]

When "voices from the margins" enter their protests against the hegemonic images of Jesus, they look for memories that have been hidden or oppressed by dominant groups. Thus, they must create an alternative discourse in order to bring forth the truth about Jesus and themselves. The philosopher Michel Foucault describes the intellectual work involved in this search for truth. First, it must describe the fractures that appear in the dominant systems of thought, and next, it must articulate alternative systems that may

---

3. Schüssler Fiorenza, *Jesus*, 7.

4. Welch, *Feminist Ethic*, 155.

5. Welch, *Feminist Ethic*, 155

operate in the political struggle. This implies the construction of what Foucault speaks of as "an alternative politics of truth."[6]

The "groups from the margins" engage in a struggle to find a Jesus with whom they can identify. In this struggle, they go back to the Jesus of Gospels and challenge the traditional, hegemonic interpretations. However, the groups on the margins are not totally without power. In his book *Power/Knowledge*, Foucault has a helpful discussion of the relations between power and knowledge. He does not accept the Marxist view of power, which ascribes power only to those on the top, working from top to bottom. Instead, Foucault holds that power is exercised in a complex web of relations. Knowledge is implicated in power and has an effect on power. Thus, through their exercise of criticism and by setting up alternative truth claims, voices from the margins also exercise power. Truth claims are formed in the struggles and conflicts for power. In Foucault's system, truth is not absolute but always a result of battle.

"In Memory of Her": Recovering the Hidden Memories of Jesus and Women

As a highly respected professor at Harvard, Elisabeth Schüssler Fiorenza can hardly be said to be on the margins. However, the study of the historical Jesus has since its beginning in the nineteenth century been dominated by men; and it is this domination that Schüssler Fiorenza criticizes in her books, most explicitly in *Jesus and the Politics of Interpretation*.

Early on, Schüssler Fiorenza applied the memory approach to the study of Jesus. Although she does not explicitly employ social and cultural memory theories, she discusses how these approaches differ from traditional historical Jesus studies.[7] She considers her Jesus research "a critical practice of *re-membering*." In contrast to historical Jesus studies that aim to produce "scientific certainty and theological normativity," she aims at "critical retrieval and articulation of memory."[8] With memory and remembering as a frame of meaning, Schüssler Fiorenza argues, there is no need to construe a dualistic opposition between history and theology, or between Jesus as an individual and Jesus as a person shaped by his community.

---

6. Foucault, *Power/Knowledge*, 131.

7. Keith, *Jesus' Literacy*, 47–48, recognizes Schüssler Fiorenza, *Jesus*; with Dunn and Hurtado as forerunners of the formal appropriation of social and cultural memory theories employed by Keith himself and his colleagues, e.g., Le Donne.

8. Schüssler Fiorenza, *Jesus*, 75.

Schüssler Fiorenza's early book *In Memory of Her* (1983) revolutionized feminist studies of Jesus and early Christianity. Instead of discussing "Jesus and women" as an addition to traditional pictures of Jesus, she rewrote the history of Jesus and the Jesus movement from a feminist perspective. She criticizes the way male scholars have constructed a picture of Jesus on the basis of the Gospel narratives. They have created an image of Jesus according to the ideals of an exceptional man and a charismatic leader (both going back to masculine ideals from the nineteenth century). These male Jesus scholars have created an impression that it is possible to bring the varied texts and ambiguous metaphors of Jesus Christ "into a single, definite discourse of meaning."[9] This male image of Jesus has become a master narrative in Western cultures, and therefore it is "already implicated in the structures of domination."[10]

Schüssler Fiorenza is critical of the hegemonic framework of historical Jesus studies that makes the traditional image of Jesus appear like historical realism. She suggests replacing it with the category of "memory," which corresponds better to what the Gospels actually do. They are not interested in "antiquarian documentation, but in the politics of meaning-making for their own audience."[11] Schüssler Fiorenza sees the task of feminist scholars as reconstructing historical Jesus discourse as an alternative discourse to domination. This implies shifting the focus from Jesus as an exceptional man and charismatic leader to a very different concept, namely, of Jesus as part of an emancipatory movement together with others. Schüssler Fiorenza introduces a model for Jesus based on wisdom, Sophia. In *Jesus: Miriam's Child, Sophia's Prophet*[12] she has explored this wisdom discourse as it was applied to Jesus in the Gospels. Schüssler Fiorenza holds that a female-personified Wisdom lies behind the earliest Christology in the Gospels (cf. Matt 11:28–30). Moreover, she specifically argues that the concept of Wisdom in early Jewish theology was influenced by the language and images of Middle Eastern and Greek goddesses.[13]

With this construction of the wisdom movement, Schüssler Fiorenza accomplishes several objectives. First, Jesus becomes part of a movement; he was not necessarily the initiator. Moreover, this movement was part of larger collection of emancipatory movements in Judaism and in antiquity in general. Thus, the Jesus movement was part of a struggle between the kyriarchal

9. Schüssler Fiorenza, *Jesus*, 5.

10. Schüssler Fiorenza, *Jesus*, 4.

11. Schüssler Fiorenza, *Jesus*, 7.

12. Schüssler Fiorenza, *Sophia's Prophet*.

13. Schüssler Fiorenza, *Jesus*, 149–53.

reality in which people lived and an egalitarian vision that characterized these emancipatory movements. The word *kyriarchy* is a neologism created by Schüssler Fiorenza to indicate a social reality that was larger than patriarchy.[14] Not only women were oppressed; Schüssler Fiorenza uses the form wo/men to indicate that the oppressed included men as well, all of whom were without power, all of whom were poor and marginalized.

When she portrays the Jesus movement as one of the emancipatory movements within Judaism fighting against kyriarchal domination, Schüssler Fiorenza also responds to a criticism often voiced by Jewish feminists. They find that Christian feminist presentations of Jesus and the Jesus movement as a liberating force paint first-century Judaism as inherently patriarchal.[15] This had made it important for Schüssler Fiorenza to portray the Jesus movement as one among a number of Jewish liberation movements, and to emphasize that Jesus and the Jesus movement struggled against kyriarchy, not against Judaism.

Thus, Schüssler Fiorenza makes a truth claim that is part of a struggle over knowledge of Jesus and over the power of interpretation. Unlike the male scholarship that she is criticizing, Schüssler Fiorenza's writing does not claim to be "neutral" or disinterested. She says that she will "investigate Historical-Jesus discourses from a critical feminist perspective committed to grass-roots wo/men's struggles and movements for survival and well being."[16] This is a general trait of all marginal groups and their readings of Jesus: they claim a similarity, even an identity, between the marginalized people whom Jesus met, and present-day marginal people.

It is no exaggeration to say that by empowering women, Schüssler Fiorenza has altered the relationship between power and knowledge in the discussion of Jesus both within academic circles and in the public square. With her criticism of presumptions and prejudices from male scholars, she has exposed the fractures in their constructions of Jesus, and she has deconstructed the dominant male picture of Jesus. Moreover, she has articulated alternative systems that take part in a political struggle for liberation today. Critics have argued that in her constructions of alternative systems, especially of the Jesus movement as an egalitarian movement with disciples as equals, she uses modern models that were not relevant in the first century.[17] However, Schüssler Fiorenza wanted to highlight the *possibility* of another way of constructing the situation around Jesus, a construction that could

14. Schüssler Fiorenza, *Jesus,* 95–101.

15. Schüssler Fiorenza, *Sophia's Prophet,* 67–96.

16. Schüssler Fiorenza, *Jesus,* 25.

17. Elliott, "Egalitarian."

challenge traditional patterns of domination and submission.[18] Schüssler Fiorenza's picture of Jesus has obvious relevance for contemporary discussions of liberation and identification with Jesus. However, her studies are historical in character; she has established an alternative historical reconstruction of Jesus, in critical confrontations with male scholars. Other groups are not so directly focused on the historical construction of Jesus; they go directly to a discussion of the meaning of Jesus today.

Mujeristas and Jesus' Kin-Dom of God

Mujerista theologians share Elisabeth Schüssler Fiorenza's commitment to grass-roots struggles and movements for survival; however, their theology comes out of a different social, political and religious experience. White, middle-class women in Europe and North America initiated the feminist movement. It became obvious that they could not speak for women everywhere; for instance, women in African American and Hispanic communities claimed that White women could not represent minority women. There are a great many feminist voices that should not be put together in one category. I will give an example from Hispanic women who speak of themselves as *mujeristas*.

In terms of social and political realities, the Hispanic community lives in a marginalized situation within the United States today. The experience of being marginalized within the most powerful country in the world has a deep influence on their way of doing theology. *Mujerista* is a relatively recent term; one of the initiators of the word, Ada María Isasi-Díaz, explains, "a *mujerista* is a Hispanic Woman who struggles to liberate herself not as an individual but as a member of a Hispanic community."[19] The basis for the reflections of the *mujeristas* is their "lived experience"; therefore their starting point is a place outside the structures of power. Their experience has been that theologians and those with power have used Jesus to marginalize them.[20] Accordingly, it is from a marginalized position that *mujeristas* raise the question, "Who is Christ for us, and how do we present Christ from the margins and to the margins?"[21] From this marginalized position, the meaning of Christ is not an issue of theories or dogmas; it is a matter of praxis in their struggle for fullness of life. This focus on praxis and the struggle

18. In her historical reconstructions, Schüssler Fiorenza has suggested using the criterion of possibility, not of plausibility. Schüssler Fiorenza, *Jesus*, 51–56.

19. Isasi-Díaz, *En la Lucha*, 4.

20. Isasi-Díaz, *En la Lucha*, 73–74.

21. Isasi-Díaz, *"Identificate con Nosotros,"* 39.

for fullness of life is implied in the term *Jesucristo*, which is a merger of "Jesus" and "Christ." In this term, the "original" Jesus and the meaning of him today, expressed by "Christ," come together. For *mujerista* theologians, this merger implies that they will move away from the idea that it is possible to reconstruct the historical Jesus, who he was and how he understood himself. They also want to move away from making christological formulas from history normative for today. Thus, the name *Jesucristo* provides an open space to express what Latinos/as believe about the message of Jesus for their present struggle for liberation and fullness of life. Interestingly, Ada María Isasi-Díaz[22] sees a parallel between the ways the Gospel writers created narratives about Jesus that responded to the issues important for the communities for whom they wrote and the work of *mujeristas* today. This observation is similar to that of Schüssler Fiorenza: that the images of Jesus in the Gospels were not "historical," but represented "the politics of meaning-making for their own audience."[23]

However, at one important point Isasi-Díaz actually enters into a historical criticism and a reconstruction of the historical Jesus. At issue is the relationship between *Jesucristo* and the Hispanic community today. Isasi-Díaz deconstructs an important part of Jesus' message in the Gospels, and articulates an alternative system that is more relevant to the present political struggle. It is generally recognized that "the kingdom of God" was the most central metaphor in Jesus' proclamation, and that Jesus was the mediator of this kingdom. However, Isasi-Díaz, suggests that he was not alone in this function. In earlier history, there were many other mediators, and today "all who commit themselves to proclaim with their lives and deeds the kingdom of God are mediators of the kingdom." This implies an identification with Jesus: Isasi-Díaz claims that "each and every one of us has the capacity and possibility of being another Christ, an *alter Christus.*"[24] Because we are all an image of God, *imago Dei*, each one of us mediates the kingdom of God in a unique way.

However, at the same time that she has defined the unique role of each one in mediating the kingdom of God, Ada María Isasi-Díaz argues that the metaphor of kingdom has become irrelevant and should be dropped. Not only has the metaphor become irrelevant, since the reality behind it, viz. monarchies, has all but disappeared, but it is also a dangerous metaphor. It refers to male sovereignty and reinforces a male image of God, and therefore it supports hierarchical and patriarchal structures that lead to systemic

---

22. Isasi-Díaz, "*Identificate con Nosotros,*" 40.

23. Schüssler Fiorenza, *Jesus,* 7.

24. Isasi-Díaz, "*Identificate con Nosotros,*" 43.

oppression. Isasi-Díaz therefore wants to go back to the original values implied by the metaphor. She finds that for Jesus, its root meaning was *shalom*, understood as fullness of life, as a communal goal. Isasi-Díaz will preserve this meaning, even with a change of the metaphor itself.

Instead of the political metaphor of kingdom, *mujerista* theology suggests a metaphor more directly related to people's personal lives: *kin-dom* (from *kinship*). "Kin-dom of God" represents the core values that Jesus lived and died for. Kinship is related to family; however, Isasi-Díaz does not give a narrow definition of family. She says that a *mujerista* theology does not "bemoan the disappearance of the traditional nuclear family."[25] Instead, family is broadly understood as including those who are united by bonds of friendship, love, and care, and of community. These represent *familia*, which is a central component of Latina communities.

Mujeristas understand theology as praxis, an integration of reflection with the struggle for liberation. However, with their discussion of kingdom as metaphor, replacing it with kin-dom, they have produced new knowledge, similar to what Schüssler Fiorenza did by replacing the masculine, heroic terms for Jesus with those of liberating movements. Both have challenged hierarchical and oppressive categories with alternative community models, inclusive of men and women. Schüssler Fiorenza works much more explicitly within established structures of New Testament scholarship; the *mujerista* theologians refer to "the precariousness of our communities" as the reason for giving priority to understandings that are useful in the work of liberation.[26]

The shift from kingdom as a political metaphor to kin-dom as a personal metaphor reflects the importance of the personal in the life of Latinas, and the centrality of relationships and the need for mutuality. This does not mean that the theology of the *mujeristas* is apolitical; an earlier work by Isasi-Díaz on Hispanic women's liberation theology bears the title *In the Struggle/En la Lucha*. However, it means that in this struggle the relations to Jesucristo are always personal. He is regarded as a companion in life, who travels with us and shares our lives. Since he appears as human-like, "like us," it is possible to recognize Christ-ways of acting in other people, to the degree that Isasi-Díaz can ask: "Is it heretical to say that salvation is not exclusively the task of Jesus? I do not think so."[27] Faith is always relational, and the kin-dom relation to *Jesucristo* is expressed in family terminology: "Christology deals with what it means that *Jesucristo* is

25. Isasi-Díaz, "*Identifícate con Nosotros*," 44.

26. Isasi-Díaz, "*Identifícate con Nosotros*," 40.

27. Isasi-Díaz, "*Identifícate con Nosotros*," 47.

our sister and our brother; discipleship deals with what it means that I am a sister or brother of *Jesucristo*."[28] The political struggle is also a question of praxis: to sustain the poor and the oppressed, to bring hope by creating the material conditions they need. Here too the aspect of mutuality dominates: it is *Jesucristo* together with the other members of the *familia* of God who participate in the struggle. Thus, a central way to describe the role of *Jesucristo*: he "simply walks with us in the midst of the ordinariness of life, that he simply walks with us."[29] Accordingly, the divine too is understood in a personal way. One example is the image of the crucified Jesus, which is central to the spirituality of Latinas. This is often not understood by others, since the suffering of Jesus appears to be a result of oppression. However, Isasi-Díaz explains this by speaking of the importance of the personal in the lives of Latinas, which in this case rests on mutuality: "It is precisely the Jesus who suffers as we suffer—who is vulnerable as we are vulnerable—that is the *Jesucristo* to whom we can relate."[30]

The conclusions that Isasi-Díaz draws from her studies and conversations with many Latinas prompt reflections. They are not trained theologians or scholars, but their issues they take up are similar to those with which theologians and philosophers have always struggled. How can we live with all the unanswered questions in life, with the dilemmas, the life problems that cannot find any solutions? Jesus does not provide an easy way out: Isasi-Díaz says, "For us Latinas, *Jesucristo* is not the one who gives us answers but the one who sustains us when there are no answers." She draws the conclusion that because of what *Jesucristo* means for Latinas, "*mujerista* theology does not seek to provide answers but rather to help us to go deeper in our questions about God and the divine presence in our lives."[31] Here, these women come across as "everyday life philosophers" who from their "lived experiences" reflect on the most important issues in life.[32]

Reclaiming Memories of a Queer Jesus

Is it possible to reclaim hidden memories of a queer Jesus? This was the project in the now-classic book by Robert Goss, *Jesus Acted Up: A Gay and Lesbian Manifesto*. In analyzing the presentations of Jesus from the margins, I have asked two questions, following a suggestion by Michel Foucault. First,

28. Isasi-Díaz, "*Identificate con Nosotros*," 49.

29. Isasi-Díaz, "*Identificate con Nosotros*," 50.

30. Isasi-Díaz, "*Identificate con Nosotros*," 53.

31. Isasi-Díaz, "*Identificate con Nosotros*," 55.

32. Gullestad, *Everyday Life Philosophers*.

how do these voices on the margins criticize and deconstruct the dominant system of thought? Second, how do these marginalized voices articulate alternative systems that may operate in the political struggle? This suggestion by Foucault has been helpful in earlier examples as well; however, Goss is the first to discuss Foucault's approach in his work.[33]

First, we need to contextualize Goss's book. During the last part of the twentieth century, when Goss was writing, gays and lesbians were still socially marginalized and ghettoized. People with HIV/AIDS faced discrimination. They were treated as "others," as suffering from a disease that had come from "outside." Act Up started as an activist organization to protest the sexual, social, and political discrimination against people with HIV/AIDS, and the group used provocative rhetoric and actions in its protests. At that time most US churches, not only evangelical and fundamentalist bodies, condemned homosexuality.

Goss's first task in *Jesus Acted Up* was to deconstruct the memories of Jesus within traditional Christologies, especially with regard to sexuality. Goss followed Foucault's genealogical method; that is, he brought to light historical knowledge of facts that have been suppressed. Goss encountered total silence about Jesus' sexuality in historical studies of him. When Jesus' sexuality was not discussed, the silence took his heterosexuality for granted. Both in Protestant and in Roman Catholic theology, Christ became a model heterosexual—someone who legitimated Christian heterosexuality, marriage, and family life. In the various mainstream Christian theologies, Jesus is presented as strongly heterosexual, as favoring asceticism, and, finally, as either implicitly or explicitly homophobic. Over the centuries as Christology evolved in the churches, many layers had accrued atop the original picture of Jesus, so that according to Goss, Christology was generally "constructed through misogyny, antisexuality, and homophobia."[34]

What was the effect of this discourse? Here, Foucault's thinking about power and knowledge comes into play. Thanks to the enormous power of the churches, the traditional "knowledge" about Jesus' sexuality that they advocated had a strong controlling effect on the bodies and sexualities of many. There seemed to be only two alternatives: to submit to the power of the churches or to extricate oneself from this power. The latter alternative made it impossible for many LGBTQ people to identify with Jesus, and many even internalized Christian homophobia.[35]

---

33. Goss, *Jesus Acted Up*, 181–90.

34. Goss, *Jesus Acted Up*, 72.

35. Goss, *Jesus Acted Up*, xxi.

With his 1993 book, Goss sought to change this situation. His first task was to deconstruct this oppressive construction of Jesus, and the next was to articulate an alternative system that would take part in the political struggle. This purpose was signaled by the book's title, *Jesus Acted Up*, which played on the name of a radical activist movement. For Goss, the only possible way to enact a queer Christology was to go back to Jesus' original praxis and to interpret it from a marginal position. What did he find? "As queer Christians retrieve the Jesus material as a source for their critical practice, they discover a powerful, subversive memory of Jesus."[36] Here Goss is tapping into the liberation theologians in Latin America, and into the *mujeristas* and African Americans and women who seek to bring forth the dangerous memories of the oppressed.[37]

Goss finds these memories in "Jesus' *Basilea* practice."[38] My own memory of the impressions that Goss's book made on me in 1993 was that it was a very effective political, activist pamphlet.[39] Rereading the book, I was struck by his thorough reading of New Testament studies and early Christian theology, and how effectively he uses these studies to present the "dangerous memories" of Jesus and his initiating a liberating *basileia* praxis. Goss focuses on Jesus' message and praxis, which "signified the political transformation of his society into a radically egalitarian, new age, where sexual, social, religious and political distinctions would be irrelevant. Jesus struggled for *basileia* liberation in siding with the humiliated, the oppressed, and the throw-away people of first-century Jewish society."[40]

There are many similarities here to the emancipatory movement of Schüssler Fiorenza, or to the kin-dom metaphor in *mujerista* theology. Schüssler Fiorenza, Isasi-Díaz, and Goss all see Jesus' proclamation and praxis of the *basileia* as an alternative system of human social relations—a system opposed to the dominant structures of the Roman Empire and Jewish society. Their interpretations are all contextual, initiated from different positions and experiences of marginality in relation to the dominant society. Like the work of Schüssler Fiorenza and the *mujaristas*, Goss's book focuses on the human body as a place of oppression and as the center of liberation. It is queer sexuality and identity that is the main marker of marginality for Goss, and this was included in Jesus' liberation. God confirmed

---

36. Goss, *Jesus Acted Up*, 109.

37 "Dangerous memories are a people's history of resistance and struggle, of dignity and transcendence in the face of oppression" (Welch, *Feminist Ethic*, 155).

38. Goss, *Jesus Acted Up*, 72–75.

39. See the evaluation of Goss's book after twenty years in Michaelson, "Queer Theology"; and Jordan, "Jesus ACTED UP."

40. Goss, *Jesus Acted Up*, 73.

this *basileia* praxis at Jesus' crucifixion. Goss does not understand Jesus'
death as a ransom for sin; he was crucified because his message and practice
of God's coming reign came into conflict with the powerful Jewish aristocracy and with Roman power in Palestine. Resurrection, Goss argues,
meant that Jesus became "God's Christ," that is, "God's power of embodied
solidarity, justice, love, and freedom."[41] Jesus becomes a parable of God,
signifying that God will not let oppression or dominating power relations
triumph. With a reference to Latin American liberation theology and its
main theme, Jesus' preferential option for the poor, Goss says, "Jesus embodied the preferential option for the oppressed."[42] Here Goss brings the
memories of Jesus and his death into direct contact with the oppression of
gays and lesbians under our present powers. When he says that the cross
is "God's invasive identification with the oppressed," he follows this up by
identifying the oppressed: "the oppressed now includes the sexually oppressed, those oppressed because of their sexual preference and identity."[43]
Therefore, Goss can say, "The cross now belongs to us. We have been crucified. We have been martyred."[44] Goss does not explicitly refer to liberation
theologian Jon Sobrino, but Goss's terminology appears to be inspired by
the way Sobrino draws parallels between Jesus as "the Crucified" and the
poor and the victims in El Salvador as "the crucified people."

In a review of the continuing relevance of Goss's book, Harvard Divinity professor Mark D. Jordan focused on what the theological sections of
the book contributed to its political program.[45] One aspect Jordan found
was the connection Goss makes between activist street theater and Jesus'
table practices, culminating in the Last Supper, which Goss calls "messianic
theatre."[46] In this way, Goss combines political activism with the inclusion
of LGBTQ people in the most sacred ritual in Christian churches. LGBTQ
participation in rituals and ceremonies (for instance, in weddings) remains
a strong visualization of the memories of a queer Jesus.

Jesus and the Poor in Latin American Liberation Theology

Latin American liberation theologians put Jesus' relationship to the poor
first. That is their most important contribution to the study of Jesus. Jesus

41. Goss, *Jesus Acted Up*, 77.

42. Goss, *Jesus Acted Up*, 82.

43. Goss, *Jesus Acted Up*, 83.

44. Goss, *Jesus Acted Up*, 83.

45. Jordan, "Jesus ACTED UP."

46. Goss, *Jesus Acted Up*, 150.

"preferential option for the poor" is one of the most memorable theological concepts of the last fifty years that many people all over the world know.[47] However, what does it mean, and how did the concept originate and evolve? It was no coincidence that it happened in Latin America in the 1960s and '70s. In the last part of the twentieth century, social and political inequalities were rampant there: poverty among the masses created extreme crises. Furthermore, many countries went from democracies to dictatorships and military rule; protesters were massacred, primarily among the poor. Traditionally, the Roman Catholic Church with its hierarchy of bishops had for the most part sided with the elite, the wealthy, and the governing classes.

As a protest and in an effort to change their own situation, local members of the churches established *base communities*, small local groups, to build consciousness and to support themselves. Theologians who identified with the situation of these base communities started to develop a theology from below, combining political analysis with studies of the Bible. They placed their presentations of Jesus in a specific geographical and socioeconomic context and interacted with contemporary economic and political issues. The theologian Gustavo Guttiérez, from Peru, presented a groundbreaking work, *A Theology of Liberation: History, Politics, and Salvation*, in which he argued that Jesus showed "preferential treatment for the poor."[48]

Already at a meeting in Medellín in 1968, Guttiérez claims, the Conferences of the bishops in Latin America and the Caribbean had supported the preferential option for the poor.[49] In the context of oppression from the governing elites and the military, this represented a "dangerous memory." Traditional Catholicism viewed poverty as an individual failure, to be alleviated by charity. In contrast, in Medellín the bishops examined poverty in its social context and called for changes in the socioeconomic structure.

The "preferential treatment of the poor" has sometimes been misunderstood to mean that Jesus cared only for the poor. However, the starting point for liberation theologians is that we live in a world divided between the haves and the have-nots. Moreover, the have-nots are in the best position to evaluate the differences in the world; they have a privileged perspective from which to evaluate reality. This does not mean that God loves only the poor, the victims of this unequal situation; he also loves the victimizers. However, God cannot be neutral about this divided situation. His love for the rich must take a different form, a call for them to convert.

47. Goizueta, "Preferential Option."

48. Guttiérez (*Theology of Liberation*, xxvi–xxvii) traces the history of the expression "preferential treatment for the poor" to the Latin American Bishops' Conference in Puebla, Mexico, in 1979, and to Pope John Paul II.

49. Guttiérez, "Option for the Poor," 317–18.

Another prominent liberation theologian, Jon Sobrino,[50] from El Salvador, uses a specific term when he speaks of the poor and their relationship to Jesus: he calls them by the name "the crucified," in parallel to Jesus, "the Crucified."[51] These terms are a direct reaction to the situation in El Salvador and to Sobrino's own experiences. Sobrino read the texts about Jesus in Galilee and his followers in light of his own Salvadoran context.[52] It was the reality of El Salvador during the 1970s and 1980s, under military rule and dictatorship, that helped Sobrino understand Jesus of Galilee. He attaches special importance to the cross of Jesus because, he says, the Salvadoran context is "above all, the reality of 'a crucified people.'"[53] The government of El Salvador and its military showed ruthlessness in killing priests and religious who spoke out on behalf of the poor. Archbishop Oscar Romero, who preached against poverty, injustice, and terrorism, was gunned down while celebrating Mass in 1980. In 1989, Sobrino narrowly escaped when six of his fellow Jesuits were killed in their sleep in their community. The martyrdom of bishops, priests, sisters, and many lay Christians is the dominant factor in Sobrino's understanding of the relationship between Jesus and today's Christians.

This is why the *location* when reading the Jesus sources is so important, and Sobrino quotes a colleague who said, "The Third World is the place of the gospel."[54] Sobrino starts by laying out the similarities between the social realities of Galilee and El Salvador: "poverty, injustice, structural oppression and repression, and slow violent death."[55] Sobrino finds a similarity between those who bring salvation, i.e. all those who have been killed in El Salvador for their faith, and Jesus; Sobrino speaks of them as carrying a "Jesus-like martyrdom."[56] In his books, Sobrino has emphasized the similarity between Jesus as "the Crucified" and the poor and victims in El Salvador as "the crucified people." Thus, it is poor countries (El Salvador, Haiti, and the like), not the rich world (e.g., Washington, DC; Paris; or Madrid) that represent a similarity to Jesus and Galilee. This leads Sobrino to criticize the church and the theologians because this poverty in the Gospel texts and in the Salvadoran context is not taken into consideration in the church's creedal confessions of who Jesus is and what he means. Instead of supporting them, the

50. Sobrino, *Christology*; Sobrino, *Jesus*.

51. Stålsett, *crucified and the Crucified*.

52. Sobrino, "Jesus of Galilee."

53. Sobrino, "Jesus of Galilee," 437.

54. Sobrino, "Jesus of Galilee," 439.

55. Sobrino, "Jesus of Galilee," 442.

56. Sobrino, "Jesus of Galilee," 445.

Vatican has criticized liberation theologians and censured many of them, stopping them from lecturing and publishing. In particular, Pope John Paul II with his Polish background was adamantly opposed to a political analysis of the situation in Latin America from a Marxist perspective.

For Sobrino, the most important elements of Jesus' life are mercy, hope, and faithfulness, all of which Sobrino interprets in light of the Salvadoran context. Archbishop Romero made a comment on how to understand mercy: "do not forget that we are human."[57] For Sobrino, this statement suggests that there is no division between merciful benefactors and those who receive help; all are human. The Salvadoran experience also means that mercy is always dialectical. In the Salvadoran context, liberation is the horizon of mercy. At the same time, liberation also means struggling against injustice. For Sobrino, the one who gives his or her life to defend the poor for the cause of justice is a martyr, like Jesus.

Hope is central to the gospel; it is part of Jesus' message that "the kingdom of God is at hand." However, how can Sobrino find hope in the Salvadoran situation? He finds it in the cross and the resurrection of Jesus. The strongest reason why the cross is a source for hope lies in the link between love and the cross. Jesus took up the cross because of love, and this love creates hope. In the Salvadoran context, the martyrs also gave their lives for love, and thereby they produced hope.

The last aspect that Sobrino brings up is following Jesus, imitating the praxis and the evangelization of Jesus. To follow Jesus is to become conformed to Jesus—to follow his story, to go through death in order to pass into life. Again, the martyrs make this faith real. Sobrino speaks of the martyrs as the most crucial reality for understanding the reality of Jesus. The material poverty of the Salvadoran context creates a situation that demands the struggle for liberation. However, the hope of liberation is linked to the martyrs, to those who gave their lives in the struggle against oppression. Archbishop Romero is the primary example of a martyr, but the same is true of the priests and religious sisters, and ultimately of all who were killed. They represent the main context for understanding who Jesus was and is. Sobrino presents Jesus as the Jesus of Galilee, i.e., a person of history. However, it is from the Salvadoran context that we understand who Jesus is, viz. "the martyr Jesus."[58]

To understand Sobrino's portrait of Jesus, and especially how he brings Jesus' followers so close to Jesus, I think we must try to grasp the extraordinary location of Sobrino's reflections. It is a place where some of his closest

57. Quoted in Sobrino, "Jesus of Galilee," 454.
58. Sobrino, "Jesus of Galilee," 459.

friends and colleagues had been killed because of their witness to Jesus and
to his solidarity with the poor. Thus, also all the poor who were killed were
included among the martyrs. There are few other locations where the identity of Jesus and of his followers in suffering could become so overwhelmingly
present. I think this is why the demonstrations of mercy, love, and hope in
the present-day martyrs and in Jesus seem to merge.[59]

Jesus as Migrant

The portrait of Jesus that is most challenging for the world as a place of
human relations is Jesus as migrant. In "El Cristo Migrante/The Migrant
Christ," Luis R. Rivera focuses on the hermeneutical challenges posed by
the experiences of global migrations, especially among the Latino/a Christians in the United States.[60] Emphasizing the close relations between Jesus
Christ and migrants, Rivera speaks of the "migrantization of Jesus Christ"
and the "Christiphication" of migrants. Rivera holds that Jesus may be
called *migrante* "because of his presence and solidarity . . . with migrants
who pray and search for hospitality and justice."[61] Matthew's Gospel presents Jesus, with his family, as a political refugee in Egypt, fleeing from the
terror of Herod's rule. Furthermore, the Gospels present Jesus as an itinerant prophet and preacher moving around different regions in Palestine.
In his migrations he becomes a guest who receives hospitality and, above
all, a host who distributes hospitality to the destitute, to the poor, and to
sinners. Rivera speaks of a "migratory and hospitality paradigm" as a key
to understanding Jesus' identity and work.[62]

Thus, Jesus represents a paradigm that is a total alternative to the policies toward migrants and refugees in the world today, which must be characterized as a "migratory and rejection paradigm." To understand the situation,
one must start with the causes of migration. Poverty, corruption, war among
drug cartels, and terrorism by the military and militias characterize the situation in El Salvador, Honduras and other Central American countries. It is
to be expected that such a situation would set large groups of migrants and
refugees moving toward Mexico and the US. This is not only happening at
the US border with Mexico; the same happens in many parts of the world, so
that the twenty-first century has been described as "the age of migration."[63]

59. See the critical discussion in Stålsett, *The crucified and the Crucified*.

60. Rivera, "El Cristo Migrante."

61. Rivera, "El Cristo Migrante," 144.

62. Rivera, "El Cristo Migrante," 144.

63. Castles et al., *Age of Migration*.

Wars, poverty, oppression and internal strife send millions of people in search of safe havens as refugees and migrants. In the Middle East, for instance, the civil war in Syria has driven millions away from their homeland, at the same time that internal warfare in Afghanistan continues. In Africa, poverty, hunger and internal warfare have caused many to flee north to the Mediterranean Europe. Most refugees have settled in poor countries neighboring Syria, especially in Jordan, Lebanon, and Turkey.

In this situation, it is depressing that the reactions from rich countries to the north and west toward migrants do not show solidarity but instead pose some of the greatest challenges to how we as humans are dependent upon one another in the world today. Many European politicians and mass-media outlets have described it as a crisis, not for people in the Middle East but for rich Europe when it was faced with an unexpectedly high number of refugees and migrants. Attempts by the central authorities of the EU to share the refugees among member states have been met with stiff resistance from several countries. Typical examples are Hungary and Poland, which in addition absolutely refused to accept non-Christian (i.e. Muslim) refugees, claiming that doing so would threaten their identity as Christian countries.

In the United States since 2016 the Trump administration dramatically stepped up policies to reduce immigration, both internationally, by Muslims from the Middle East and Africa, and especially from Mexico and Central America, where many flee to the US from internal terrorism and poverty. Trump wanted to reduce immigration by such means as strengthening the physical border (the "wall against Mexico"), increasing the number of border patrol agents, and stepping up deportations of noncriminal undocumented immigrants. The arguments for immigration control and boundary-making are based on the distinction between citizens and noncitizens. Support for these policies, not only in the USA but also in Europe, has spread from ultraright political parties to mainstream, even leftist parties. In many countries, there has been an increase in nativism (i.e., opposition to foreigners) and ethnonationalism (i.e., defining national identity in terms of ethnicity).

The United Nations High Commissioner on Human Rights warns, "Human rights violations against migrants, including denial of access to fundamental rights such as the right to education or the right to health, are often closely linked to discriminatory laws and practices, and to deep-seated attitudes of prejudice and xenophobia against migrants."[64] This makes it difficult to see how migrants and refugees can be included in our common humanity.

64. "Migration and Human Rights."

Jesus as a symbol of migration and hospitality expresses his solidarity with migrants; he joins them in their struggle for life. This makes them more than objects of Christian compassion, love, and service: "They are subjects and agents in the company of Christ."[65] Luis Rivera even says that "Jesus Christ's presence among us for migrants turns them into *alter Christ.*"[66] This term brings to mind Saint Francis, who was called "the second Christ," since in him the poverty of Christ became visible.[67] Vulnerable and marginal migrants reveal Christ's presence and identity both among the migrants themselves and to those who host them.

In this way, Christ as migrant encourages human relatedness between the migrants and those who engage in hospitality and justice. To be hospitable to migrants means not just caring for their immediate needs; the struggle for justice means being agents of God to create an alternative society, the kin(g)dom of God, based on hospitable communion. This vision of an alternative society must necessarily include a criticism of any worldview that excludes migrants from human relatedness and defines them as "foreign" in relation to "us." Indeed, migrants point towards a better future for the world, they "give us a new way of understanding how to live and to be in the world. Like Jesus, they critique society by the very way they live and move in the world."[68]

Where Did Jesus Happen?

My goal in this chapter has been to see if there were some commonalities to the approach to Jesus from groups at the margins. One common element was the marginalized group's need to counter hegemonic presentations of Jesus, and the fact that those on the margins clearly represented an alternative image of Jesus. For all of the marginalized, their own location, the place from which they interpreted Jesus, is significant. Such locations are without privileges, characterized by poverty, alienation, or even sociopolitical situations of terror and oppression. The experience of living in marginal locations was hermeneutically significant; it made possible an identification with the people surrounding Jesus: the poor, the sick, and the possessed. Even more significantly, it also opened the way to an identification with Jesus, who himself suffered and was crucified. For some, this identification with Jesus also makes possible a sharing not only of Jesus' suffering but also of his work of liberation.

65. Rivera, "El Cristo Migrante," 143.
66. Rivera, "El Cristo Migrante," 143.
67. See chapter 4. [x-ref]
68. Groody, "Christology," 258–59.

Memory is a central term in many of these writings; these writers identify their own stories about Jesus as "dangerous memories"—that is, as memories of resistance and struggle, in contrast to dominant memories, which defend privileges and the status quo. In addition, those who do not explicitly speak of memories present their picture of Jesus as an alternative and a challenge to the common, hegemonic picture of him. They all share the understanding of memory as combining history and the quest for meaning in their presentation of Jesus. This is most explicitly expressed in the *mujerista* term *Jesucristo*.

9

From Memory to History?

The Prophet Who Would Change Galilee

IF THE GOSPELS ARE memories of Jesus, is it possible to find the historical Jesus? In this book, I have tried to follow the memories of Jesus through various phases of history and in different social and cultural contexts. The memories were ways of making sense of Jesus for a particular community; they expressed the identity of groups who were formed around following Jesus. In addition, the memories of Jesus and his first followers were told as representations of the origin of Christian societies and nations. The historical study of Jesus, which started at the time of the Enlightenment, was in one sense a continuation of a central aspect of memory, namely, to provide meaning for the present. However, there was a distinct difference in that history had a critical dimension to it; its results questioned the memories of Jesus. Memories were often ideal pictures of the past, and told from the perspective of faith. In contrast, the purpose of historical study was to expose the myths and the religious beliefs that were part of the memories of Jesus.

We saw a significant example of such criticism in the discussion of the responsibility for the death of Jesus. The memories of the Gospels and their retellings through later periods clearly served ideological purposes, by putting blame on Jewish leaders at the time of Jesus. During periods of religious polemics, they were even used to accuse all Jews throughout history. In this case, critical historical studies, initiated by Jewish scholars in the nineteenth century, performed a necessary task. These studies were based on historical information about Rome's rule, its power, and its method of ruling through subservient clients.

This is an example of how historical studies can place the memories of Jesus in a broader context. Many different studies may help us to understand the social contexts of memories: for instance, literature, languages, and hermeneutics, as well as social sciences, such as social anthropology, sociology, social psychology, and economics. As a result, we may move memories of Jesus out from a separate religious sphere into larger contexts.

Placing Jesus: Was Jesus a Galilean?

Studies of Jesus have been concerned with his social context, with the groups and people who surrounded him. However, there has been less interest in the place in which he lived, which was a geographical place as well as a social and ideological place. In *Putting Jesus in His Place*, I have argued that *place* is an important part of a person's identity. It is more than just a reference, or mere background; a place is an active part of a person.[1] A focus on Jesus situated in place will give a more comprehensive picture of him.

One of the most persistent memories of Jesus was that he was a Galilean. Mark starts by introducing Jesus as coming from Nazareth in Galilee. In the birth story in Luke's Gospel, Nazareth in Galilee is the hometown of Mary and Joseph, and this is where Jesus grows up. In Matthew's Gospel, Bethlehem is Jesus' hometown and the place of his birth. King Herod forces Joseph with Mary and Jesus to take refuge in Egypt for a period; it is only via various signs from God that they end up in Nazareth in Galilee. It was obviously important to bring Jesus to Galilee, since in memory he was known as "Jesus the Galilean" (Matt 26:69). That is true in John's Gospel too, even if John has a different story line, in which most memories about Jesus are localized in other regions, and most often in Jerusalem.

In the Synoptic Gospels, most of Jesus' activities are localized in Galilee. Thus, they establish Galilee as the main location of Jesus, and place it in contradistinction to Jerusalem. This is the dominant geographical memory that has been taken over by most scholars as "history."

In nineteenth-century scholarship, Jesus was identified as a Galilean. In chapter 6, above, we saw how significant that identity was for the anti-Jewish interpretation of Jesus. Race was an important aspect of identity, and in order to present Jesus as (almost) a European, scholars separated a non-Jewish Galilee from the Jewish Jerusalem and Judea. Thus, in this first phase of the quest for the historical Jesus, the issue of Galilee played an important part.[2]

In the second phase of historical Jesus research, from the 1950s, however, there was little interest in Galilee. Judaism as the context of Jesus

1. Moxnes, *Putting Jesus in His Place*, 1–21.
2. Moxnes, "Construction of Galilee."

was primarily understood as a religious system, and geography or different regions did not play a significant role. Judaism was contrasted with
Jesus and emerging Christianity. Within this history-of-ideas perspective,
there was little interest in local contexts or possible differences between
Galilee and Jerusalem.

With the so-called Third Quest for the historical Jesus came a renewed
interest in Galilee, as part of a move from a history of religious ideas to an
integration of religion into social history. This occurred while a range of
interdisciplinary approaches to the study of Galilee (calling upon, e.g., sociology, social anthropology and archaeology) broadened the perspective.
This move was part of a paradigm shift in writing history, which expanded
from a focus on great powers to an interest in local communities and regions.
As a result, the discussion has turned back to some of the same questions
that preoccupied nineteenth-century scholars: Was there something in the
identity of Galilee that could explain Jesus, his message, and his activities?
However, the identity of Galilee was no longer discussed in terms of race,
as in the nineteenth century, but in terms of *ethnicity*. After World War II,
ethnicity became a central category to classify people; it replaced race, which
after the Holocaust and the end of colonialism had been delegitimized. However, ethnicity could be understood in different ways. One traditional view
emphasized language, ancestry, and religion as central aspects of ethnicity.
Another position saw ethnicity as a form of social interaction, of defining
boundaries against other groups.[3] In this case, social behavior was important,
for instance, with regard to purity rules or food customs.

Can we say as a historical fact that Jesus was a Galilean? Since all
the Gospels say that he was called a Galilean, this label may be regarded
as trustworthy. However, in terms of Jesus' public life, the memories in the
Synoptic Gospels on the one hand and in John's Gospel on the other do not
agree on the central locations of his activities. In the end, we may have to
choose between them. More importantly, even if we accept that Galilee was
the primary place of Jesus' activity, the memories of Jesus in Galilee must be
interpreted in light of different understandings of the identity of Galilee.[4]
Memories are not permanently fixed; they will always be understood in light
of the cultural context of those who listen to the memories.

When scholars have asked about the importance that his Galilean
background had for Jesus, they have thought about how Galilee influenced
Jesus. However, I will turn the question around and ask in what ways Jesus
had an impact upon and may have influenced Galilee. Jonathan Z. Smith

---

3. Barth, ed., *Ethnic Groups.*
4. Moxnes, "Construction of Galilee."

has said that "human beings are not placed, they bring place into being."[5] The identity of a place is not a given. Humans also shape place, for instance, by the way they cause social structures to interact with one another. Galilee was shaped by the cultivation of land and by fisheries on the Sea of Galilee, which created economic opportunities. However, peasants and fishermen did not have full control over the results of their work.[6] Herod Antipas, who ruled over Galilee at the time of Jesus, as well as the temple bureaucracy, exacted taxes and dues, and estate owners made demands of the peasants. In addition, religious rules and laws provided ideological justification for this system. It was this system that Jesus knew and experienced, and that he reacted against with his teaching.[7] Many of his parables reflect life in peasant households and in villages, and some of them show that these were spaces under the domination of external forces.

There may be additional support for a Galilean context for Jesus' teachings in the sayings material in the Q source. Scholars have suggested that the Q collection of sayings originated in Galilee, and that it therefore might throw light on Jesus' teaching in Galilee.[8] Place-names in the sayings provide specific references to Galilee; it is possible to establish a social map from these names: Capernaum, at the north end of the Sea of Galilee, followed by Bethsaida and Korazin, nearby (Q 10:13–16). The Phoenician towns of Tyre and Sidon are at a distance, and Jerusalem is far away (Q 13:34). When Jesus is engaged in conflicts with Pharisees, they take place in private houses or in courtyards or marketplaces—typical village settings lacking public buildings, which were found in towns. Archeological excavations confirm these suggestions.[9] The mention of houses and households gives additional support that Galilean villages are plausible places for Jesus' sayings.

Was There a "Galilee of the Gentiles"?
Archaeology as a Source for History

The memory of Galilee in Jewish tradition was of "Galilee of the Gentiles" (Isa 9:1; Matt 4:15). In the nineteenth century, one of the main historical "facts" about Galilee was that it had a mixed population due to an influx of non-Jewish people moved there by foreign rulers. This was a commonly accepted

5. Smith, *To Take Place*, 30.

6. Hanson, "Galilean Fishing Economy."

7. Moxnes, *Putting Jesus in His Place*, 155–56.

8. Reed, *Archaeology*, 170–96.

9 Richardson, *Building Jewish in the Roman East*, 17–110.

historical hypothesis. However, it was turned into ideology with the claim that Jesus might have belonged to this mixed population; he might even have been an Aryan! This hypothesis has now been seriously weakened by archeological explorations in Galilee over the last generation.

In *Archaeology and the Galilean Jesus,* Jonathan L. Reed presents the results of recent excavations and their relevance for our understanding of Jesus.[10] Reed emphasizes, however, that while archeology can tell us little directly about Jesus, it can tell us much about the conditions of the society in which he lived. Archaeological studies show few traces of a permanent population in Galilee in the first centuries after the Assyrian occupation.[11] For instance, excavations have not brought to light examples of Assyrian-style pottery. It was not until the Hasmoneans established a Jewish state in Judea during the second and first centuries BCE that we find traces of an increased population in Galilee. This was most likely a result of Judean inhabitants moving north.

Archaeologists therefore find it most plausible that the inhabitants in Galilee were primarily Jews. To test that hypothesis, they studied the material culture inside domestic space to find traces of social behavior. They were looking for material from four different groups that would imply Jewish behavior: (1) Most importantly, large numbers of stone vessels for eating and drinking indicated a Jewish population. According to the purity laws in the Mishnah, stone vessels would not transmit ritual impurity. (2) Excavations revealed many *miqwaot,* stepped immersion pools, that were used for the required ritual washing. They were found in many Galilean villages, smaller ones in private houses, larger ones near olive presses and synagogues. Two other indicators were more rare. (3) Ossuaries are small chests that were used for "second burials." One year after a person had died and had been placed in a burial chamber; the bones were collected and put into an ossuary. (4) Excavations of garbage dumps may reveal the dietary habits of the inhabitants in a house or village. Finds of animal bones were of special interest; the absence of pig bones was a strong indication that the inhabitants were Jews. Within all groups in Galilee, archaeologists found a great deal of correspondence to similar finds in Judea; thus, Reed concluded that the religious mentality and cultural identity in Galilee and Judea were quite similar.[12]

From this, we may conclude that Jesus grew up in a Jewish environment in Galilee. That he was a Galilean did not mean that he was not a

10. Reed, *Archaeology.*

11. Reed, *Archaeology,* 23–61.

12 Reed, Archaeology, 23–61.

Jew; however, there were local and historical characteristics that made him a "Jewish Galilean."[13]

A Life-Writing of Jesus

We started this book by arguing that Greek and Latin biographies were the main models for the evangelists writing their gospels. When historical Jesus scholarship started in the nineteenth century, scholars likewise chose the biography as the genre for their studies of Jesus,[14] in contrast to the dogmatic presentations of the divine Christ. At the time, this was a controversial decision since biography was regarded as a genre that reflected a critical attitude to the teachings of the church.

Today few scholars would speak of writing a biography of Jesus. That is not because they consider it improper on the grounds that Jesus was divine rather than human. From a contemporary view of biographies, the problem is that there are not adequate sources for a biography of Jesus. The aim of a biography is to cover the life span of a person, based on sources. However, for Jesus there are no reliable sources for the years before his short public life. Even for that period, the sources are fragmentary, and this makes it impossible to write a biography of Jesus in a traditional sense. What is possible, however, is what the British biographer Hermione Lee calls *"life-writing."*[15] On the basis of the fragments or relics that are left after a life, she suggests that it is possible to reconstruct certain activities, sayings, and thematic aspects of a life. In the case of Jesus, there are enough sources in the Gospels to give a profile of his activities, his sayings, and his relationships with other people.

There are similarities between discussions of biographies and of the trustworthiness of memories. Dale Allison, an authority on the historical Jesus, employs modern memory studies to construct a history of Jesus.[16] However, he is critical of how much memory can contribute to knowledge of the historical Jesus and speaks of "the frailty of human memory." According to Allison, we cannot use memories to establish specific historical events; however, they may provide general impressions of Jesus, typical ways of his acting or speaking. Allison suggests that "certain themes, motifs and rhetorical strategies recur again and again throughout the primary sources; and it must be in those themes and motifs and rhetorical strategies—which, taken together, leave some distinct impressions—if it

---

13. Freyne, *Jewish Galilean*.

14. Moxnes, *Jesus and the Rise of Nationalism*, 17–38.

15. Lee, *Body Parts*.

16. Allison, *Constructing Jesus*, 1–30.

is anywhere, that we will find history."[17] Scholars who work with literary approaches to the gospels have found the same: if the same themes, events, or words appear in several sources from different genres (e.g., parables, stories, or sayings), it is likely that these memories give a reliable picture of Jesus.[18] Allison concludes that even if one cannot firmly establish historical evidence, "I find it very difficult to come away from the primary sources doubting that I have somehow met a strikingly original character."[19] Therefore, in this chapter, I will try to give a character profile of Jesus, enough to recognize him and to say, "This is Jesus!"

As a basis for a "life-writing" of Jesus, I suggest that the Gospels provide sufficient material to give a profile of his activities, his sayings and his relations to other people. I will use these three areas to structure the following presentation. I take it for granted that Jesus was Jewish; that has been demonstrated by the history-of-Jesus research I discussed in chapter 6. In this chapter, I have emphasized that Jesus was a Galilean Jew. Thus, the fact that Jesus was a Jew was the basis for who he was; it was against this background that he developed his characteristics: (1) Jesus was homeless. (2) He proclaimed the kingdom of God as the new household. (3) He was a healer in a sick society. (4) He gathered around him a band of unusual followers. (5) He was a charismatic movement leader, and he was crucified. (6) From an early stage, his resurrection was a central part of the memory about Jesus.

Jesus as Homeless:
From Household to Itinerancy

Was Jesus a vagabond? Even to suggest this possibility appears to be in total contrast to the presentations in the Gospels and the presuppositions of Jesus scholars. They often portray Jesus surrounded by poor, hungry, sick, and marginalized people, while he is reaching out to them, healing them, and including them in fellowship meals. This image of the loving and caring Jesus always preserves the distinction between Jesus and groups of people he serves, between the helper and the needy, between the savior and the destitute.

So how can it be that the distinctions blur between "Him" and "them," that Jesus himself is included among the outcasts, the poor, and the homeless, and that such categories express who Jesus is?[20] This is both historically and hermeneutically a challenging question, since it breaks both

17. Allison, *Constructing Jesus*, 15.
18. Dahl, "Historical Jesus," 95; Le Donne, *Jesus*, 175–76.
19. Allison, *Constructing Jesus*, 23.
20. Myles, *Homeless Jesus*.

with traditional images of Jesus in the Gospels and with the consensus of historical Jesus scholars.

I think all scholars accept that Jesus grew up in a household in Galilee. There are a few mentions in the Gospels of Jesus' household of origin—maybe reflecting memories from people in his village—which mention that folks knew his mother, maybe his father, his brothers (mentioned by name), and his sisters (Matt 13:55–56; Mark 6:3). Family, household, and village provided the social context for people's lives; Jesus' sayings about households refer to this social situation. A saying attributed to Jesus describes a three-generational family, where "house" and "fields" frame the list of members (Mark 10:29–30). This list tells us the importance of the house and the fields that provided a living. The household provided the individual with material and social support, as well as with an identity and a place in the village community. Although not specifically about Jesus, this saying describes the "first socialization" of Jesus, growing up in an ordinary household in Galilee.

Against the background of strong ties to household and village, Jesus' leaving this social context to join John the Baptist must have been a dramatic rupture. However, this is often overlooked in presentations about the beginning of Jesus' public activity.[21] Did Jesus choose this homelessness voluntarily, or was there also socioeconomic and political pressure behind it?[22] We may start by examining how the Gospels explain the circumstances around the start of Jesus' mission. Matthew says, "Now when Jesus heard that John had been arrested, he withdrew to Galilee. He left Nazareth and made his home in Capernaum by the sea" (Matt 4:12–13). John's arrest has often been taken to represent an opportunity for Jesus to move from being a disciple of John the Baptist to starting out on his own. However, this reference to John also points to the circumstances of John's death and to the danger it represented to be close to him. Thus, Jesus' move might be seen as a flight from the forces of Herod Antipas.

Even if Jesus chose to be homeless, he was also under pressure from social sanctions. Luke's story of the reactions that Jesus faced when he returned to his village, Nazareth, after having healed and preached in Capernaum is a case in point. After initially receiving a positive response to his message of salvation to the poor, Jesus provokes people by proclaiming that in times of famine and illness, God helped only Gentiles. The result is a conflict with the people of Nazareth that turns into a dangerous situation:

> All in the synagogue were filled with rage.[29] They got up, drove
> him out of the town, and led him to the brow of the hill on which

21. Moxnes, *Putting Jesus in His Place*, 46–71.
22. Myles, *Homeless Jesus*, 10.

their town was built, so that they might hurl him off the cliff.[30] But
he passed through the midst of them and went on his way.[31] He
went down to Capernaum, a city in Galilee. (Luke 4:28–31)

With their violent acts, the villagers force Jesus to leave Nazareth. If,
therefore, the conflict is caused by Jesus' proclamation, it is the attack by the
villagers that causes him to leave.

The ultimate homelessness that Jesus suffered is reflected in his saying
in Luke 9:57–59: "As they were going along the road, someone said to him,
'I will follow you wherever you go.' And Jesus said to him, 'Foxes have holes,
and birds of the air have nests; but the Son of Man has nowhere to lay his
head.'" This is a description of Jesus as a vagabond, sleeping outside, with no
house.[23] The "son of man" was dislocated from civilized society, from a place
where he was at home and that secured his identity. Jesus shared the position
of the homeless and the vagabonds; he was pushed outside: he represented
a challenge to the structures of society. Jesus was not only a man without a
place; he was now outside human community.

Thus, Jesus experienced the situation of poor people exposed to the
pressures from wealthy elites. In Galilee, there was a growing tendency toward higher taxes, higher rents, and other rising duties for peasants. Such
expenses might force them to give up ownership to their land to larger landowners; some peasants might be evicted for insolvency, and others might
leave their villages to get away from their creditors. The powerful might also
use other means to take the land from poor peasants, like illegal encroach-
ment, violence, robbery, and threats.[24] A situation with a growing number
of landless peasants might result in banditry, a way for poor peasants to
protect themselves from the establishment.

However, even if we emphasize these external pressures, the gospel
stories also portray Jesus as making controversial utterances, criticizing
social institutions, and breaking with cultural norms. Thus, in some sense
he provoked the reactions that put him into the position of being homeless and vagrant.

Jesus called at least some of the people he met to leave their household
and to follow him into homelessness to proclaim the kingdom of God (Luke
9:60). Several Jesus sayings emphasize the conflicts that could result from
following him and leaving one's household. In many instances, Jesus mentions no alternative to the household; the call was simply to follow Jesus.
However, it is obvious that over time the group established some form of
social structure. Jesus rejected and criticized the household that he had left;

23. Vaage, *Galilean Upstarts*, 89–90.
24. Hamel, *Poverty and Charity*, 159–60.

however, the model itself was so strong that even the new group of disciples was described *as if* it was a household. This is the case in the well-known story of how Jesus' mother and his siblings come to bring him home. Jesus rejects them and says to his disciples who are gathered around him, "Here are my mother and my brothers! Whoever does the will of God is my brother and sister and mother" (Mark 3:34–35). This is an example of what social anthropologists speak of as "social kinship," that is, people who are not biological kin or family and are nevertheless described as kin and family. However, this is not a complete family; in no instances does Jesus speak of a father in his new family gathered around him.

The Kingdom of God as the New Household

Jesus challenged people to leave the security and community in their households to follow him into an uncertain future, without any security for what they needed to live or social support. Instead, Jesus proclaimed that their new household was the kingdom of God, and that God was a father who would provide for his household.

This was an unconventional way to speak of the kingdom of God. There can be no doubt that the proclamation of the kingdom of God, more than anything else, characterized the message of Jesus. However, the meaning of the term itself is disputed. It appears that "kingdom of God" was a well-known term among Jews, since Jesus never explains its meaning. But Jesus' use of this term distinguishes him, his vocabulary, and his teaching from writings in the Bible and other Jewish texts. The Hebrew scriptures make frequent use of the term "king" in reference to God, but they rarely employ the term "kingdom of God." Jesus, however, speaks frequently of the "kingdom of God," whereas he rarely uses the term "king" in reference to God.[25] "Kingdom" is a translation of the Greek term *basileia*, which is derived from *basileus*, the word for "king" or "emperor." Therefore, *basileia* belongs to political terminology, and "the kingdom of God" represents a contrast to the kingdoms of kings and emperors. However, in many instances Jesus combines the notion of the kingdom of God with sayings about God as Father. He speaks of God not as a king but as a caring father. Thus, the kingdom of God appears to be like a household marked by caring relationships between its members.

Thus, Jesus speaks of the kingdom of God as a physical place and as a social arena. Understood in this way, we break with a long tradition in biblical scholarship that interpreted the kingdom of God in terms of *time*: "When

25. Moxnes, *Putting Jesus in His Place*, 113–18.

does it come?" The result of this temporal emphasis has been little interest in the place aspect of the kingdom of God. We can compare what Jesus does when he proclaims the kingdom of God with the literary genre of imaginary places or fantasy worlds.[26] For instance, *Utopia* (1516) by Thomas More and *Gulliver's Travels* (1726) by Jonathan Swift present famous examples of imaginary places. These authors were critical of the political and social situation in England when they were writing, and they therefore made up descriptions of imaginary societies that represented qualities that they found lacking in England. I suggest that we can compare Jesus' presentations of the kingdom of God with such fantasy literature; thus, Jesus set up an alternative to the social and political situation in Galilee. When Jesus proclaimed a kingdom ruled by a God who acts as a caring father does, he criticized the dominant economic and social structures that benefited the elite.

Jesus' teaching about the kingdom of God as a household was above all directed to those who were homeless, poor, and discriminated against because they had followed him. The Beatitudes in Matt 5:2-12 and Luke 6:20-26 may refer to the situation of the followers of Jesus; they are the ones who are poor, who mourn, who hunger and are persecuted. The first promise of the Beatitudes speaks to the poor: "theirs is the kingdom of heaven" (Matt 5:2).

In the Lord's Prayer (Matt 6:9-13), Jesus brings together the images of the kingdom of God and of the household, with God as father. Jesus directs his prayer to his "Father" and combines this form of address with the petitions "Your kingdom come" and "Give us this day our daily bread." Thus, Jesus describes God as a caring father who provides bread for his children, not as a patriarch who rules over his household. We find the same images in Jesus' words against worry; they are also addressed to his disciples: "Therefore I tell you, do not worry about your life, what you will eat, or about your body, what you will wear" (Luke 12:22). Jesus' words describe a situation where the disciples are excluded from their households of origin, which provided shelter, food, and clothing. Jesus compares their situation to that of birds and flowers; however, his point is not to paint a nature symbolism. Instead, the point that he makes several times is that God cares about the birds, and even more about the disciples. It is because they have a Father who knows their needs that they need not worry (Luke 12: 29-30).

However, Jesus was not only concerned to comfort the disciples in their suffering; he also directed his criticism at the large inequalities among people in Galilee. The Hellenistic economic model in Galilee during the rule of Herod Antipas (4 BCE-39 CE) was based on reciprocity between

---

26. Moxnes, *Putting Jesus in His Place*, 108-11.

equals, those who had property. It was against this system of reciprocity, which offered no support for the poor, that Jesus directed his criticism and launched a new system. Some of his parables describe how small peasants and tenant farmers incurred debts to landowners.[27] As a result, many of them lost their land and were reduced to day laborers. From many of the parables we can detect a criticism of this system: for instance in the contrast between "rich" and "poor" (Luke 16:19–31) or in the relations between patron and clients (Matt 20:1–15; Luke 16:1–9). Some of these parables subvert the system of domination and exploitation—for instance, the parable of the dishonest steward (Luke 16:1–9). Other parables are more straightforward in the way they imagine a place with a new social structure free from domination (Luke 14:7–24). Jesus demanded that money should be lent out without any expectation of a return, and that the poor should be invited to dinners without expectation of a return invitation.[28] Jesus' parables put forth a vision of a new social order. I have suggested that this could be called the *Economy of the Kingdom*.[29]

Healer in a Sick Society

Jesus not only spoke of the kingdom of God; he also acted to bring about the kingdom. His healings pointed to new social relations. In all societies, especially in poor societies, we find that poverty, illnesses, malnutrition, and psychiatric problems are linked. Illness is not simply a problem for the individual; it is a societal problem: illnesses may reflect disparity, injustice, and social pressures. This comes across when we read the stories of Jesus who encounters village folk and large crowds gathering around him. There are people who suffer from various conditions and illnesses; they are blind, paralyzed, deaf, and diseased. In his sayings, Jesus quotes passages from Scripture that combine poverty and illness (Isa 61:1–2; cf. Luke 4:18–19). We must start with these structural connections when we ask about the meaning of the stories of Jesus as a healer or an exorcist.

From the time of Jesus there are many stories of healers, so Jesus was not exceptional. However, Jesus is an exception in the number of stories told about his healings. Thus, this must have been a central theme in the memories told about him, already from an early stage. There are many memories of Jesus as healer, especially in Mark's Gospel. The first part of the gospel is made up of a series of stories about how Jesus travels around Galilee and heals

27. Luke 7:41–42; 16:1–9.
28. Luke 6:34; 14:12–14; Moxnes, *Economy of the Kingdom*, 22–98; 127–38.
29. Moxnes, *Economy of the Kingdom*.

the sick, exorcises demons and feeds the hungry crowds.[30] Such healings are reported so often, also by opponents, and in different types of material, that we must suppose that the authors of the Gospels and their contemporaries must have believed that they really happened.

These stories have presented a problem for students of the historical Jesus, who often just left them alone and concentrated on the teaching of Jesus.[31] It was embarrassing that Jesus was associated with such primitive forms of healing that were not historically trustworthy. However, in recent years there has been a renewed interest in Jesus' healings and exorcisms.[32] Many attempts have been made to explain these stories of healing. Modern medicine has come in for criticism, since it looks at healing only as a physical, biological phenomenon. With a more holistic perspective on the person who is ill, healing may include integrating the person into a social community, improving the person's self-confidence, and helping the person find new meaning in life. However, these perspectives cannot explain everything; there seems now to be a greater willingness to accept that people may have experienced physical healings that cannot find a medical explanation. Demonic possessions may have different causes—e.g., a defense mechanism against extreme outside pressures in an overwhelmingly difficult social situation.

An Unusual Movement?

What was the link between Jesus' proclamation of the kingdom of God and the movement he started? Jesus proclaimed the kingdom of God as a household for the marginalized, and he healed those who were weakest in society. How was this reflected in the composition of the group? This is a different perspective from the most common way to discuss the Jesus movement, which often follows the sequence in the Gospels. Mark and Matthew represent, so to speak, the hegemonic model, starting with Jesus' calling the twelve disciples, who together with Jesus occupy the primary position in the story. Obviously, in the cultural memory of the movement they have a special place, pointing towards the future of the Jesus movement. They are described according a fixed pattern called a "pilgrim type," that is, as people who make a dramatic break with social roles in a household in order to start a new life.[33] In order to gain access to the larger group around Jesus from a historical

---

30. Mark 1:21–3; 5–9.

31 Typically, Bornkamm, *Jesus of Nazareth.*

32. Henriksen and Sandnes, *Jesus as Healer,* 25–63.

33. Valantasis, "Constructions of Power."

perspective, I will look at those who gathered around Jesus without becoming "followers" in the exclusive sense (i.e., the disciples).

Among these we find women; the description of them in the Gospels may provide glimpses into the role of women in a traditional society. An encounter with Jesus did not have such dramatic consequences for them as for the men; rather, they integrated their new vocation into their traditional roles in the household—roles of caring and providing food.[34] Consequently, these women are not easily visible in the main story line; however, they appear in stories at the margins, as disciples in a household (Luke 10:38–42), or as providers of support for Jesus and his male disciples (Luke 8:1–3). However, women become more visible as the Jesus story approaches its climax: the week in Jerusalem moves toward the crucifixion, the burial, the anointment ritual, and finally the commission to become witness of the resurrection. In this last phase of the Jesus story, women followers seem to replace the male disciples, who have gone into hiding.

"Tax collectors and sinners" were the most controversial groups that Jesus brought into his fellowship, thereby including people who were regarded as marginal or outside the boundaries of society. Tax collectors were associated with taxes and tolls, which were very unpopular with people. The ruler of Galilee, Herod Antipas, oversaw the collections; however, he subcontracted them to tax collectors. This task gave many opportunities for a tax collector to enrich himself, and tax collectors had a bad reputation and were looked down upon as "sinners." *Sinner* was a term that had different connotations: sinners took up occupations with bad reputations, such as tax collecting and also shepherding; but sinners also trespassed religious and moral norms.[35]

That Jesus included "tax collectors and sinners" in his fellowship meals and treated them as "friends" is documented in many different types of texts—in stories about Jesus, in his sayings, and in accusations leveled at him.[36] Thus, this tradition most likely goes back to Jesus himself. Although forgiveness of sins was possible according to both Jewish and early Christian texts, Jesus' attitude appears to have been so radical that he provoked anger and protest among many. Moreover, Jesus emphasized that his mission was directed especially toward "the poor, the crippled, the lame, and the blind" (Luke 14:13). This was an old tradition in Jewish scriptures;

34. Valantasis, "Constructions of Power," 805–10.

35. Donahue, "Tax Collectors and Sinners."

36. Mark 2:13–17; Matt 9:9–13; Luke 5:27–32; Luke 15:1–2; 19:1–10; Matt 21:31–32; Q 7:31–35.

however, Jesus turned it into criticism of social relations in society during his time, and this made his attitude controversial.

Jesus' relationships to people on the border of or outside of Jewish society is an issue under discussion. Here, the different gospels provide conflicting memories. In Matt 10:6, Jesus tells his disciples not to go to the Gentiles and Samaritans but only to the "lost sheep" of Israel. In Luke 4:25–6, on the other hand, Jesus provokes people in the synagogue with the story of how, during a famine, the prophet Elijah gave food to a widow in Sidon rather than to the Israelites. In the end, both Matthew and Luke tell how Jesus, after the resurrection, commands his disciples to proclaim to "all nations" (Matt 28:16–20; Luke 24: 46–47). Stories of how Jesus healed non-Jews appear trustworthy. In a well-known story, Jesus heals the daughter of a Syrophoenician woman who challenged him after he had refused to help her. This story reflects so badly on Jesus that it is unlikely somebody would have come up with such a story when the Gospels were being written, at a time when the mission to non-Jews was expanding.

When we consider the groups that Jesus attracted, it is obvious that they did not make up a normal cross-section of society. Rather, they represented a new model for society; for instance, Jesus' words about children as the first in the kingdom of God (Matt 19:14; Mark 10:14; Luke 18:16) overturned accepted hierarchies. The same is true of Jesus' praise of barren women (Luke 23:28–31); they were otherwise looked down upon as unlucky since they were not able to produce children. Jesus' words on children may also have another aspect. Children represented a presexual stage, and therefore they were symbols of the ascetic side of the Jesus movement. In a society that was based on marriage and procreation, Jesus' proclamation of an ascetic way of life in the world to come, that is, without marriage (Mark 12:24–25), could not fail to provoke. In Luke's version, asceticism is an ideal already in this life (Luke 20:34–36). Even more challenging was Jesus' saying about those "who have made themselves eunuchs for the sake of the kingdom of heaven" (Matt 19:12).[37] It is unclear whether the saying refers to castration or sexual abstinence; either way, it rejected marriage and praised an ascetic lifestyle. Moreover, having been castrated, a eunuch was regarded as a "half man." Thus, the saying was a rejection of the masculine ideal in Jewish society and other societies in the Greco-Roman world.[38] When we also notice that in Jesus' sayings about the "new" family, there are no father figures, it becomes obvious that the Jesus movement had departed from the

37. Moxnes, *Putting Jesus in His Place*, 72–90.

38 A eunuch was an ambiguous figure, regarded as neither man nor woman; therefore sometimes described as "half man," in Latin *semivir* (Apuleius, *Golden Ass*, 8. 26–29).

traditional household structure, headed by the father, the main authority. It is significant that Jesus did not speak of himself as a father. This title that was reserved for God, as the father in the kingdom of God.

Based on all these elements, I suggest that Jesus and his followers made up a "queer movement." I do not use *queer* in a sexual sense, in the meaning of "gay," but in a broader sense: of breaking with traditional social norms. These norms are based on a system of binaries, with clear divisions between men and women, masters and slaves. It was especially in its earliest period that the Jesus movement broke with social norms. This is typical of the first phase of protest movements. Many scholars argue that Jesus and the Jesus movement represented a strong pro-family structure.[39] This is true of later periods and is reflected, for instance, in the Pastoral Letters. However, at the same time, asceticism and the rejection of marriage and procreation was a strong trend for several centuries.[40]

Was Jesus a Charismatic Leader?[41]

How can we best characterize Jesus? Attempts to describe him usually take one of two forms. Some use categories from antiquity like prophet or teacher; others use modern categories like ascetic or social revolutionary. The latter categories are of course anachronistic; however, by using a social model they help us to understand what type of person Jesus was. One of the most common models has been that of a charismatic leader, inspired by Max Weber's works from the first part of the twentieth century.[42] Weber used charisma in his discussion of authority; he developed the idea of three types of legitimate authority: legal, traditional, and charismatic. The prophets in ancient Israel and Jesus were examples of charismatic leaders.

Weber outlines two strands in the understanding of charisma. One finds that charisma, its power and authority, resides in the individual. For instance, when he introduces Jesus of Nazareth as a prophet, as one of the classic types of a charismatic leader, Weber describes him as a "purely individual bearer of charisma, who by the virtue of his mission proclaims a religious doctrine or divine commandment."[43] This understanding of charisma comes close to the ideas of the Great Man and the unique personality, which were dominant in the nineteenth century.

39. Elliott, "Family-Oriented."
40. Brown, *Body and Society.*
41. The following section draws on Moxnes, "Charismatic Leader?"
42. Weber, *Economy and Society.*
43. Weber, *Economy and Society* 1, 439.

However, I suggest that Jesus did not represent this form of individualized charisma. Elisabeth Schüssler Fiorenza has strongly criticized this model from a feminist perspective.[44] To use the Great Man or heroic figure as a model creates an image of Jesus that only men can identify with. Instead, she suggests that Jesus was not a unique leader; rather, he was part of a movement. Thus, instead of Jesus as a single authority, I suggest that it is more relevant to portray Jesus within the Jesus movement. Charisma then becomes an expression of the relationship between a leader and his group. This is in line with a different perspective on Weber's concept of charisma, one that sees the charismatic quality not as inherent in a person but as attributed by his followers. The sociologist Peter Worsley has developed this understanding in a study of the cargo cults in Melanesia: "To the sociologist, charisma . . . can only be that which is recognized, by believers and followers, as 'charismatic' in the behavior of those they treat as charismatic . . . Charisma, therefore, sociologically viewed, is a social relationship, not an attribute of individual personality or a mystical quality."[45] This sociological perspective helps us make sense of the memories of how people recognized Jesus as a charismatic healer and preacher. Charisma was part of the social relationships between Jesus, his followers, and the crowds that gathered around him.

THE DEATH OF THE CHARISMATIC

The American Jesus scholar Marcus Borg has developed this perspective on Jesus as a charismatic leader within a relationship with his followers. Partly in contrast to the well-known image of Jesus as an eschatological prophet, he presents a more comprehensive picture that includes many more aspects of Jesus' activities. Borg suggests that we understand Jesus as "a charismatic who was a healer, sage, prophet and revitalization movement founder."[46] He presents Jesus and his movement more in terms of a renewal than of a return to old peasant traditions that preserved hierarchical and patriarchal patterns. Borg presents the Jesus movement and Jesus' vision as an "alternative culture." Jesus' vision of society was based on a compassion that included outcasts, women, and the poor. In this way, Jesus represented a radical criticism of the present situation of his society. His criticism was directed at societal institutions, especially the temple and its politics centered on holiness and purity, which affected villages and local culture. As a result, Jesus represented a challenge to the Jerusalem

44. Schüssler Fiorenza, *Politics of Interpretation*.
45. Worsley, *Trumpet Shall Sound*, XII.
46. Borg, *Jesus*, 15.

leadership as well as to the Romans and their rule. Borg argues that it was this challenge that led to the crucifixion of Jesus.

Borg thus raises a historical question: Was there a *purpose* to the journey of Jesus to Jerusalem that led to his death? This is a different question from the one the Gospels ask, which from a postresurrection perspective are concerned with the meaning of the death of Jesus. When Jesus went with his disciples to Jerusalem for the Passover, he came in order to participate in the celebration of liberation from Egypt of the Jewish people. This was the foundational narrative of the Jewish people. Therefore, Passover always brought expectations of the arrival of a time of liberation, and fomented a strong group fervor. Jesus' central message—the kingdom of God, that God would establish his reign—took on a political meaning of liberation from Roman rule and increased the tension already present in Jerusalem.

Two central events show how Jesus must deliberately have challenged Jerusalem and the Romans. The first is his entry into Jerusalem. The description in the Gospels clearly reflects biblical tradition, with Jesus riding on a colt (Zech 9:9; cf. Mark 11:1–11). This may be an example of how proof texting from the Bible was told as a story of something that actually happened. Jesus' disciples followed him, and the people who came out to meet him acclaimed him with praise as the "Son of David" and "King of Israel." From the perspective of Jesus as a charismatic leader, this episode illustrates how charisma functioned as a social relationship between leader and people. Jesus' form of entry may well have sparked the enthusiasm; however, it was the crowds of pilgrims coming to Jerusalem for the Passover who proclaimed Jesus as Messiah.

This is the main point in Paula Fredriksen's discussion of the events that led up to the crucifixion of Jesus.[47] Fredriksen follows John's Gospel in the reconstruction of the life of Jesus. Therefore, she holds that Jesus was known in Jerusalem from earlier Passovers. However, it was the relations between the crowds and Jesus that made Jesus' last Passover extraordinary. Fredriksen does not attribute the identification with the Messiah to Jesus himself; rather, the crowds had a strong enthusiasm for the coming kingdom and associated that with the coming of the Messiah. They made Jesus into the charismatic leader of a movement that could not be controlled. The tumult around Jesus and his disciples made the Romans aware of the prophet from Galilee, and made them follow him during the next days. The crowds hailed Jesus as the Messiah; and shortly afterwards he was executed by the Romans as a messianic pretender, as "King of the Jews" (Mark 15:26).

47. Fredriksen, *Jesus of Nazareth*, 235–59.

Paula Fredriksen draws the conclusion that the fervor and enthusiasm of the crowds that led directly to Jesus' death.[48]

The controversy in the temple (Mark 11:15–18) was the other event that challenged leadership of the temple and the Jewish elite in Jerusalem.[49] Jesus' turning of the tables of the moneychangers and vendors of sacrificial animals has been interpreted in many different ways, e.g., as a purification of temple worship. The best suggestion is provided by the way the temple action is directly linked to the high priest's accusations against Jesus. Jesus is accused (falsely, the evangelists say) of planning to destroy the temple, and to build a new one (Mark 14: 57–59). Jesus' action against the temple, and against the authority and power of the Jerusalem leadership, is a much more plausible reason for their turning against him than accusations of blasphemy. Jesus prophesied the destruction of the temple as part of apocalyptic events before the coming of the Messiah (Mark 13:1–2, 24–27). Jesus' symbolic action was linked to his proclamation of the kingdom and to his own role in the coming eschatological events.[50]

Thus, the temple elite and the Romans shared a concern that if the people gathered in Jerusalem flocked around him, Jesus represented a danger for political stability. John's Gospel presents a saying by the chief priests that is an accurate description of the situation for local leaders under Roman supremacy: "If we let him go on like this, everyone will believe in him, and the Romans will come and destroy both our holy place and our nation" (John 11:48). The temple leadership and Jerusalem elite were not independent rulers; they had their power only as long as they had the confidence of the Romans. In the case of Jesus, both groups had partially overlapping reasons to want to stop Jesus from stirring up protests and possible revolts. However, only the Romans had the power to crucify Jesus; this is why Pontius Pilate, the Roman governor in Judea, bore the responsibility for Jesus' crucifixion. In the context of his rule in Judea, this small matter did not make a big impact at the time.

However, in the memory of the Christian church, Pilate is forever linked to Jesus death, in the words of the Apostles' Creed: "He suffered under Pontius Pilate, was crucified, died, and was buried." This statement is brief, mentioning only the simple facts of Jesus's death. At the same time, however, Jesus' death was remembered, retold, and interpreted in a variety of ways;[51] it is summed up in the memory of the Christian church in the words of the Nicene Creed: "*For our sake* he was crucified under Pontius Pilate; he suffered death and was buried."

48. Fredriksen, *Jesus of Nazareth*, 257.

49. Sanders, *Jesus*, 61–90.

50. Fredriksen, *From Jesus to Christ*, 111–14.

51. Sloyan, *Crucifixion of Jesus*, 45–122.

Memories of Resurrection

The end of the history of Jesus was his death on a cross and his burial in a tomb. That is as far as historical studies can go. However, the memories of Jesus continue, with stories of an empty tomb, of how he appeared to women at the tomb and to male disciples in various locations over a period. For the gospel writers—and for their audiences—these stories continued the story of Jesus as a prophet in Galilee and Jerusalem and belonged in the same sense to the memories of Jesus. Some of these stories also suggest a social location for the memories. Both Luke and John's Gospels tell stories of how the disciples recognized Jesus as risen from the dead and alive in the setting of a meal (Luke 24:29–31; John 21:12–13). These meal scenes clearly point to the sacred meal of the Jesus followers, the Eucharist. In this way, the memories of how Jesus appeared to his disciples are not dependent only on the transmission of authoritative stories. They become communicative memories that disciples can later participate in when they encounter Jesus in the Eucharist.

From Memory to History

I started out by raising the question of whether it is possible to make a transition from memories to a history of Jesus. At the end of the book, I feel tempted to rephrase the question: how has the historical study of Jesus been influenced by memories? The last chapters have brought up memories of Jesus told from the perspectives of gender, race and class, and from people in marginal positions. Common for these memories is that they are concerned with the meaning of Jesus for their lives. This is not something new. Scholars in the nineteenth century were studying Jesus as an ideal for national unity; Jesus was portrayed as "a great man" who shaped European history. These scholars from male, white elites had a hegemony in studies of the historical Jesus. Now new groups of scholars who bring with them new experiences and new memories have broken this hegemony. Without women's experiences and memories there would have been no feminist perspectives on the study of the historical Jesus. Experiences of migration and homelessness opens up questions of Jesus' homelessness. People at economic and political margins will more easily recognize the political aspects of Jesus in his historical context. Thus, memories can open up new questions and new perspectives in historical studies of Jesus.

Conclusion

Jesus—Memories for the Future?

I WRITE THIS CONCLUSION on August 6, 2019, the anniversary of the day the atomic bomb was dropped on Hiroshima. That day showed what catastrophes humans can make, that we have the capacity to destroy societies, the earth, and our common future. The frightening possibility of an "Apocalypse Now" is very real. How does this situation affect the memories we can tell about Jesus?

The stories and the historical traditions told about Jesus have always sought to respond to the questions and needs of every new generation of people and their relationships with Jesus. New questions and new needs bring about reinterpretations of the first memories of Jesus. When I try to raise some of today's questions, I am in fact exploring "communicative memories"—that is, memories of an individual shared with his or her contemporaries.[1] Thus, rather than sharing scholarly insights, which I hope the earlier chapters have provided, in this brief section I hope to enter into a dialogue with my readers.

The memory of August 6, 1945, and the fear of atomic weapons in the background of contemporary life helps us to recognize fears that haunted contemporaries of Jesus—fears of illness, plague, and demon-possession. When Jesus healed the sick and exorcised demons, as the Gospel of Mark relates time and again, these acts took on cosmic significance; these healings and exorcisms had a deeper meaning than they do in our time, given our modern medicine and psychiatric clinics. People suffered from real fears that demons, even the devil himself, would destroy the world. Today atomic weapons and the threats to deploy them make us realize the similarities to apocalyptic pictures in Jesus' teaching. Furthermore, we should not write off as mere myths the stories in the apocryphal gospels of Jesus fighting the

1. Assmann, "Communicative and Cultural Memory."

devil in Hades. True, they are myths; nevertheless, they reveal the powers that first-century people feared, and that Jesus stood up against. Thus, the date August 6 brings to mind that we can tell memories of Jesus as the one who cares for the individual as well as the one who fights the destructive powers that threaten to annihilate the world.

The August 6 date also recalls another contemporary threat against humanity, viz the danger of destroying humanity as a community, as a fellowship. War is the end result of powers that aim to divide people; it is the total collapse of human solidarity. The memories of Jesus' proclamation of the kingdom of God present a renewed solidarity. When Jesus talked about the kingdom of God, *kingdom* was a well-known word in political discourse, which described dominion over people by their rulers. However, Jesus surprised his audience when he did not speak of God as king; instead, he used an image from the household and spoke of God as a father who cared for his children and who provided for them. Jesus' alternative to the rule of princes, which was violent and oppressive, was a fellowship of solidarity and intimacy.

From our own recent history, the concept of the Third Reich represents the absolute perversion of what a state ought to be, namely, rule for the good of the people. Today, too, many rulers exercise absolute power over their people; they employ nationalism to divide people; they pressure the world in a dangerous direction toward wars and military destruction. Moreover, faceless, global forces also divide the world. Global capitalism facilitates the free movement of money and profit-making activities by multinational corporations, powers at work across the world for the good of some but for the disenfranchisement of many. The problem with the free movement of money is that there is no corresponding free movement of people. When poor people try to move in order to secure better opportunities for themselves and their children, their movements are stopped, sometimes by border checkpoints, sometimes by intimidation, and sometimes by threats.

What memories of Jesus come to mind when I enter a passport control in Europe? I have a privileged place in the line for "Citizens of the EU / European Economic Area," while travelers from Africa and Asia end up in the long line for "All Others." My privileged place becomes even more evident when I consider refugees trying to cross the Mediterranean in dangerous boats, or refugees desperately, hope against hope, trying to cross the US-Mexico border to flee violence and poverty.

The memories of Jesus in the Gospels offer a vision of our common humanity, of a Jesus who commissions his followers to spread the gospel to "all nations" (Matt 28:19), who begins a movement reaching "to the ends of the earth" (Acts 1:8). The memories of Jesus' sayings of fellowship in a household, can become a vision of humanity as one family, of solidarity present in close relationships spread to a larger society. Instead of protecting the boundaries around "our own people," is it possible to imagine "a world people"? Some of the earliest memories of Jesus point in this direction. In his exchange with the Samaritan woman, Jesus builds bridges across divides based on ethnicity, gender, and morality. In the parable of the good Samaritan, Jesus breaks down ethnic and religious divisions; it is the foreigner who reflects "What would Jesus do?" not the privileged insiders.

The catastrophe of August 6, 1945, reminds us also of another threat to our common humanity. Because of mass destruction, individuals disappear in a loss of memory; they lose not only their lives but also their identity. Many people experience this catastrophe while they are still alive, when they are forced to become refugees from their homes and homesteads. They have lost not only all their possessions but also their identities, their own selves. A young Syrian woman, a refugee in Norway, puts it in this way: "I have no official name; I have no address. I have no identity; I am a refugee and live in hiding in Norway."[2] In one of his parables, Jesus provides an identity for those who have been made invisible:

> "For I was hungry and you gave me food, I was thirsty and you gave me something to drink, I was a stranger and you welcomed me, I was naked and you gave me clothing, I was sick and you took care of me, I was in prison and you visited me." Then the righteous will answer him, "Lord, when was it that we saw you hungry and gave you food, or thirsty and gave you something to drink? And when was it that we saw you a stranger and welcomed you, or naked and gave you clothing? And when was it that we saw you sick or in prison and visited you?" And the king will answer them, "Truly I tell you, just as you did it to one of the least of these who are members of my family, you did it to me." (Matt 25:35–40)

In a world where so many are in real danger of losing their identity, the strongest memory we can tell about Jesus is how he is the face of all who have become faceless, how he gives himself to all who have lost themselves.

---

2. This quotation from an anonymous Syrian woman was documented as part of a photo exhibition by André Clemetsen and Halvor Moxnes called *Hvor skjer Jesus?* (*Where Does Jesus Happen?*), held in Oslo Cathedral from February 27 to March 18, 2018.

Suggested Readings

Jesus in Early Christian Memory

The Gospels as Biographies of Jesus

Burridge, Richard A. *What Are the Gospels? A Comparison with Graeco-Roman Biography*. 2nd ed. Biblical Resource Series. Grand Rapids: Eerdmans, 2004.

————. *Four Gospels, One Jesus? A Symbolic Reading*. Grand Rapids: Eerdmans, 2005.

Conway, Colleen M. *Behold the Man: Jesus and Greco-Roman Masculinity*. Oxford: Oxford University Press, 2008.

Hägg, Tomas. *The Art of Biography in Antiquity*. Cambridge: Cambridge University Press, 2012.

Stanton, Graham. *The Gospels and Jesus*. 2nd ed. Oxford Bible Series. Oxford: Oxford University Press, 2002.

Memory Studies and Reception History

Allison, Dale C. *Constructing Jesus: Memory, Imagination, and History*. Grand Rapids: Baker Academic, 2010.

Le Donne, Anthony. *The Historiographical Jesus: Memory, Typology, and the Son of David*. Waco, TX: Baylor University Press, 2009.

————. *Jesus: A Beginners Guide*. London: One World, 2018.

Pelikan, Jaroslav. *Jesus through the Centuries: His Place in the History of Culture*. New Haven: Yale University Press, 1985.

Taylor, Joan E. *What Did Jesus Look Like?* London: Bloomsbury, 2019.

Growing Memories:
The Apocryphal Jesus

Aasgaard, Reidar. *The Childhood of Jesus. Decoding the Apocryphal Infancy Gospel of Thomas.* Eugene, OR: Cascade Books, 2009.

Ehrman, Bart D. *Lost Christianities: The Battles for Scripture and the Faiths We Never Knew.* Oxford: Oxford University Press, 2003.

Elliott, J. K. *The Apocryphal Jesus: Legends of the Early Church.* New York: Oxford University Press, 1996.

Kasser, Rodolphe, et al., eds. *The Gospel of Judas.* Washington, DC: National Geographic, 2006.

King, Karen L. *The Gospel of Mary of Magdala: Jesus and the First Woman Apostle.* Santa Rosa, CA: Polebridge, 2003.

Patterson, Stephen J. *The Gospel of Thomas and Jesus.* Sonoma, CA: Polebridge, 1993.

Counterhistories about Jesus:
Jesus' Narratives in Jewish Sources and in the Quran

Khalidi, Jarif. *The Muslim Jesus.* Cambridge: Harvard University Press, 2001.

Leirvik, Oddbjørn. *Images of Jesus Christ in Islam.* 2nd ed. New York: Continuum, 2010.

Meerson, Michael, and Peter Schäfer, trans. and eds. *Toledot Yeshu: The Life Story of Jesus.* 2 vols. Texts and Studies in Ancient Judaism 149. Tübingen: Mohr/Siebeck, 2014.

Robinson, Neil. *Christ in Islam and Christianity: The Representation of Jesus in the Qurān and the Classical Muslim Commentaries.* London: Macmillan, 1991.

Schäfer, Peter. *Jesus in the Talmud.* Princeton: Princeton University Press, 2007.

The Second Christ:
Saint Francis and the Human Jesus in the Middle Ages

Armstrong, Regis J. et al., eds. *The Founder.* Francis of Assisi: Early Documents 2. Hyde Park, NY: New City, 2000.

————, et al., eds. *The Saint.* Francis of Assisi: Early Documents 1. *The Founder.* Hyde Park, NY: New City, 1999.

Bynum, Caroline Walker. *Jesus as Mother: Studies in the Spirituality of the High Middle Ages.* Publications of the Center for Medieval and Renaissance Studies, UCLA 16. Berkeley: University of California Press, 1982.

Vauchez, André. *Francis of Assisi: The Life and Afterlife of a Medieval Saint.* Translated by M. F. Cusato. New Haven: Yale University Press, 2012.

When Did Jesus Become "Historical"?
Jesus in the Enlightenment and Modernity

Sources

Chubb, Thomas. *The True Gospel of Jesus Christ Asserted.* 1738. Whitefish, MT: Kessinger Legacy Reprints, 2010.

Jefferson, Thomas. *The Life and Morals of Jesus of Nazareth.* St. Louis: Thompson, 1902. https://en.wikisource.org/wiki/The_Life_and_Morals_of_Jesus_of_Nazareth/.

Reimarus, Herman Samuel. *Fragments.* Edited by Charles H. Talbert. Translated by Ralph S. Fraser. Lives of Jesus Series. Philadelphia: Fortress, 1970.

Renan, Ernest. *Vie de Jésus.* Paris: Michel Lévy, 1863. English translation: *The Life of Jesus.* New York: Modern Library, 1927.

Schleiermacher, Friedrich. *The Life of Jesus.* Edited and with introduction by Jack C. Verheyden. Translated by S. Maclean Gilmour. Lives of Jesus Series. Philadelphia: Fortress, 1975.

Strauss, David Friedrich. *The Life of Jesus Critically Examined.* Translated by George Eliot. 1846. Reprint, Edited and introduced by Peter C. Hodgson. Lives of Jesus Series. Philadelphia: Fortress, 1972.

Toland, John. *Christianity not Mysterious.* British Philosophers and Theologians of the 17th & 18th Centuries. New York: Garland, 1978.

History

Birch, Jonathan. *Jesus in an Age of Enlightenment: Radical Gospels from Thomas Hobbes to Thomas Jefferson.* London: Palgrave Macmillan, 2019.

Brown, Colin. *Jesus in European Protestant Thought 1778–1860.* Grand Rapids: Baker, 1988.

Dawes, Gregory W., ed. *The Historical Jesus Quest: Landmarks in the Search for the Jesus of History.* Louisville: Westminster John Knox, 2000.

———. *The Historical Jesus Question: The Challenge of History to Religious Authority.* Louisville: Westminster John Knox, 2001.

Fox, Richard Wightman. *Jesus in America.* San Francisco: Harper, 2004.

Moxnes, Halvor. *Jesus and the Rise of Nationalism: A New Quest for the Nineteenth Century Historical Jesus.* London: Tauris, 2012.

Prothero, Stephen. *American Jesus: How the Son of God Became a National Icon.* New York: Farrar, Straus & Giroux, 2003.

Schweitzer, Albert. *The Quest of the Historical Jesus.* Translation of the 2nd German ed. Translated by Susan Cupitt. Edited by John Bowden. Minneapolis: Fortress, 2001.

Histories of Hate Speech

History of Scholarship

Bishops' Committee for Ecumenical and Interreligious Affairs, United States Conference of Catholic Bishops. *The Bible, the Jews, and the Death of Jesus: A Collection of Catholic Documents.* US Conference of Catholic Bishops, Washington, DC, 2004.

Cohen, Jeremy. *Christ Killers: The Jews and the Passion from the Bible to the Big Screen.* New York: Oxford University Press, 2007.

Heschel, Susannah. *Abraham Geiger and the Jewish Jesus.* Chicago Studies in the History of Judaism. Chicago: University of Chicago Press, 1998.

———. *The Aryan Jesus: Christianity, Nazis and the Bible.* Princeton: Princeton University Press, 2007.

Kaufmann, Thomas. *Luther's Jews: A Journey into anti-Semitism.* Oxford: Oxford University Press, 2017.

The Jewish Jesus

Flusser, David, with R. Steven Notley. *Jesus.* Rev. ed. Jerusalem: Magnus, 1997.

Fredriksen, Paula. *Jesus of Nazareth, King of the Jews: A Jewish Life and the Emergence of Christianity.* London: Macmillan, 2000.

Klausner, Joseph. *Jesus of Nazareth.* Translated by Herbert Danby. 1925. Reprint, New York: Bloch, 1989.

Levine, Amy-Jill. *The Misunderstood Jew: The Church and the Scandal of the Jewish Jesus.* New York: Harper, 2006.

Sanders, E. P. *Jesus and Judaism.* Philadelphia: Fortress, 1985.

Vermes, Geza. *Jesus the Jew: A Historian's Reading of the Gospels.* Philadelphia: Fortress, 1973.

———. *Jesus and the World of Judaism.* Riddell Memorial Lectures. Philadelphia: Fortress, 1983.

———. *The Religion of Jesus the Jew.* Minneapolis: Fortress, 1993.

Jesus and Gender, Class, and Race: Memories of Jesus in Modern Conflicts

Blum, Edward J., and Paul Harvey. *The Color of Christ: The Son of God and the Saga of Race in America.* Chapel Hill: University of North Carolina Press, 2012.

Cleage, Albert B., Jr. *The Black Messiah.* New York: Sheed & Ward, 1968.

Cone, James H. *Black Theology and Black Power.* New York: Seabury, 1969.

Greene, Naomi. *Pier Paulo Pasolini: Cinema as Heresy.* Princeton: Princeton University Press, 1990.

Hall, Donald E. ed., *Muscular Christianity: Embodying the Victorian Age.* Cambridge Studies in Nineteenth-Century Literature and Culture 2. Cambridge: Cambridge University Press, 1994.

Hawkins, Russell, and Phillip Luke Sinitiere, eds. *Christians and the Color Line: Race and Religion after Divided by Faith*. New York: Oxford University Press, 2014.
Reinhartz, Adele. *Jesus of Hollywood*. Oxford: Oxford University Press, 2007.
Tatum, W. Barnes. *Jesus at the Movies: A Guide to the First Hundred Years*. 2nd ed. Santa Rosa, CA: Polebridge, 2004.
Yancy, George. *Christology and Whiteness: What Would Jesus Do?* New York: Routledge, 2012.

Jesus from the Margins:
The Power of "Dangerous Memories"

Goss, Robert. *Jesus Acted Up: A Gay and Lesbian Manifesto*. San Francisco: Harper, 1993.
Lassalle-Klein, Robert, ed. *Jesus of Galilee: Contextual Christology for the 21st Century*. Maryknoll, NY: Orbis, 2011.
Recinos, Harold J., and Hugo Magallanes, eds. *Jesus in the Hispanic Community. Images of Christ from Theology to Popular Religion*. Louisville: Westminster John Knox, 2009.
Schüssler Fiorenza, Elisabeth. *Jesus and the Politics of Interpretation*. New York: Continuum, 2000.
———. *Jesus: Miriam's Child, Sophia's Prophet: Critical Issues in Feminist Christology*. New York: Continuum, 1994.
Sobrino, Jon. *Jesus in Latin America*. Translated by Robert R. Barr. Maryknoll, NY: Orbis, 1987.

From Memory to History? The Prophet
Who Would Change Galilee

History of Scholarship and Methods

Ehrman, Bart D. *Did Jesus Exist? The Historical Argument for Jesus of Nazareth*. New York: HarperOne, 2012.
Le Donne, Anthony. *Historical Jesus: What Can We Know and How Can We Know it?* Grand Rapids: Eerdmans, 2011.
Schüssler Fiorenza, Elisabeth. *Jesus and the Politics of Interpretation*. New York: Continuum, 2000.
Powell Mark Allan. *Jesus as a Figure in History: How Modern Historians View the Man from Galilee*. 2nd ed. Louisville: Westminster John Knox, 2013.
Theissen, Gerd, and Annette Merz. *The Historical Jesus: A Comprehensive Guide*. London: SCM, 1998.

Jesus in a Galilean Context

Freyne, Sean. *Jesus, a Jewish Galilean: A New Reading of the Jesus-Story*. London: T. & T. Clark, 2004.

Moxnes, Halvor. *Putting Jesus in His Place: A Radical Vision of Household and Kingdom*. Louisville: Westminster John Knox, 2003.

Reed, Jonathan L. *Archaeology and the Galilean Jesus: A Re-examination of the Evidence*. Harrisburg: Trinity, 2000.

Vaage, Leif E. *Galilean Upstarts: Jesus' First Followers according to Q*. Valley Forge, PA: Trinity, 1996.

Bibliography

Aasgaard, Reidar. *The Childhood of Jesus. Decoding the Apocryphal Infancy Gospel of Thomas*. Eugene, OR: Cascade Books, 2009.

Adams, Dickenson W., ed. *Jefferson's Extracts from the Gospels*. The Papers of Thomas Jefferson, 2nd ser. Princeton: Princeton University Press, 1983.

Allison, Dale C. *Constructing Jesus: Memory, Imagination, and History*. Grand Rapids: Baker Academic, 2010.

——. *The New Moses. A Matthean Typology*. Minneapolis: Fortress, 1993.

Ansaldi, G. R. "Christo e Lavoratori nell'arte dell'800." In *Christo Lavoratore*, edited by P. G. Rovella, 61–82. Rome: Società grafica romana, 1955.

Apuleius, Lucius. *The Golden Ass*. Translated by Sara Ruden. New Haven: Yale University Press, 2011.

Armstrong, Regis J., et al., eds. *Francis of Assisi: Early Documents*. 4 vols. Hyde Park, NY: New City, 2001.

Assmann, Aleida. *Cultural Memory and Western Civilization: Functions, Media, Archives*. Cambridge: Cambridge University Press, 2011.

Assmann, Jan. *Cultural Memory and Early Civilization: Writing, Remembrance, and Political Imagination*. Cambridge: Cambridge University Press, 2011.

——. "Communicative and Cultural Memory." In *Cultural Memory Studies: An International and Interdisciplinary Handbook*, edited by Astrid Erll and Ansgar Nünnin, 109–18. Berlin: de Gruyter. 2008.

Assmann, Jan, and John Czaplicka. "Collective Memory and Cultural Identity." *New German Critique* 65 (1995) 125–33.

Baldwin, James. *The Fire Next Time*. New York: Penguin, 1962.

Baltzer, Klaus. *Die Biographie der Propheten*. Neukirchen-Vluyn: Neukirchener, 1975.

Barth, Fredrik, ed. *Ethnic Groups and Boundaries: The Social Organization of Cultural Difference*. Oslo: Universitetsforlaget, 1969.

Benedict XVI, Pope. *Jesus of Nazareth*. Vol. 2, *Holy Week—from the Entrance into Jerusalem to the Resurrection*. Translated by Philip J. Whitmore. San Francisco: Ignatius, 2011.

Berggrav, Eivind. *Mannen Jesus*. Oslo: Norges Kristelige Studenterbevegelse, 1921.

Biale, David. "Counter-History and Jewish Polemics against Christianity; the *Sefer toledot yeshu* and the *Sefer zerubavel*." *Jewish Social Studies* 6 (1999) 130–45.

Bignami, Silvia, et al., eds. *Galleria d'arte contemporanea della Pro Civitate Christiana di Assisi*. Florence: Giunti, 2015.

Birch, Jonathan C. P. *Jesus in an Age of Enlightenment: Radical Gospels from Thomas Hobbes to Thomas Jefferson*. London: Palgrave Macmillan, 2019.

Bishops' Committee for Ecumenical and Interreligious Affairs, United States Conference of Catholic Bishops. *The Bible, the Jews, and the Death of Jesus: A Collection of Catholic Documents*. Washington, DC: United States Conference of Catholic Bishops, 2004.

Blum, Edward J., and Paul Harvey. *The Color of Christ: The Son of God and the Saga of Race in America*. Chapel Hill: University of North Carolina Press, 2012.

Boff, Leonardo. *Saint Francis: A Model for Human Liberation*. Translated by John W. Diercksmeier. New York: Crossroad, 1982.

Bonaventure. *The Major Legend of Saint Francis*. In *Francis of Assisi: Early Documents*, edited by Regis J. Armstrong et al., 2:525–649. 4 vols. Hyde Park, NY: New City, 2000.

Borg, Marcus. *Jesus: A New Vision: Spirit, Culture, and the Life of Discipleship*. San Francisco: Harper & Row, 1987.

Bornkamm, Günther. *Jesus of Nazareth*. Translated by Irene and Fraser McLuskey with James M. Robinson. London: Hodder & Stoughton, 1960.

Brandes, Georg. *Det Moderne Gjennembruds Mænd*. Copenhagen: Gyldendal, 1883.

Bremmer, Jan N., ed. *The Apocryphal Acts of John*. Studies on the Apocryphal Acts of the Apostles 1. Kampen: Pharos, 1995.

Brooke, Rosalind B. *The Image of St Francis: Responses to Sainthood in the Thirteenth Century*. Cambridge: Cambridge University Press, 2006.

Brown, Peter. *The Body and Society: Men, Women, and Sexual Renunciation in Early Christianity*. Lectures on the History of Religions, n.s. 13. New York: Columbia University Press, 1988.

Brown, Colin. *Jesus in European Protestant Thought, 1778–1860*. Grand Rapids: Baker, 1988.

Brown, Raymond E. *The Birth of the Messiah*. New, updated ed. ABRL. New York: Doubleday, 1993.

Brun, Lyder. *Jesu billede*. Copehagen: Gyldendal, 1904.

Bruun, Christopher. *Om Jesus som menneske*. Kristiania: Steenske, 1898.

Burridge, Richard A. *Four Gospels, One Jesus? A Symbolic Reading*. 2nd ed. Grand Rapids: Eerdmans, 2005.

———. *What Are the Gospels? A Comparison with Graeco-Roman Biography*. 2nd ed. Biblical Resource Series. Grand Rapids: Eerdmans, 2004.

Bynum, Caroline Walker. *Jesus as Mother: Studies in the Spirituality of the High Middle Ages*. Publications of the Center for Medieval and Renaissance Studies, UCLA 16. Berkeley: University of California Press, 1982.

Carillo, Elisa A. "The Italian Catholic Church and Communism, 1943–1963." *CHR* 77 (1991) 644–57.

Cartlidge, David R., and J. Keith Elliott. *Art and the Christian Apocrypha*. London: Routledge, 2001.

Castles, Stephen et al. *The Age of Migration: International Population Movements in the Modern World*. 5th ed. Basingstoke, UK: Palgrave Macmillan, 2014.

Chagall, Marc. White *Crucifixion*. 1938. The Art Institute of Chicago. https://www.artic.edu/artworks/59426/white-crucifixion/.

Chamberlain, Houston S. *Foundations of the Nineteenth Century.* New York: Lane, 1912.

Chiesi, Roberto. *Cristo mi chiama, ma senza luce, Pier Paolo Pasolini e Il Vangelo secondo Matteo.* Genoa: Le Mani, 2015.

Chubb, Thomas. *The True Gospel of Jesus Christ Asserted.* 1738. Reprint, Whitefish, MT: Kessinger Legacy Reprints 2010.

Cleage, Albert B., Jr. *The Black Messiah.* New York: Sheed & Ward, 1968.

Cohen, Jeremy, *Christ Killers: The Jews and the Passion from the Bible to the Big Screen.* New York: Oxford University Press, 2007.

Cone, James H. *Black Theology and Black Power.* An Original Seabury Paperback. New York: Seabury, 1969.

Conway, Colleen M. *Behold the Man: Jesus and Greco-Roman Masculinity.* Oxford: Oxford University Press, 2008.

Crossan, John Dominic. *In Parables: The Challenge of the Historical Jesus.* New York: Harper & Row, 1973.

Culpepper, R. Alan. *Anatomy of the Fourth Gospel: A Study in Literary Design.* Foundations and Facets. New Testament. Philadelphia: Fortress, 1983.

———. *The Gospel and Letters of John.* Interpreting Biblical Texts. Nashville: Abingdon, 1998.

Dahl, Nils A. "The Historical Jesus." In *Jesus the Christ,* edited by Donald H. Juel, 81–111. Minneapolis: Fortress, 1991.

Dawes, Gregory W., ed. *The Historical Jesus Quest: Landmarks in the Search for the Jesus of History.* Louisville: Westminster John Knox, 2000.

———. *The Historical Jesus Question: The Challenge of History to Religious Authority.* Louisville: Westminster John Knox, 2001.

Dencik, Lars, and Karl Marosi. "Different Antisemitisms: On Three Distinct Forms of Antisemitism in Contemporary Europe. With Special Focus on Sweden." *Nordisk Judaistik / Scandinavian Jewish Studies* 27 (2016) 61–81.

Donahue, John R. *The Gospel in Parable: Metaphor, Narrative, and Theology in the Synoptic Gospels.* Fortress: Minneapolis, 1988.

———. "Tax Collectors and Sinners: An Attempt at Identification." *CBQ* 33 (1971) 39–61.

Dube, Zorodzai. *Storytelling in Times of Violence: Hearing the Exorcism Stories in Zimbabwe and in Mark's Community.* Acta Theologica 41. Oslo: University of Oslo, 2012.

Dunn, James D. G. *Jesus Remembered.* Grand Rapids: Eerdmans, 2003.

Eco, Umberto, *The Name of the Rose.* Translated by William Weaver. New York: Harcourt, 1983.

Ehrman, Bart D. *Did Jesus Exist? The Historical Argument for Jesus of Nazareth.* New York: HarperOne, 2012.

———. *Lost Christianities: The Battles for Scripture and the Faiths We Never Knew.* New York: Oxford University Press, 2003.

———, ed. *Lost Scriptures: Books that Did Not Make It into the New Testament.* New York: Oxford University Press, 2003.

Ehrman, Bart, and Zlatko Plese, eds. and trans. *The Apocryphal Gospels: Texts and Translations.* New York: Oxford University Press, 2011.

Elliott, John H. "The Jesus Movement Was not Egalitarian but Family-Oriented." *BibInt* 11 (2003) 173–210.

————. "Jesus Was not an Egalitarian: A Critique of an Anachronistic and Idealist Theory." *BTB* 32 (2002) 75–91.

Elliott, J. K. *The Apocryphal Jesus: Legends of the Early Church.* New York: Oxford University Press, 1996.

European Commission. "Combatting Antisemitism." https://ec.europa.eu/newsroom/just/item-detail.cfm?item_id=50144/.

Evans, Curtis J. "White Evangelical Protestant Responses to the Civil Rights Movement." *HTR* 102 (2009) 245–73.

Fishbane, Michael. *Song of Songs.* JPS Bible Commentary. Philadelphia: Jewish Publication Society, 2015.

Fladmoe, Audun, and Marjan, Nadim. "Silenced by Hate? Hate Speech as a Social Boundary to Free Speech." In *Boundary Struggles: Contestations of Free Speech in the Norwegian Public Sphere,* edited by Arnfinn Haagensen Midtbøen et al., 45–75. Oslo: Cappelen Damm, 2017.

Fletcher, Jeannine Hill. "Christology." In *The Strength of Her Witness: Jesus Christ in the Global Voices of Women,* edited by Elizabeth A. Johnson, 284–98. Maryknoll, NY: Orbis, 2016.

Flusser, David, with R. Steven Notley. *Jesus.* Rev. ed. Jerusalem: Magnus, 1997.

Foucault, Michel. *Power/Knowledge: Selected Interviews and Other Writings, 1972–1977.* Translated and edited by Colin Gordon. Brighton, UK: Harvester, 1980.

Fox, Richard Wightman. *Jesus in America.* San Francisco: HarperSanFrancisco, 2004.

Fredriksen, Paula. *From Jesus to Christ: The Origins of the New Testament Images of Jesus.* New Haven: Yale University Press, 1988.

————. *Jesus of Nazareth, King of the Jews: A Jewish Life and the Emergence of Christianity.* London: Macmillan, 2000.

Freyne, Sean. *Jesus, a Jewish Galilean: A New Reading of the Jesus-Story.* London: T. & T. Clark, 2004.

Funkenstein, Amos. "History, Counterhistory, and Narrative." In *Probing the Limits of Representation: Nazism and the "Final Solution,"* edited by Saul Friedlander, 66–81. Cambridge: Harvard University Press, 1992.

Goizueta, Roberto S. "The Preferential Option for the Poor: Christ and the Logic of Gratuity." In *Jesus of Galilee: Contextual Christology for the 21st Century,* edited by Robert Lassalle-Klein, 175–86. Maryknoll, NY: Orbis, 2011.

Goss, Robert. *Jesus Acted Up: A Gay and Lesbian Manifesto.* San Francisco: HarperSanFrancisco, 1993.

Graetz, Heinrich. *Geschichte der Juden.* Vol. 3, *Von dem Tode Juda Makkabi's bis zum Untergang des jüdischen Staates.* 2nd ed. Leipzig: Leiner, 1863.

Greene, Naomi. *Pier Paulo Pasolini: Cinema as Heresy.* Princeton: Princeton University Press, 1990.

Groody, Daniel. "Christology at the U.S./Mexico Border." In *Jesus of Galilee: Contextual Christology for the 21st Century,* edited by Robert Lassalle-Klein, 249–61. Maryknoll, NY: Orbis, 2011.

Grundmann, Walter. *Jesus der Galiläer und das Judentum.* Veröffentlichungen des Instituts zur Erforschung des jüdischen Einflusses auf das deutsche kirchliche Leben. Leipzig: Wigand, 1940.

Gullestad, Marianne, *Everyday Life Philosophers: Modernity, Morality, and Autobiography in Norway.* Oslo: Scandinavian University Press, 1996.

Guttiérez, Gustavo. *A Theology of Liberation: History, Politics, and Salvation.* Translated and edited by Sister Caridad Inda and John Eagleson. London: SCM, 1974.

———. "The Option for the Poor Arises from Faith in Christ." Translated by Robert Lassalle-Klein et al. *TS* 70 (2009) 317–26.

Hägg, Tomas. *The Art of Biography in Antiquity.* Cambridge: Cambridge University Press, 2012.

Halbwachs, Maurice. *On Collective Memory.* Edited and translated by L. A. Coser. The Heritage of Sociology. Chicago: University of Chicago Press, 1992.

Hall, Donald E., ed. *Muscular Christianity: Embodying the Victorian Age.* Cambridge Studies in Nineteenth-Century Literature and Culture 2. Cambridge: Cambridge University Press, 1994.

Hamel, Gildas. *Poverty and Charity in Roman Palestine, First Three Centuries C.E.* Near Eastern Studies 23. Berkeley: University of California Press, 1990.

Hanson, K. C. "The Galilean Fishing Economy and the Jesus Tradition." *BTB* 27 (1997) 99–111.

Hawkins, Russell, and Phillip Luke Sinitiere, eds. *Christians and the Color Line: Race and Religion after Divided by Faith.* New York: Oxford University Press, 2014.

Henriksen, Jan-Olav, and Karl Olav Sandnes. *Jesus as Healer: A Gospel for the Body.* Grand Rapids: Eerdmans, 2016.

Heschel, Susannah. *Abraham Geiger and the Jewish Jesus.* Chicago Studies in the History of Judaism. Chicago: University of Chicago Press, 1998.

———. *The Aryan Jesus: Christianity, Nazis and the Bible.* Princeton: Princeton University Press, 2008.

———. "Jesus in Modern Jewish Thought." In *The Jewish Annotated New Testament,* edited by Amy-Jill Levine and Marc Zvi Brettler, 582–85. New York: Oxford University Press, 2011.

Hill, C. E. *Who Chose the Gospels? Probing the Great Gospel Conspiracy.* Oxford: Oxford University Press, 2010.

Hill, Mike. *After Whiteness: Unmaking an American Majority.* Cultural Front. New York: New York University Press, 2004.

Hoff, Svein, et al. *Henrik Sørensen: Fragmenter av et kunstnerliv.* Oslo: Gyldendal, 1992.

Isasi-Diaz, Ada María. *En la Lucha: In the Struggle; Elaborating a Mujerista Theology.* Minneapolis: Fortress, 1993.

———. "Identificate con Nosotros: A Mujerista Christological Understanding." In *Jesus in the Hispanic Community: Images of Christ from Theology to Popular Religion,* edited by Harold J. Recinos and Hugo Magellanes, 38–57. Louisville: Westminster John Knox, 2009.

Jaffé, Dan. *Jésus sous la plume des historiens juifs du XXe siècle: Approche historique, perspectives historiographiques, analyses méthodologiques.* Patrimoines judaïsme. Paris: Cerf, 2009.

Jeanrond, Werner G. *Theological Hermeneutics: Development and Significance.* London: SCM, 1994.

Jefferson, Thomas. *The Life and Morals of Jesus of Nazareth.* St. Louis: Thompson, 1902. https://en.wikisource.org/wiki/The_Life_and_Morals_of_Jesus_of_Nazareth/.

———. "Syllabus of an Estimate of the Doctrines of Jesus, Compared with Those of Others." http://www.sacred-texts.com/bib/jb/jb04.htm.

Jordan, Mark D. "Jesus ACTED UP and Any Possible Future of 'Queer Theology.'" *Theology and Sexuality* 21 (2015) 198–204.

Julian of Norwich. *Revelations of Divine Love.* Translated by Elizabeth Spearing. With an introduction and notes by A. C. Spearing. Penguin Classics. London: Penguin, 1998.

Justin Martyr. *The Dialogue with Trypho.* Translated by A. Lukyn Williams. Translations of Christian Literature, ser. 1, Greek Texts. London: SPCK, 1930.

———. *The First and Second Apologies.* Translated by L. W. Barnard. Ancient Christian Writings 56. New York: Paulist, 1997.

Käsemann, Ernst. "The Problem of the Historical Jesus." In *Essays on New Testament Themes,* 15–47. Translated by W. J. Montague. Studies in Biblical Theology 1/41. London: SCM, 1964.

Kasser, Rodolphe, et al., eds. *The Gospel of Judas.* Washington, DC: National Geographic, 2006.

Kaufmann, Thomas. *Luther's Jews: A Journey into Anti-Semitism.* Oxford: Oxford University Press, 2017.

Khalidi, Jarif. *The Muslim Jesus.* Cambridge: Harvard University Press, 2001.

Keith, Chris. *Jesus' Literacy: Scribal Culture and the Teacher from Galilee.* London: T. & T. Clark, 2011.

———. "Memory and Authenticity: Jesus Tradition and What Really Happened." *ZNW* 102 (2011) 155–77.

Kelley, Shawn. *Racializing Jesus. Race, Ideology and the Formation of Modern Biblical Scholarship.* London: Routledge, 2002.

King, Karen L. *The Gospel of Mary of Magdala: Jesus and the First Woman Apostle.* Santa Rosa, CA: Polebridge, 2003.

———. *What Is Gnosticism?* Cambridge: Harvard University Press, 2003.

Klausner, Joseph. *Jesus of Nazareth.* Translated by Herbert Danby. 1925. Reprint, New York: Bloch, 1989.

Kleist, James A., trans. *The Didache, the Epistle of Barnabas, the Epistles and the Martyrdom of St. Polycarp, the Fragments of Papias, the Epistle to Diognetus.* Ancient Christian Writers 6. Cork: Mercier, 1948.

Kosloski, Philip. "Why Is There a Feast for St Joseph the Worker?" *Aleteia.* https://aleteia.org/2017/05/01/why-is-there-a-feast-for-st-joseph-the-worker/.

Kwok, Pui-Lan. "Engendering Christ." In *The Strength of Her Witness: Jesus Christ in the Global Voices of Women,* edited by Elizabeth A. Johnson, 255–69. Maryknoll, NY: Orbis, 2018.

———. "Jesus/the Native: Biblical Studies from a Postcolonial Perspective." In *Teaching the Bible: The Discourses and Politics of Biblical Pedagogy,* edited by Fernando F. Segovia and Mary Ann Tolbert, 69–85. Maryknoll, NY: Orbis, 1998.

Lagarde, Paul de. *Deutsche Schriften: Gesammtausgabe letzter Hand.* Göttingen: Dieterische Verlagsbuchhandlung, 1878.

Lassalle-Klein, Robert, ed. *Jesus of Galilee: Contextual Christology for the 21st Century.* Maryknoll, NY: Orbis, 2011.

Le Donne. Anthony. *Historical Jesus: What Can We Know and How Can We Know It?* Grand Rapids: Eerdmans, 2011.

———. *The Historiographical Jesus: Memory, Typology, and the Son of David.* Waco: Baylor University Press, 2009.

———. *Jesus: A Beginners Guide.* Oneworld Beginners' Guides. London: Oneworld, 2018.

Lee, Hermione. *Body Parts: Essays in Life-Writing.* London: Chatto & Windus, 2005.

Leirvik, Oddbjørn. *Images of Jesus Christ in Islam*. 2nd ed. New York: Continuum, 2010.

Levine, Amy-Jill. *The Misunderstood Jew: The Church and the Scandal of the Jewish Jesus*. New York: HarperOne, 2006.

Levine, Amy-Jill et al., eds. *The Historical Jesus in Context*. Princeton Readings in Religions. Princeton: Princeton University Press, 2006.

Lipton, Sara. "'The Sweet Lean of His Head': Writing about Looking at the Crucifix in the High Middle Ages." *Speculum* 80 (2005) 1172–1208.

Lutheran World Federation, and the International Jewish Committee for Interreligious Consultation. *Luther, Lutheranism, and the Jews*. July 1, 1983. https://ccjr.us/dialogika-resources/documents-and-statements/interreligious/lwfijcic1983/.

Meeks, Wayne A. *Christ Is the Question*. Louisville: Westminster John Knox 2006.

Meerson, Michael, and Peter Schäfer, trans. and eds. *Toledot Yeshu: The Life Story of Jesus*. 2 vols. Texts and Studies in Ancient Judaism 149. Tübingen: Mohr/Siebeck, 2014.

Martínez, Jessica, and Gregory A. Smith. "How the Faithful Voted: A Preliminary 2016 Analysis." *FactTank: News in the Numbers*, November 9, 2016. Pew Research Center. https://www.pewresearch.org/fact-tank/2016/11/09/how-the-faithful-voted-a-preliminary-2016-analysis/.

Michaelson, Jay. "Queer Theology and Social Transformation Twenty Years after Jesus ACTED UP." *Theology and Sexuality* 21 (2015) 189–97.

Montefiore, C. G. *The Synoptic Gospels*. 2 vols. London: Macmillan, 1909.

Moxnes, Halvor. "The Construction of Galilee as a Place for the Historical Jesus (2 parts)." *BTB* (2001) 26–37, 64–77.

———. "Does the History of the Canon Matter? Contextualizing the Debate over the Authority of the New Testament Canon." *BTB* 45 (2015) 108–15.

———. *The Economy of the Kingdom: Social Conflicts and Economic Relations in Luke's Gospel*. OBT 23. 1988. Reprint, Eugene, OR: Wipf & Stock, 2004.

———. "Honor and Shame." *BTB* 23 (1993) 167–76.

———. *Jesus and the Rise of Nationalism: A New Quest for the Nineteenth-Century Historical Jesus*. London: Tauris, 2012.

———. "Jesus in Discourses of Dichotomies: Alternative Paradigms for the Historical Jesus." *JSHJ* 11 (2013) 130–52.

———. *Putting Jesus in His Place: A Radical Vision of Household and Kingdom*. Louisville: Westminster John Knox, 2003.

———. "Was Jesus a Charismatic Leader? The Use of Social Models in the History of the Jesus Movement." In «*Lampada per i miei passi è la tua parola, luce sul mio cammino*» (*Sal 119,105*). *Studi offerti a Marcello Del Verme in occasione del suo 75 compleanno*, edited by Pasquale Giustiniani and Francesco del Pizzo, 51–72. Supplementum . . . di Bibbia e oriente 27. Bornato: Sardini, 2017.

Murray, Lauren Donna. "Elite Father and Son Relationships in Republican Rome." PhD diss., University of Edinburgh, 2015.

Myles, Robert J. *The Homeless Jesus in the Gospel of Matthew*. The Social World of Biblical Antiquity 2/10. Sheffield: Sheffield Phoenix, 2014.

Nasr, Seyyed Hossein, et al., eds. *The Study Quran: A New Translation and Commentary*. New York: HarperOne, 2015.

Newman, Hillel I. "The Death of Jesus in the Toledoth Yeashu Literature." *JTS* 50 (1999) 59–79.

Nicodemi, Giorgio. "La figura di Gesú divino lavoratore nel pensiero e nella realizzazione di otto artisti contemporanei." *La Rocca* 11/17 (1952) 10–12.

Norwegian Government. Strategi mot hatefulle ytringer 2016–2020 (Strategies against hate speech). English summary, 9–10. https://www.regjeringen.no/contentassets/72293ca5195642249029BF6905ffo8be/hatefulleytringer_uu.pdf/.

Oxford Constitutional Law (website). "Hate Speech." https://oxcon.ouplaw.com/view/10.1093/law-mpeccol/law-mpeccol-e130/.

Pageau, Jonathan. "The Ox and the Ass in the Nativity Icon." *Orthodox Art Journal*, 24 December 2012, http://www.orthodoxartsjournal.org/why-an-ass-and-an-ox-in-the-nativity-icon/.

Park, Wongi. "Christological Discourse as Racial Discourse." *Religion & Theology* 23 (2016) 213–30.

Pasolini, Pier Paolo, dir. *The Gospel according to St. Matthew*. Starring Enrique Irazoqui et al. DVD. West Conshohocken, PA: Alpha Video, 2019.

Patterson, Stephen J. *The Gospel of Thomas and Jesus*. Foundations & Facets. Reference Series. Sonoma, CA: Polebridge, 1993.

Pelikan, Jaroslav. *Jesus through the Centuries: His Place in the History of Culture*. New Haven: Yale University Press, 1985.

Peters, F. E. *Jesus and Muhammad: Parallel Tracks, Parallel Lives*. New York: Oxford University Press, 2011.

Philo of Alexandria. *On Abraham. On Joseph. On Moses*. Translated by F. H. Colson. Philo's Works 6. LCL 289. Cambridge: Harvard University Press, 1935.

Powell, Mark Allan. *Jesus as a Figure in History: How Modern Historians View the Man from Galilee*. 2nd ed. Louisville: Westminster John Knox, 2013.

Prothero, Stephen. *American Jesus: How the Son of God Became a National Icon*. New York: Farrar, Straus & Giroux, 2003.

Recinos, Harold J., and Hugo Magallanes, eds. *Jesus in the Hispanic Community: Images of Christ from Theology to Popular Religion*. Louisville: Westminster John Knox, 2009.

Reed, Jonathan L. *Archaeology and the Galilean Jesus: A Re-examination of the Evidence*. Harrisburg: Trinity, 2000.

Reimarus, Herman Samuel. *Fragments*. Edited by Charles H. Talbert. Translated by Ralph S. Fraser. Lives of Jesus Series. Philadelphia: Fortress, 1970.

Reinhard, Kathryn L. "Joy to the Father, Bliss to the Son: Unity and the Motherhood Theology of Julian of Norwich." *ATR* 89 (2007) 629–45.

Reinhartz, Adele. *Jesus of Hollywood*. Oxford: Oxford University Press, 2007.

———. "The Jews of the Fourth Gospel." In *The Oxford Handbook of Johannine Studies*, edited by Judith M. Lieu and Martinus C. De Boer, 121–39. Oxford Handbooks. Oxford: Oxford University Press, 2018.

Religion News Service. "Exit polls show few changes in the religious vote." November 5, 2020. https://religionnews.com/2020/11/05/exit-polls-show-few-changes-in-the-religious-vote/.

Renan, Ernest. *An Essay on the Age and Antiquity of the Book of Nabathæan Agriculture: To which is Added an Inaugural Lecture on the Position of the Shemitic Nations in the History of Civilization*. ATLA Monograph Preservation Program, ATLA fiche 1986–2855. London: Trübner, 1862.

———. *The Life of Jesus*. Modern Library of the World's Best Books. New York: Modern Library, 1927.

————. "Nouvelle lettre à M. Strauss." In *Ouevres completes*, edited by H. Psichari, 1:449–62. 10 vols. Paris: Calmann-Lévy, 1947.

Richardson, Peter. *Building Jewish in the Roman East.* JSJSup 92. Leiden: Brill, 2004.

Rivera, Luis R. "El Cristo Migrante/The Migrant Christ." In *Jesus in the Hispanic Community: Images of Christ from Theology to Popular Religion*, edited by Harold J. Recinos and Hugo Magellanes, 135–54. Louisville: Westminster John Knox, 2009.

Robinson, James M. *The Nag Hammadi Library in English.* 4th ed. Leiden: Brill, 1996.

Robinson, Neil. *Christ in Islam and Christianity: The Representation of Jesus in the Qurān and the Classical Muslim Commentaries.* London: Macmillan, 1991.

Rossi, Giovanni. "Un motive nuovo nell'aarte sacra: Gesu' divino lavoratore." In *Gesu il divino lavoratore*, edited by Mario Marino, 11–17. Rome: Istituto Beato Angelico di Roma, 1959.

Runesson, Anders. *Divine Wrath and Salvation in Matthew: The Narrative World of the First Gospel.* Minneapolis: Fortress, 2016.

Said, Edward W. *Orientalism.* New York: Vintage, 1978.

Sanders, E. P. *Jesus and Judaism.* Philadelphia: Fortress, 1985.

————. *Paul and Palestinian Judaism: A Comparison of Patterns of Religion.* London: SCM, 1977.

Schäfer, Peter. *Jesus in the Talmud.* Princeton: Princeton University Press, 2007.

————. "Jesus' Origin, Birth, and Childhood according to the Toledot Yeshu and the Talmud." In *Judaea-Palaestina, Babylon and Rome: Jews in Antiquity*, edited by Benjamin Isaac and Yuval Shahar, 139–61. Texts and Studies in Ancient Judaism 147. Tübingen: Mohr/Siebeck, 2012.

Schleiermacher, Friedrich. *Das Leben Jesu.* Berlin: Reimer, 1864.

————. *The Life of Jesus.* Edited and with introduction by Jack C. Verheyden. Translated by S. Maclean Gilmour. Lives of Jesus Series. Philadelphia: Fortress, 1975.

————. *On Religion: Speeches to Its Cultured Despisers.* Translated and edited by Richard Crouter. Cambridge Texts in the History of Philosophy. Cambridge: Cambridge University Press, 1996.

Schreckenberg, Hans. *The Jews in Christian Art: An Illustrated History.* New York: Continuum, 1996.

Schröter, Jens. *Jesus of Nazareth: Jew from Galilee, Savior of the World.* Translated by W. Coppins and S.-B. Pounds. Waco, TX: Baylor University Press, 2014.

Schüssler Fiorenza, Elisabeth. *In Memory of Her: A Feminist Theological Reconstruction of Christian Origins.* London: SCM Press, 1983.

————. *Jesus and the Politics of Interpretation.* New York: Continuum, 2000.

————. *Jesus: Miriam's Child, Sophia's Prophet: Critical Issues in Feminist Christology.* New York: Continuum, 1994.

Schwartz, Barry. *Abraham Lincoln and the Forge of National Memory.* Chicago: University of Chicago Press, 2000.

Schweitzer, Albert. *The Quest of the Historical Jesus.* Translation of 2nd German ed. Edited by John Bowden. Translated by Susan Cupitt et al. Fortress Classics in Biblical Studies. Minneapolis: Fortress, 2001.

Sebastian, Joseph. *God as Feminine: A Dialogue.* European University Studies Series 23. Theology Series 523. Frankfurt: Lang, 1995.

Seo, Pyung Soo. *Luke's Jesus in the Roman Empire and the Emperor in the Gospel of Luke.* Eugene, OR: Pickwick Publications, 2015.

Sloyan, Gerard S. *The Crucifixion of Jesus: History, Myth, Faith.* Minneapolis: Fortress, 1995.

Smith, Jonathan Z. *To Take Place: Toward Theory in Ritual.* Chicago Studies in the History of Judaism. Chicago: University of Chicago Press, 1987.

Sobrino, Jon. *Christology at the Crossroads: A Latin American Approach.* Translated by John Drury. London: SCM, 1978.

————. *Jesus in Latin America.* Translated by Robert R. Barr. Maryknoll, NY: Orbis, 1987.

————. *Jesus in Latin America.* Translated by Robert R. Barr. 1987. Reprint, Eugene, OR: Wipf & Stock, 2004.

————. "Jesus of Galilee from the Salvadoran Context: Compassion, Hope, and Following the Light of the Cross." *TS* 70 (2009) 437–60.

Sørensen, Sven Oluf. *Søren: Henrik Sørensens liv og kunst.* Oslo: Andresen & Butenschøn, 2003.

Stålsett, Sturla J. *The crucified and the Crucified: A Study in the Liberation Christology of Jon Sobrino.* Studies in the Intercultural History of Christianity 127. Bern: Lang, 2003.

Stanton, Graham. *The Gospels and Jesus.* 2nd ed. Oxford Bible Series. Oxford: Oxford University Press, 2002.

Stinton, Diane B. *Jesus of Africa: Voices of Contemporary African Christology.* Faith and Cultures Series. Maryknoll, NY: Orbis, 2004.

Strauss, David Friedrich. *Das Leben Jesu für das deutsche Volk bearbeitet.* Leipzig: Brochaus, 1864.

————. *Das Leben Jesu kritisch bearbeitet.* Tübingen: Osiander, 1835–36.

————. *The Life of Jesus Critically Examined.* Translated by George Eliot. Originally published 1846. Reprint, Edited and introduced by Peter C. Hodgson. Lives of Jesus Series. Philadelphia: Fortress, 1972.

Sugirtharajah, R. S. *Jesus in Asia.* Cambridge: Harvard University Press, 2018.

Sullivan, K. E. *Pre-Raphaelites.* Discovering Art. London: Brockhampton, 1996.

Tatum, W. Barnes. *Jesus at the Movies: A Guide to the First Hundred Years.* 2nd ed. Santa Rosa, CA: Polebridge, 2004.

Taylor, Joan E. *What Did Jesus Look Like?* London: Bloomsbury, 2019.

Theissen, Gerd, and Annette Merz. *The Historical Jesus: A Comprehensive Guide.* Minneapolis: Fortress, 1998.

Thomas of Celano. *The Life of Saint Francis.* In *Francis of Assisi: Early Documents,* edited by Regis J. Armstrong et al., 1:171–297. 4 vols. Hyde Park, NY: New City, 1999.

Toland, John. *Christianity Not Mysterious.* British Philosophers and Theologians of the 17th & 18th Centuries. New York: Garland, 1978.

Seim, Turid Karlsen. *The Double Message: Patterns of Gender in Luke–Acts.* T. & T. Clark Academic Paperbacks. London: T. & T. Clark, 2004.

United Nations Human Rights, Office of the High Commissioner. "Migration and Human Rights." https://www.ohchr.org/en/issues/migration/pages/migrationandhumanrightsindex.aspx/.

Vaage, Leif E. *Galilean Upstarts: Jesus' First Followers according to Q.* Valley Forge: Trinity, 1994.

Valantasis, Richard. "Constructions of Power in Asceticism." *JAAR* 63 (1995) 775–821.

Vatican II. *Nostra Aetate: The Relation of the Church to Non-Christian Religions.* http://
www.vatican.va/archive/hist_councils/ii_vatican_council/documents/vat-ii_
decl_19651028_nostra-aetate_en.html.

Vauchez, André, *Francis of Assisi. The Life and Afterlife of a Medieval Saint.* Translated by
M. F. Cusato. New Haven: Yale University Press, 2012.

Vermes, Geza. *Jesus the Jew: A Historian's Reading of the Gospels.* Philadelphia: Fortress,
1981.

———. *Jesus and the World of Judaism.* Riddell Memorial Lectures. London: SCM,
1983.

———. *The Religion of Jesus the Jew.* London: SCM, 1993.

Weber, Max. *Economy and Society.* 2 vols. Edited by Guenther Roth and Claus Wittich.
Translated by Ephraim Fischoff et al. Berkeley: University of California Press,
1978.

Welch, Sharon D. *A Feminist Ethic of Risk.* Minneapolis: Fortress, 1990.

Winter, Bruce W. *Divine Honours for the Caesars: The First Christians' Responses.* Grand
Rapids: Eerdmans, 2015.

Winter, Paul. *On the Trial of Jesus.* 2nd ed. Revised and edited by T. A. Burkill and Geza
Vermes. Studia Judaica 1. Berlin: de Gruyter, 1974.

Worsley, Peter. *The Trumpet Shall Sound: A Study of "Cargo" Cults in Melanesia.* 2nd,
augmented ed. New York: Schocken, 1968.

Yancy, George, ed. *Christology and Whiteness: What Would Jesus Do?* London:
Routledge, 2012.

Index

Page numbers in *italics* indicate
an illustration.

Lightning Source UK Ltd.
Milton Keynes UK
UKHW012158160821
388948UK00002B/698

9 781532 684746